D1201443

The English Library
before 1700

Bodleian Library, Oxford: Arts End, 1610–12
(*see page* 237)

The English Library before 1700

STUDIES IN ITS HISTORY EDITED BY

FRANCIS WORMALD

Professor of Palaeography in the University of London

AND

C. E. WRIGHT

*Deputy Keeper, Department of Manuscripts,
British Museum*

UNIVERSITY OF LONDON
THE ATHLONE PRESS
1958

Published by
THE ATHLONE PRESS
UNIVERSITY OF LONDON
at 2 Gower Street, London WC1
Distributed by Constable & Co Ltd
12 Orange Street, London WC2

Canada
University of Toronto Press
Toronto, 5

U.S.A.
Essential Books Division
Oxford University Press Inc
New York

Printed in Great Britain by
WESTERN PRINTING SERVICES LTD
BRISTOL

PREFACE

THE CHAPTERS that make up this volume are, with two exceptions, based upon lectures delivered in the spring of 1952 and 1954 under the auspices of the School of Librarianship and Archives of University College, London. The original courses, arranged by Professor Raymond Irwin as Director of the School, were devoted to 'The Mediaeval English Library' and 'The English Renaissance Library' respectively. Subsequently the School of Librarianship suggested and the Athlone Press Board of Management agreed that in printed form the lectures might prove useful to a wider circle. At this point the Press Board invited us to undertake the task of editing them for publication and *The English Library before 1700* is the result.

A word is necessary about the manner in which the contents and arrangement of the printed text differ from that of the lecture courses. In place of the introductory lectures with which he inaugurated each series, Professor Irwin has kindly consented to write a General Introduction. Subsequently, in order that the contents of the mediaeval library might be more fully covered, Professor R. M. Wilson of the University of Sheffield (who has made a special examination of the mediaeval library catalogues in connection with his researches into the 'Lost Literature' of the Middle Ages in this country) accepted an invitation to contribute a chapter on this subject. The second series of lectures in 1954 covered a more extended field chronologically than that represented in the version published here. A very sharp change of character occurs, however, in the history of book-collecting and librarianship at the close of the seventeenth century, as may be very easily seen by a study of the activities of such notable collectors as Charles Spencer, earl of Sunderland, and the two Harleys, Robert and Edward, first and second earls of Oxford (though

Robert Harley, active in the first decade of the eighteenth century, was closer to the old tradition), or on a more limited scale Thomas Coke, Viscount Coke and later earl of Leicester, who was the real originator of the library at Holkham. For this reason it was thought best to preserve the homogeneous character of the published volume by confining it to the period before 1700. Only in the case of chapter xi, where special circumstances in the story of the Oxford libraries necessitated special treatment, is this date limit exceeded.

In view of what has been said the reader will appreciate that the book as it now appears does not profess to offer a comprehensive treatment of the whole history of the earlier growth of the English library. To have attempted this (even were the time yet ripe for it) would have involved a quite impracticable amount of re-casting and expansion of the lectures. We have been content to present this material in the form of a group of related individual studies, with only such minor editorial revision and additions as seemed essential.

The original lecture series were not illustrated but it was thought that the value of the printed version would be greatly increased if plates were provided, and this has been done.

March 1958   F.W.
                                                        C.E.W.

CONTENTS

ACKNOWLEDGEMENTS

The editors and publishers wish to thank the following persons and bodies for courteous permission to reproduce photographs: the Controller, Her Majesty's Stationery Office; the Ministry of Works; the Dean and Chapter of Durham; the Master and Fellows of University College, Oxford; the Master and Fellows of Magdalene College, Cambridge; the Curators of the Bodleian Library; the Syndics of the Cambridge University Library; the Curators of the Durham University Library; the Trustees of the British Museum; and the National Buildings Record.

LIST OF PLATES

Frontispiece. The Bodleian Library, Oxford: Arts End, 1610–12.

1. Press in the Pepysian Library, Magdalene College, Cambridge.

2. Pepys's Library as it originally was in his house in York Buildings, from a drawing in the Pepysian Library, Magdalene College, Cambridge.

3. Carrells in the cloister of Gloucester Cathedral.
   Copyright, National Buildings Record.

4a. Lanercost Priory, Cumberland. View of the north-east corner of the cloister. The small round-headed embrasure in the middle of the picture is a book cupboard.
   Photograph, Dr C. E. Wright.

4b. Iron Grill in the Spendement in Durham Cathedral behind which some of the books were housed.
   Photograph, Daisy R. Edis.

5. Page of the fourteenth-century catalogue of the library of Lanthony Priory, near Gloucester. The heading to the second paragraph reads 'Primus Gradus Secundi Armarii'. Note halfway down the words 'quaternus rubeus' after an entry.
   B.M. Harley MS 460, f. 4b.

6a. Memorandum, thirteenth-century, recording the gift in 1248 of the MS by Caerleon Abbey, Monmouth, to Hailes Abbey, Glos., founded in 1246.
   B.M. Add. MS 48984. Crown copyright.

6*b*. Laurence, monk of Durham, writing.
>   Durham, University Library, Cosin MS V. iii. 1 (late twelfth-century).

7. An unbound MS.
>   Durham Cathedral, Dean and Chapter Library, MS A. iv. 34.

8*a*. A note, at the foot of the page, early fourteenth-century, from the scribe to the illuminator indicating the subject to be drawn into the initial. It reads: 'Episcopus in cathedra et paulus loquens sibi coram eo' (A bishop in a chair and Paul before him speaking to him).
>   Durham, University Library, Cosin MS V. i. 8, f. 102.

8*b*. Tacitus, *De Oratoribus*, written in Italy for John Tiptoft, earl of Worcester, fifteenth-century. His arms are in a wreath at the foot of the page.
>   B.M. Harley MS 2639, f. 2.

9. Memorandum relating to the borrowing of a pecia. At the bottom of the left-hand page is the thirteenth-century note: 'Sequentem quaternum habet Frater W de Wynton'.
>   Durham, University Library, Cosin MS V. v. 3, f. 111b.

10. Catalogue of the library of Christ Church, Canterbury, made under Prior Henry of Eastry (1285–1331). In the left-hand column a number of books in English are mentioned.
>   B.M. Cotton MS Galba E. iv, f. 134.

11. Pseudo-Dionysius, *De Hierarchia*, in Greek, written in the West by a Western scribe, thirteenth-century. The first two marginal notes are in the hand of Robert Grosseteste, bishop of Lincoln, 1235–53.
>   Oxford, Bodleian MS Canon. gr. 97, f. 86vo.

12. List of manuscripts seen by John Leland in Lincolnshire monastic houses, ? c. 1534. The annotation is in Henry VIII's hand.
>   B.M. Royal MS Appendix 69, f. 2b.

13. Cotton's list of MSS loaned from his library and of the persons to whom the loans had been made; the part illustrated bears the heading: 'such Books as I have before this 23 April lent out of my Study'. Note the loan to Ben Jonson.
>   B.M. Harley MS 6018, f. 149.

I

General Introduction

RAYMOND IRWIN

THE LITERARY HERITAGE

IT is likely that the enquirer, considering this question for the first time, will be struck by the continuity of the tradition which lies behind the growth of our libraries. He will realise at once that the English library tradition is only a small part of the history of Western libraries, and that this is itself but a part of the history of Western civilisation. His subject is thus linked closely with the history of scholarship. The continuity of the tradition is important: it gives both significance and perspective to our view of English libraries; it reminds us of the debt we owe to other ages and other nations, and of our responsibility to those who come after us. In a real sense our English libraries have their roots in the libraries of Greece and Alexandria; of Rhodes, Cos, Pergamum, Antioch, Macedonia and Constantinople; of the villas of cultured Romans and the universities of Southern Gaul; of Arab cities from Bagdad to Cordova; and of the great chain of religious strongholds from Caesarea, Patmos and Mount Athos to Monte Cassino, Bangor, Wearmouth, York, Bobbio and Fulda. All these and many other sources have contributed something to our library history; and we in these islands from the time of St Columban, Alcuin and St Boniface onwards, have ourselves contributed not a little to the librarianship of other nations.

In the present work the impact of the classical tradition on the contents of our libraries is surveyed in chapters vi and vii.[1] Our interest in this tradition will naturally however take us behind the titles that happen to lie on our library shelves at a given period. One feature of the mediaeval dependence on the classical tradition lies in the language in which books were written. Classical Latin changed gradually into its post-classical, ecclesiastical and mediaeval forms, but it remained in essence Latin. If Boethius (as Gibbon suggested) was the last Roman whom Cicero would have been prepared to recognise as a compatriot, nevertheless Cicero would have been able to interpret, with distaste perhaps but without much difficulty, the writings of, say, Bede or John of Salisbury or Erasmus. To write and read the same language is a powerful bond that has cemented Western scholarship for two thousand years. The strongest factor in securing the continuity of a written language is the teaching of grammar and rhetoric in the schools, and in Western Europe there was an unbroken tradition of such teaching throughout our period in the monastic, cathedral and grammar schools. The separation of the written language of scholarship from the spoken forms of Anglo-Saxon or Middle English also helped to maintain the stability of written Latin. Still another cause that contributed to this was the use of Latin for Church services, without which it would certainly have perished as a living language. Christianity introduced to Europe a new learned class for whom a knowledge of Latin was a professional qualification; indeed learning and sanctity were both comprehended in the word *clericus*. Unlike most creeds, Christianity has always been essentially a bookish religion, and scholarship owes a great debt to it, if only for this reason. We can note too that the use of Latin for writing involves a certain measure of bilingualism. As Grosseteste wrote, there were in England two languages—Latin for the clergy, French for the ignorant. Many however used both, and this always provides a healthy intellectual discipline. It did so in Cicero's day, when every cultured Roman knew Greek; equally it must have had its effect in the Middle Ages. There was a time in the twelfth and thirteenth centuries when trilingualism was not uncommon. Abbot Samson of Bury was not only 'eloquens Gallice et Latine' but was well able to preach in his own Norfolk dialect. The Jewish business man of this period, such as Aaron of Lincoln, was very probably fluent in four languages, adding Hebrew to the other three.

To the librarian the use of Latin in one respect proved a hindrance rather than a blessing, namely, in the sphere of arithmetic.

The need for calculating in Roman notation must surely have deterred mediaeval scholars from mathematical experiment. The pupils of Rabanus Maurus, for example, were driven to employ a most complicated method of counting up to a million on the fingers; this perhaps being simpler than working on paper in Roman numerals. The introduction of the Arabic decimal system in the twelfth century, with its zero and nine integers, helped not only the mathematician, but the librarian and bibliographer, by simplifying the pagination of books, the citation of references, and the compilation of indexes: a very necessary aid as compilations and epitomes increased in number and size.

The organisation of the mediaeval library owes little to that of classical libraries except a few simple technical terms such as *armarium* (aumbry, Fr. *armoire*) which was common in both periods. There are no records of the chaining of books in classical antiquity, and other equipment such as lecterns, stalls and carrells are essentially mediaeval developments.

The similarity between the monastic cloister and the classical colonnade (both of which were associated with libraries) naturally attracts attention, but it is probable that the resemblance is accidental, rather than deliberate. It may be noted however that the ruins of many colonnaded buildings would be familiar to the designers of early monastic buildings in Gaul. Odilo of Cluny brought Roman columns of marble up the Rhône and the Saône to adorn his new cloisters; and Bede tells us that Benedict Biscop built St Peter's, Wearmouth 'after the Roman style', using masons and glaziers from Gaul. Even the cloisters were apparently glazed.[2]

However important the continuity of language may be, the actual continuity of record is even more important. When our links with the Latin tongue began to weaken in the sixteenth century, continuity of record was strengthened by the influence of humanism on the 'new learning', by the retention of Latin teaching in schools, and by the growing stream of translations into the vernacular. Dr C. E. Wright in chapters viii and ix describes how the threatened break in the tradition caused by the dispersal of the monastic and academic libraries in 1536–50 was averted by the zeal of the Elizabethan antiquaries.

THE RELIGIOUS BASIS

No study of the history of libraries can neglect the part they have played as instruments of authority over an unlettered or partly educated people. From the earliest times, civilisation has been founded in some form on religious symbolism (whether it be a holy place, or a grove, or a stone circle or a mound) which serves to hold the tribe together. If, as has been maintained,[3] the art of communication is a vital step in our history, the art of recording communication is doubly important; for only by written records can man communicate with man over distances of time and space. Libraries, which are indeed repositories of recorded communications, are thus seen in a true sense as one of the foundation stones of human society. It will cause no surprise therefore to find that libraries in the ancient world were always associated with temples, shrines or holy places, or indeed with the royal palace, which shares in the divinity of the king; and in the Christian world the association of libraries with ecclesiastical institutions has been equally close. In this country, from the coming of St Augustine to the fifteenth century, it would be hard to find any library that was not directly or indirectly connected with the Church; and the same is true of institutional libraries for the next three centuries at least. For both, pagan and Christian, learning and religion have always been inseparably connected, and there is a real sense in which their libraries have been religious institutions: storehouses in which national traditions are enshrined in stone or wood or papyrus or parchment, and from which there radiates the intellectual and spiritual power or superstition or magic that binds the nation together into a unity. The spiritual power of the book has always been a force to be reckoned with. For the Christian in particular, books were primarily weapons of aggression or defence in a world of strife. Until the eighteenth century indeed, a disinterested love of scholarship is as rare as a disinterested library. Matthew Parker's great collection, Bodley's library at Oxford, and the parish libraries that sprang up in the seventeenth and eighteenth centuries, were all expressly formed for religious purposes.[4]

READING IN THE FIFTEENTH CENTURY

The existence of libraries and their proper use depends not merely on the ability to read and write, but on the development of the habit of reading. An enquiry into the rise and progress of this habit at different periods of our history will shed light on the history of our libraries; particularly of course on the history of the private working collection in which this habit is commonly exercised.

It is well known that it was mainly during the fifteenth century that the lay population of England (more particularly southern and eastern England) became literate. Before the fifteenth century, even clerical collections were far from common. Only one collection belonging to a parish priest is known in the thirteenth century: a library of forty-eight volumes, owned by Geoffrey de Lawath, rector of St Magnus, London, a list of whose books occurs in a *Liber Decretorum* at Pembroke College, Cambridge.[5] Most of the volumes concerned theology, grammar or dialectic, but there were three medical works.[6] Even episcopal libraries were limited in numbers, though there were notable exceptions such as those of Richard de Bury, Simon Langham, William of Wykeham, William Reed, Adam Easton, Richard Gravesend and Thomas Bradwardine.[7] Many bishops lived a nomadic life, moving from manor to manor, or on diocesan visitations, and these are not the sort of conditions to encourage the growth of private libraries.[8]

From Chaucer's day onwards, a gradual change came over England. The case for the spread of literacy in the fifteenth century has been ably argued.[9] The main points can be mentioned briefly. Sir Thomas More's estimate, made in 1533, that more than half the population could read English (i.e. perhaps two and a half millions out of four or five millions) is well known. Over a century earlier, another estimate suggests that over 85 per cent were illiterate.[10] Both these estimates were guesses, but many considerations support the increase in literacy in this period. Lay people were beginning to own books, to set a proper value on them and to mention them in their wills; some fair-sized collections are revealed in this way.[11] English was being used freely for business and personal correspondence; this is of course the time of the Paston, Cely and Stonor letters. The earliest domestic libraries belong to this period,

B

ranging from Chaucer's library in the gatehouse at Aldgate, where
he loved to retire among his books, to the Paston and Fastolf collections[12] and to Sir Thomas More's library at Chelsea—perhaps
the first great working collection owned by a lay scholar. Some of
his books More took with him to the Tower; at the last fateful
interview with Sir Richard Rich, they were taken away from him
in a sack. Not least among English libraries in the years prior to
the Reformation was that owned by More's friend John Fisher,
bishop of Rochester, which was tragically plundered by Thomas
Cromwell at the time of the bishop's martyrdom. It is described as
the 'notablest Library of Books in all England, two long galleries
full, the Books were sorted in stalls & a Register of the names of
every Book at the end of every stall'. The collection had been
intended for St John's College, Cambridge.[13]

The kinds of books that were in demand in the fifteenth century
often suggest the existence of home libraries such as that possessed
by the Paston family. Translations into English, from Chaucer
and John de Trevisa onwards, increased steadily in number, till by
1600 most of Virgil, Horace, Ovid, Seneca, Cicero, Pliny and
some Greek literature was available in English; still more was of
course accessible in French or Italian. The popularity of courtesy
and conduct books, and of the commonplace book or scrapbook,
implies domestic rather than academic use; the latter was a useful
way of providing a library *in parvo*.[14] The increasing interest in
personal religion brought in addition a demand for many devotional works intended for home use. By the middle of the century,
manuscript books were being copied in large numbers for lay
readers. Some families such as the Pastons might occasionally employ a scribe of their own; but there were publishing firms such as
that of John Shirley (1366–1456), which produced work in quantity. Shirley seems to have lent, as well as sold, manuscripts to his
customers,[15] anticipating the later combination of bookseller and
circulating library. It is evident therefore, that when Caxton came
to issue his printed books, there was a wide reading public wait-
ing for the productions of his press. Certain other changes bearing
on this development can be noted. Paper, mostly imported from
France, was proving a convenient and cheap substitute for parchment. Posters and handbills were becoming a common method of

public information. Manors were being enlarged to provide private apartments for the lord and lady, who (as Langland records in *Piers Plowman*) now dine by themselves 'in a chambre with a chymnye', instead of in the great hall; without such a development, little private reading would have been possible. And in parish churches, pews with book rests were for the first time becoming common, while windows began to grow wider, and clerestory windows were being added, to provide more light in the nave.[16]

Lastly, the fifteenth century was the first great age of English humanism, when collectors such as John Tiptoft, earl of Worcester, and Humphrey, duke of Gloucester ('potential Maecenases', as R. R. Bolgar calls them) are said to have 'spoiled the libraries of Italy to enrich England'.[17] Let it be said here that, however great was their contribution to English scholarship, the impression they made on academic circles was very slight; and most of the imported books were lost in the troubles of the succeeding century. Nevertheless, there are unmistakable signs of a change of outlook. Poggio, writing about 1422, had complained bitterly of the absence of anything but the works of modern scholasticism in English libraries. In 1497, Erasmus drew a kinder picture of Oxford: 'There is so much erudition, not vulgar but recondite, accurate, ancient, both Latin and Greek, that you would not seek anything in Italy but the pleasure of travelling.' And in 1514, when Corpus Christi College, the first Renaissance foundation at Oxford, was established by Bishop Foxe, Erasmus was moved to extravagance once again over its *Trilinguis Bibliotheca*, its beautiful new library which, he said, would attract more students to Oxford than in times gone by had been drawn to Rome. But in a few years' time, the movement received a check from which it was slow to recover, and the term 'new learning' acquired a meaning which would have been strange to the earlier collectors.

LIBRARIES IN THE TUDOR AND STUART PERIOD

The unhappy events of 1535–50, and the endeavour of the Elizabethan antiquarians to retrieve the dispersed books, are examined in chapters viii and ix and the rebirth of the libraries at Cambridge and Oxford in chapters x and xi. Meanwhile the domestic working libraries of English scholars and writers began slowly to assume a more familiar shape and appearance. There is no record of any movable presses, designed with a view to elegance as well as utility, before the Restoration. The few large collections were probably arranged on sloping shelves, sides up, or on horizontal wall shelving, but the average domestic library was still very small, and the books would be kept in an oak chest or perhaps piled on a table. Much research is still needed on this problem, but some information can be gleaned from the changes in binding styles.[18] Bindings with elaborate designs on their sides, or with bosses or cameos, were evidently intended to lie on sloping shelves, but this must have entailed an extravagant use of the space available. As collections grew in size, volumes were arranged upright on shelves, showing only their fore-edges or spines, and seventeenth-century designs on spine and fore-edge suggest this new method of storage. Really large collections appeared earlier in France than in England; except for Dr John Dee's library there was nothing in sixteenth-century England to rival the 3000 volumes collected by Grolier, and the 8000 printed books and 1000 manuscripts of the historian Jacques de Thou far exceeded anything in this country. Montaigne, in his essay *Of three commerces*, gives a pleasant account of his own library, which was fitted with five rows of wall shelving. And it is safe to say that nobody in the England of this period had the imagination to picture anything like the abbey of the Thelemites, which Rabelais provided with 'six fair great libraries' in six several languages (which did not incidentally include English).

In 1556 Sir William More of Loseley House in Surrey drew up an inventory which reveals the contents of his library.[19] The walls were hung with maps, an almanack and a picture, but no shelving is mentioned; there was a globe and various items of writing and counting equipment. There were 140 volumes in the collection, including nearly 100 in English. This must have been a much richer collection than the average manor of the period could boast. A more typical one is perhaps revealed in the papers of the Johnson family at Glapthorn. The parlour at this manor, which was expensively furnished for the time, was provided with a single shelf of books, including a Froissart, a Bible and some devotional works.[20]

There were of course scholarly collections of larger size, such as those of the statesman and classical scholar Sir Thomas Smith (1513–77) amounting to about a thousand volumes; the larger collection made by the astrologer Dr John Dee at Mortlake, said to have included about 3000 printed books and 1000 manuscripts, which was famous enough to have drawn a visit from the queen;[21] and the finely bound collection of Thomas Wotton (1521–87), the father of Sir Henry Wotton. Izaak Walton tells us a little about the library of Richard Hooker, which was valued after his death at £1092 9s. 2d., and must therefore have been substantial; and rather more about that of John Donne, as it appeared just before his death in 1631. This included '1,400 authors, most of them abridged and analysed in his own hand', besides 'six score of his sermons and a great collection of business documents'.[22] We have a very inadequate idea however of its arrangement: there were pictures on the walls, but the books must surely have been on fixed wall shelving.

Of all the books published in this period, none suggests research in a library so forcibly as *The Anatomy of Melancholy*, in which nearly a thousand different authors are actually cited. Burton's own collection was indeed a large one, and is said to have amounted to 2000 volumes, about half of which went to the Bodleian and to Christ Church at his death. And in Bodley's library it supplied some of the pamphlets and plays carefully excluded by the founder: 'new books every day, pamphlets, currantoes, stories, whole catalogues of volumes of all sorts . . .' in Burton's own words.

But these collections were still exceptional. Doubtless there were others as large, and there were many writers who must have owned substantial libraries, though we can only imagine their size and value from the sources they used in their writings. A writer's sources and his library are not necessarily equivalent, but there was at least more likelihood of approximation then than now. Shakespeare,[23] Spenser, Sidney[24] and Milton may be taken as instructive examples in this period; but in the case of Shakespeare we have, for instance, no information as to what use he made of the library at Southampton House in Holborn, and any picture we form of his library at the New Place in Stratford must be largely guesswork.

The Commonwealth period is distinguished by the largest English collection yet recorded: that of the jurist John Selden. Over 8000 of his books reached the Bodleian after his death in 1654. As Selden was instrumental in arranging the transfer of the Lambeth library to Cambridge and perhaps also in preserving the Royal Library from dispersal by the Puritans, he must be regarded as one of the great benefactors of English libraries in the seventeenth century.

THE RESTORATION PERIOD

The use of paper in place of parchment and the invention of printing resulted in a substantial increase not only in the number of books published, but in the size of the libraries in which they were accommodated. For the first time since the Alexandrian libraries, the librarian was compelled to face the problem of quantity, with all those consequent questions of selection and arrangement and routine which constitute what we now know as library economy. This development made itself felt in France earlier than in England, where it was delayed by the political and religious changes of the sixteenth century.

The feeling that there should be a national collection of books was expressed at various times by men of vision. Dr Wright has described in chapter ix how Leland, Dee and Sir Robert Cotton were moved by this ideal. Something very similar was in the mind of Sir Humphrey Gilbert, whose plan, published in 1572, for a university of London to be known as Queen Elizabeth's Academy, included a great library under a salaried keeper, and with certain deposit rights;[25] and of Edmund Bolton, who in 1617 proposed to the king a fanciful, though intriguing, scheme for transforming Windsor Castle into an English Olympus, with a governing body which was to review and license for publication all non-theological works, to provide the vulgar people with indexes expurgatory and expunctory of all secular books, to build up a national historical collection, and to produce a history and large-scale map of London.

While Bolton was working out the elaborate details of this plan, Bacon was writing his *New Atlantis* and describing the college of scientific research which he called Solomon's House. This institution was both the island's university and its national library,[26] and some of its fellows were engaged in collecting books and abstracts for it; this is probably the first use of the term 'abstract' in its modern, technical sense. These fellows were called 'merchants of light' (which today would be translated as documentalists or information officers), and 'depredators' (which seems an unkind expression for a research librarian). Bacon's scheme served as a blue-print for the Royal Society, which was established forty years later; in 1726 Swift satirised it in the *Voyage to Laputa*.

In 1627 Gabriel Naudé published his *Avis pour dresser une bibliothèque*, the first attempt to produce a systematic textbook of library economy. Later Cardinal Mazarin appointed him to organise and establish the Mazarine library, for which he collected 40,000 books[27] from Italy, Germany, Flanders and England, having them all bound in morocco and stamped with the cardinal's arms. The library was dedicated with commendable tolerance 'to all who desired to come there to study'. He regarded the collection with some justice as the eighth wonder of the world.

Naudé's work today seems an admirably sane attempt to design a system of librarianship. Throughout he emphasises that quality in books is more important than quantity; yet, 'There is nothing which renders a Library more recommendable, than when every man findes in it that which he is in search of, and could nowhere else encounter; this being the perfect Maxime, that there is no Book whatsoever, be it never so bad or decried, but may in time be sought for by some person or other . . .' The *Avis* was translated into English by John Evelyn in 1661 for the benefit of English book collectors whose libraries were then beginning to increase rapidly in size.

Two English contributions to the subject were made in this period. In 1650 *The Reformed Library Keeper* was published by John Durie, the Protestant divine who became keeper of the Royal Library in that year; in this he put forward the ideal of a national library 'to keep the publick stock of learning, to increase it and to propose it to others in the waye which may be most helpful to all'. And in 1697, a later keeper of the Royal Library, Richard Bentley, published as a broadside his *Proposal for building a Royal Library*, in which he urged the establishment of a truly national library in a new building to be built out from St James's into St James's Park. Both Naudé's ideas and Durie's contributed something to the work of Leibnitz, who, besides being a great philosopher and mathematician, was also the greatest librarian of his age; he was the first to have a real vision of an organised, comprehensive and scholarly research library, with adequate endowments, regular acquisitions, and with the emphasis always on quality rather than on variety or cost.[28]

The period from 1660 to 1730 in England saw the rise of many famous private collections and many scholarly working libraries. The first landmark is the library of Samuel Pepys, accommodated in the independent movable presses which he had made for him in 1666–8, when (as he said) his books were growing numerous and lying one upon the other. They are the earliest examples of a type of furniture which soon became an almost universal feature of the gentleman's study. These same presses still hold his books at

Plate 1 Cambridge. No other English domestic library is more justly famed than the one collected and arranged with such loving care by Pepys; no other collector took such pains to ensure its 'unalterable preservation and perpetual security'. The library consisted of about 3000 volumes in eleven cases of carved mahogany with doors made of small panes of glass, and the lower doors con-

Plate 2 structed so as to lift up. The books were arranged in double rows, with the smaller ones in front so that all titles were visible, and some very short ones standing on stilts so as not to break the line.[29] There may have been other libraries at this time furnished with equal elegance, but information is lacking. It would for example be hard to believe that Sir Thomas Browne's library, which Evelyn saw and admired on his visit to Norwich in 1671, was anything but well-arranged and displayed.

NOTES TO CHAPTER I

1. For general studies of the progress of humanism, see R. R. Bolgar, *The Classical Heritage and its Beneficiaries*, Cambridge, 1954, and the introduction to C. S. Lewis, *English Literature in the Sixteenth Century*, Oxford, 1954.

2. For a further discussion of this topic, see the present writer's article in *The Library Association Record*, 4th ser., xxi (1954), pp. 117–21.

3. J. Z. Young, *Doubt and Certainty in Science*, Oxford, 1951.

4. See for example John Evelyn's comments on Tenison's library at St Martin's in the Fields (*Diary*, 15 Feb. 1684). Evelyn regarded St Paul's Cathedral as the proper place for a public library in London.

5. Cambridge, Pembroke College, MS 162. See also chapter iv, p. 73.

6. J. R. H. Moorman, *Church Life in England in the Thirteenth Century*, Cambridge, 1945, p. 99.

7. See also chapter vi.

8. Moorman, op. cit., quotes one case of a bishop who in a period of 296 days moved his household eighty-one times.

9. See for example J. W. Adamson, 'The Extent of Literacy in England in the 15th and 16th Centuries', *The Library*, 4th ser., x (1929–30), pp. 163–93; H. S. Bennett, 'The Production and Dissemination of Vernacular MSS in the 15th Century', *The Library*, 5th ser., i (1946), p. 175.

10. William Thorpe in 1407 said that in any batch of twenty pilgrims, less than three could repeat one of the commandments or say the Pater Noster, Ave Maria or Credo readily in any language. We can guess that most men who could at this time read at all would pass such a test. See A. W. Pollard, *Fifteenth Century Prose and Verse*, Oxford, 1903, p. 139.

11. The will of Henry le Scrope in 1415 refers to nearly eighty volumes; that of Walter Crome, rector of St Benet Shorhog, in 1452 mentions ninety-three. See C. L. Kingsford, *Prejudice and Promise in 15th Century England*, Oxford, 1925, p. 40.

12. See H. S. Bennett, *The Pastons and their England*, Cambridge, 1932, App. I.

13. W. Y. Fletcher, *English Book Collectors*, London, 1902, p. 17.

14. H. S. Bennett, *Chaucer and the Fifteenth Century*, Oxford, 1947, p. 164, suggests as a good example of this type B.M. Egerton MS 1995 (c. 1470) which in 450 pages combines some fifteen items of romance, history, medicine, etiquette and sport, together with various lists and notes for quick reference.

15. See prefatory verses in B.M. Add. MS 16165, quoted by H. S. Bennett, *Chaucer and the Fifteenth Century*, Oxford, 1947, p. 116.

16. Before the 15th century there was rarely any seating in the nave, except for a few stone benches along the walls of the aisles. The nave was then used for various secular purposes such as church ales, plays, fairs, etc., and as a warehouse for goods placed in sanctuary or received in pledge by the churchwardens.

17. See also chapter vi, below.

18. See the valuable article on this subject by Graham Pollard in *The Library*, 5th ser., xi (1956), pp. 71–94.

19. J. Evans, 'Extracts from the private account book of Sir W. More', *Archaeologia*, xxxvi (1855), pp. 284–92; H. S. Bennett, *English Books and Readers*, *1475–1557*, Cambridge, 1952, pp. xiii, xiv.

20. B. Winchester, *Tudor Family Portrait*, London, 1955, p. 113.

21. See M. R. James, *Lists of Manuscripts Formerly Owned by Dr John Dee*, Bibl. Soc., Supp. to Trans. i, 1921.

22. About 100 volumes have been identified, some in the Bodleian and others in the Middle Temple Library. See Geoffrey Keynes' *A Bibliography of Dr John Donne*, Cambridge, 1932, and John Sparrow in *Times Literary Supplement*, 29 July 1955.

23. There is a useful discussion of Shakespeare's library in *Shakespeare's England*, Oxford, 1916, i, p. 279.

24. See Lewis, *English Literature in the Sixteenth Century*, pp. 333, 355.

25. *Queene Elizabethes Achademy* (ed. F. J. Furnivall, E.E.T.S., E.S. viii, 1869), pp. 1–12.

26. It is significant that More's Utopia had nothing comparable. Raphael Hythlodaye took with him on his fourth voyage a library (a 'pretty fardel of books') consisting of Greek works, some in 'Aldus' small print'. He taught the Utopians how to make paper and how to print; they had previously used skins, bark and reeds for writing.

27. It may be noted that Bodley's library, which began with 2000 books, reached 16,000 by 1620, and in 1714 had only 30,000, with 6000 MSS.

28. See A. L. Clarke, 'Leibnitz as a Librarian', *The Library*, 3rd ser., v (1914), pp. 140–54.

29. See also chapter x, below

II

The Monastic Library

FRANCIS WORMALD

EADING was enjoined by St Benedict as one of the activities
to be practised by his monks. He says, 'Otiositas inimica est
animae; et ideo certis temporibus occupari debent fratres in
labore manuum, certis iterum horis in lectione divina', and in the
summer two hours are set apart to it as well as a further period if
the monk so wishes.[1] Indeed St Benedict's rules for reading are
quite considerable, indicating that he regarded this activity as
important for the welfare of the monk. If men are to read they
must have books. At the same time a monk must own no property. Therefore from the earliest days of monasticism there must
have been books, but books owned in common, a corporate collection. These corporate collections belonging to the ecclesiastical
institutions whether monastic or secular are the ancestors of the
monastic and cathedral libraries. It seems that the subject falls into
three main divisions. Where did they keep the books; where did
they get the books; how did they produce them themselves? It
may appear from this threefold category that the most important
item of all has been left out: what was in the libraries? This omission has been made quite purposely, for the history of the contents
of the mediaeval libraries of England would be the history of
English mediaeval learning which is a long and important subject
of its own.[2] It will be necessary sometimes to mention the general
contents of a library, but this will be all. The question of the home
production of manuscripts has been treated by Dr Ivy in the
following chapter.

To return then to the first question: where were books kept in
monasteries and religious establishments? The answer to this is
of course governed by the answer to a second question—where

were books read? In the Rule of St Benedict three kinds of reading are mentioned. First the reading at the services in choir, second the reading in the refectory at meal times, and thirdly the private reading which the monk did as part of his duty as a monk.[3] There is a fourth category which, though not mentioned by St Benedict in his Rule, must have been of some importance. This was reading done in the infirmary, a part of the abbey which was nearly always housed in special buildings of its own. It was in fact inconvenient to have books which were for use in one place kept in another. It was desirable that they should be kept somewhere near the place where they were to be used, and in practice this meant the sacristy of the church, the refectory and the library proper.

The sacristy was, and is, situated in a place both convenient for entrance to the church and as secure as possible. Some books must also have been kept permanently in the church, particularly large books such as the choir books with music which stood on great lecterns in the centre of the choir. Other books may have stood on the desks of the abbots and lesser dignitaries. It is difficult to imagine that the great missal made for Nicholas Lytlington, abbot of Westminster, in 1383-4 or the even larger Whitefriars Missal now in the British Museum (Add. MSS 29704 and 29705, etc.) can have had anything but a very permanent home. St Albans Abbey had in fact a cupboard in the choir where liturgical books were kept. A breviary, now Royal MS 2 A.x in the British Museum contains an inscription in it 'De armariolo in choro' and a psalter (British Museum Royal MS 2 B.vi) contains a similar inscription. An even more secure place was the high altar itself, and it was here and in the treasury that the most precious books were kept. This arrangement applied particularly to books which by tradition were associated with saints. Thus, in a drawing of the high altar at St Augustine's, Canterbury, preserved in a fifteenth-century manuscript of Thomas of Elmham's Chronicle[4] a number of books are labelled 'libri missi a gregorio ad Augustinum'.[5] Other books such as the Liber Vitae of Durham were kept on the altar for liturgical purposes, and there were at least two Gospel books at Glastonbury which were kept amongst the reliquaries because relics formed part of the decoration of their bindings.[6] Gospel books belonged primarily to the church or liturgical library and were kept in the sacristy or treasury. In Reading in the twelfth century two psalters were chained in the church, though the catalogue unfortunately does not tell us exactly whereabouts in the church.[7] Certain books in this liturgical category may have been kept in close proximity to the shrine of a local saint. Thus British Museum Cotton MS Tiberius B. ii, a fine copy of Abbo of Fleury's life of St Edmund, king and martyr, contains an inscription 'Liber feretrariorum' which means that it belonged to those who were in charge of the shrine of the saint. These considerations throw some light on the interesting fact that in a great number of cases books of this class did not, when the time came to give them such things, receive press-marks. They formed in fact a small sub-library of their own, and even when they do appear in book lists tend to be found in a separate category by themselves.

Besides these liturgical books there were those which were in use in the refectory. Thus at Reading there was a volume of sermons marked as being 'in refectorio', and at Bury two manuscripts, a Haymo and a Prosper, are both marked as belonging to the refectory.[8] There would also be kept in such places the lives of the saints and homilies which formed a considerable portion of the pious public reading. The books in the refectory may have belonged to the main library and have only been kept there for the sake of convenience, but they form a definite category of book. In the case of the two Bury St Edmunds manuscripts which have just been mentioned, they have both the inscription 'de refectorio', and also a press-mark which seems to indicate that books of this kind could be moved about. The books of the refectory were in fact much more closely related to the main library than the books kept for use in choir, which were in constant demand and could not be changed, in the manner in which books in use at meal-times could be changed.[9]

By far the largest collection of books in any monastery or cathedral were those which formed the general library of the community. In the great days of monasticism these were nearly always kept in the cloister. We have actually no knowledge where books were kept in the period of the Dark Ages, but on the evidence of certain lives of saints it is possible that they may have been kept in some of the cells. But as soon as the cloister became a really important centre of community life it was natural that books should not only be read but also kept there. It seems clear from the monastic customs that the cloister was the place where reading was done. The Cluniac Customs refer to the brethren reading there and it was of course the general meeting-place of the community. The growth of private rooms is a later development. The portion of the cloister which was most usually employed for reading was the walk which lay nearest the side of the great church. It will not be out of place to quote here the famous description of the cloister at Durham found in the *Rites of Durham*:

In the north syde of the Cloister, from the corner over against the church dour to the corner over againste the Dorter dour was all fynely glased, from the hight to the sole within a litle of the growhd into the Cloister garth. And in every wyndowe iii Pewes or Carrells, where everyone of the old Monks had his carrell, severall by himselfe, that when they had dyned, they dyd resorte to that place of Cloister, and there studyed upon there books, every one in his carrell, all the afternonne, unto evensong tyme. This was there exercise every day. All there pewes and carrells was all fynely wainscotted and verrie close, all but the forepart, which had carved-wourke that gave light in at their carrell doures of wainscott. And in every carrell was a deske to lye there books on. And the carrells was no greater from one stanchell of the window to another. And over against the carrell against the church wall did stand sertain great almeries or cupboards of waynscott all full of Bookes, wherein did lie as well the old ancient written Doctors of the Church as other prophane authors, with dyverse other holy mens wourks, so that everyone dyd studye what Doctor pleased them best, having the Librarie at all times to go
Plate 3   studie in besydes there carrells.[10]

Cloister garth = the open court enclosed by a cloister; wainscott = panelling; stanchell = stanchion, an upright bar between the mullions of a window.

To this long description there should be added a rather shorter extract from the Customs of St Augustine's, Canterbury, made at the beginning of the fourteenth century. This says that the precentor shall have his seat in front of the cupboard in the cloister and his carrell nearby. The succentor shall have his seat and carrell on the bench near the cupboard so that both or one of them shall be at hand ready to answer any questions that the brethren may put to them. If the information given by these two passages is

combined, we find an efficient library system in operation including not only proper book storage, but also comfort for the readers
as well as the necessary arrangements for their supervision. These
passages do in fact supply us with most valuable indications as to
the general arrangement of the monastic libraries before the provision of special rooms for library purposes, which is a late development unknown in England in the twelfth century.[11]

As has already been said the normal place for keeping the books
was on the side of the cloister nearest the church. This was
normally the warmest place in the monastery where the brethren
could sit and do their reading. Books were also frequently kept in
the east walk of the cloister on the side nearest the church. The
arrangements at Westminster Abbey, as far as they may be de-
duced from the surviving structure, provide interesting and easily
accessible evidence. If you walk down the north walk of the
cloister you notice that the stone bench which runs round the
whole cloister has been cut away towards the east end of the walk,
and again in the east walk in the bay which stands nearest to the
north-east entrance to the church, the wall-arcade instead of being
brought down by shafts which come down to the bench is stopped
short with corbels.[12] Both these arrangements seem to indicate
that there were large cupboards or Almeries set up against the
wall. Such an arrangement would be similar to those found at
Durham, and the Customs of St Augustine's, Canterbury, and
Westminster Abbey were intimately related to each other. Other
monasteries also used this system, for we occasionally find noted
in books such phrases as 'De Armario claustri' or 'De claustro', as
in the case of certain manuscripts from Bury St Edmunds. An
extension of this kind of arrangement may be inferred from the
manuscripts from Waltham Abbey in Essex. Here there are
fourteenth-century notes which not only mention the press-mark,
but also the particular cupboard to which they belong, namely,
'almarium canonicorum', 'almarium prioris' and 'almarium sup-
prioris'.[13] Whether these last two categories were really reserved
for the prior and sub-prior is not clear. It is possible that originally
they may have been so designated.

In certain monasteries the books were kept in a store which
stood on the east side of the cloister between the church and the

Plate 4a   chapter house door. It is interesting to notice that this is very nearly
the same position as was occupied by the large cupboard which
stood in the cloister of Westminster Abbey. The practice has been
found in a number of Cistercian houses, and a description of the
arrangements at Meaux in Yorkshire still exists.[14] In this case the
room, for it certainly was a room, was called the 'commune
almarium claustri' and presumably took the place of a whole
series of cupboards in the cloister. The actual description of the
Meaux arrangements was made in the fifteenth century, so that
they may not be of primitive origin. The remains of a similar
room at Kirkstall Abbey, also in Yorkshire, indicate, however,
that it was a practice already in existence in the twelfth century,
and there are other examples from the continent.[15] What is important to remember is that these rooms were book stores and not
libraries where books were studied. If anyone wished to read a
book the proper place to do it was the cloister and this was and
remained so, particularly in such houses as Westminster Abbey,
Gloucester and Durham, where the carrell system was in operation. A separate room devoted to study is a very late arrangement,
and even when it was introduced it is interesting to observe the
influence of earlier practice. For instance, when Prior Wessyngton built a library at Durham in about 1446 its position was between the chapter house and the south transept. At Gloucester
there was the same arrangement. At Lincoln, Salisbury, St Paul's,
London, and Wells, all secular cathedrals, the library was built
over the eastern part of the cloister. In all these instances there is
an obvious conservatism of design to be seen, the libraries being
put up over the place where the 'commune armariolum' often
stood or immediately above the book room. It should, however,
be remembered that these libraries are usually not earlier than the
fifteenth century.

It appears that the precentor of an abbey was normally in charge
of the library, though in the case of the nuns of Barking there was
a librarian.[16] At St Augustine's, Canterbury, as we have already
seen, he was assisted by the succentor. The choice of the precentor
is by no means surprising, for he was normally placed in charge of
the music and the arrangements for the services. This would mean
that it was his business to see that the service books were in good

condition and kept properly. He would also have to replace them when they became worn out. Thus, he would naturally be connected with the scriptorium and with the library. In a very large monastery it is possible that his place was taken by a deputy, but normally he must have had a good deal to do with the library, and it may be presumed that he supervised the lending of books.

In all monasteries on the first Monday in Lent there took place the solemn distribution of books in the chapter house. Certain books were given out to all the monks for their reading during the year.[17] Many descriptions of this ceremony exist. The Constitutions of Lanfranc, the Customary of Norwich and the Customary of St Augustine's, Canterbury, all refer to it. The Customary of Barking has a particularly good account.

After Terce on the first Monday in Lent the librarian shall spread a carpet in the middle of the chapter house and place on it the books from the cupboard, and at a sign from the abbess she shall rise and sitting in the middle of the chapter house shall read out in the lists and indicate which person had which book in the past year. The reader should read slowly so that between each name there may be a pause until she who has been named shall return the book. When anyone shall hear her name called out she shall rise at once and bring her book to the carpet and if she has read the whole work she shall bow to the cross and retire. Those who have not read through their book shall prostrate themselves before the abbess and ask her pardon.[18]

Perhaps the most valuable account of all is to be found in the Customs of the Augustinian Canons of Barnwell dating from the end of the thirteenth century. Here the librarian was also the precentor and his duties are very carefully set out. Amongst other things it is clear that at Barnwell there was a very careful system of registering the books taken out by the brethren. The passage reads as follows:

He [the librarian] ought also to hand to the brethren the books which they see occasion to use, and to enter on his roll the titles of the books and the names of those who receive them. These when required are bound to give surety for the volumes they receive; nor may they lend them to others whether known or unknown, without having first

C

obtained permission from the librarian. Nor ought the librarian to lend books, unless he receive a pledge of equal value.[19]

It will perhaps be well to sum up what we have found out so far. The books were read and kept in three places—the church, the frater (refectory) and the cloister. By far the most usual arrangement was for the books to be kept in cupboards in the cloister, particularly on the side nearest the church. If other accommodation was necessary, it appears that rooms off the cloister were used as *Plate 4b* book stores and not as libraries. If the monks were to have any special place to work it would be in the carrells in the cloister. This arrangement must have remained in use at any rate until the fifteenth century when libraries in the more modern sense begin to appear. The books themselves were placed in cupboards, which, according to the Barnwell Customs, ought to be lined inside with wood, so that the walls might not moisten or stain the books. These presses, the Customs continue, should be divided vertically as well as horizontally by sundry shelves on which the books may be ranged so as to be separated from one another; for fear they be packed so close as to injure each other or delay those who want them.

How far all these requirements were carried out in all monastic houses it is quite impossible to say, but probably in most there was a press for what books they had and there was some arrangement for their surveillance, which as we have seen was usually in the hands of the precentor. In connection with this it is well to remember that, by comparison with modern standards, a mediaeval library was small. In the great library of Christ Church, Canterbury, in the fourteenth century there were probably thirteen hundred volumes, which could be kept in a comparatively few cupboards. Numbers such as this one, are of course most misleading, on account of the mediaeval habit of binding several works between two covers. A book list of a mediaeval house is often a very deceptive document, since frequently only the first item in the volume was noted. This leads us to consider the question of the mediaeval press-marks and book lists.

From quite early times it had been the custom for librarians to insert on the fly-leaves of books the *ex libris* of the particular monastery to which the book belonged.[20] This was sometimes accompanied by a note of where it came from. Thus, in the books presented by Æthelstan to a number of monasteries there will be found a note at the beginning recording the fact.[21] I cannot recall ever having seen a real English *ex libris* dating from before the twelfth century, since the Æthelstan notes are perhaps in a class by themselves, the books being royal presents and, therefore, probably not designed for the ordinary library of the monastery. On the other hand from the twelfth century onwards it became increasingly common to record the ownership of the book. Sometimes the contents of the volume are also written at the beginning,[22] but in English manuscripts at any rate we do not encounter press-marks until the thirteenth century, though there is one case of marking books in the twelfth century.

At Christ Church, Canterbury, the books acquired before the middle of the twelfth century were marked with a series of small letters or symbols, which Dr James found to coincide with an early book list of the house still in existence today in the University Library at Cambridge.[23] Each book appears to have been marked on the recto of the first leaf with a small symbol which looks rather like the letters and symbols which are found in manuscripts and refer the reader from the main text to the commentaries in the margin. These letters and symbols cannot, I think, be called press-marks. They are much rather the marks which enabled anyone with the list to verify a particular manuscript. One wonders whether these marks were not noted down by the librarian on his borrowing list. The same consideration applies to many so-called press-marks which are normally marks enabling a book to be found in or from a catalogue. The placing of these press-marks is late and belongs to the fourteenth century rather than the thirteenth. This practice seems to go with the beginning of the setting apart of special rooms for the keeping of books and also with the appearance of much more systematic catalogues. The old habit of giving the note of ownership on the fly-leaf still continued, and this was combined with the press-mark or the press-mark was added to it. Usually there are two marks, a letter of the alphabet followed by a numeral. At St Augustine's, Canterbury, the arrangement is indicated in a slightly different manner. The library was divided into a series of *distinctiones*, these being in some way determined by the subject, and indicated by a numeral preceded by the letters *Di*. There may have been separate cupboards for each *distinctio*, but it is improbable, as some *distinctiones* were quite small. The *distinctiones* were subdivided into *gradus* to which was also attached a number. Each monastery or library used its own system, though occasionally the systems are extraordinarily similar and we have to be careful to see that the right kind of book is in the right *distinctio* for any given house.[24]

It is not at all easy to say which monasteries had the best organised libraries. As we have already seen, the two monasteries of Christ Church and St Augustine's, Canterbury, had very important collections. That at St Augustine's must have been particularly interesting because it had the most continuous existence of all the houses. On the other hand the surviving catalogues indicate that there were large collections in other places. So we come then to the question of catalogues of the monastic libraries. The earliest that we have from England date from the twelfth century, but they are very unlike the modern catalogue and might be more correctly termed book lists. These are nevertheless the ancestors of our catalogues. The earliest ones are by no means always found as separate documents. They are quite frequently found written on the fly-leaves of books. The mid-twelfth-century catalogue from Rochester is written into the Textus Roffensis, and the rather later list of the Reading Abbey books is written in the Chartulary amongst the copies of charters and the relic list.[25] It is in fact an inventory of possessions rather than a catalogue which could assist anyone to use the library. Anyone who wanted to find a particular work from this list would have some difficulty in so doing, since the books are given neither distinctive mark nor name. On the other hand the Canterbury list of about 1170 does give some help by the addition of the distinctive marks which have been mentioned before. Nevertheless these early lists do show that there was some classification of the books by means of their contents, though at the end they sometimes wander off into irrelevancies. The catalogues nearly always begin with bibles, particularly the glossed books which were so popular in the twelfth century. These were usually followed by the works of the Fathers, headed normally by St Augustine, and then, with a greater degree of variation, subjects such as philosophy, law, grammar. Medicine normally came at the end. It was also customary to complete a catalogue by including the various donations the library had received, arranged under the name of the donor. The library catalogue therefore very often presented the form of a shelf-list which continued as a list of benefactions. The discovery of a rare volume would be a hard task, unless one had some idea of the kind of subject. If one knew this, it might be possible in a well-regulated establishment to discover the book, since within their subject headings, volumes were occasionally arranged in a rough alphabetical order.

Catalogues of the mediaeval collections are on the whole rare, though catalogues do exist for a number of very important libraries. There are, for instance, catalogues of St Augustine's and Christ Church, Canterbury, Durham and Glastonbury.[26] On the other hand little is known of the library of such an important monastery as Malmesbury which must have contained many treasures. Two most important catalogues are those of Lanthony and Titchfield, both Augustinian houses.[27] The former was made in the middle of the fourteenth century, the latter in 1400. The Lanthony library consisted of five armaria, each of these being divided into a number of *gradus*. Three out of the four armaria were concerned with biblical matters, the Fathers and theology. The fourth cupboard contained law, philosophy, grammar and mathematics, while the fifth, which consisted of only one *gradus*, was probably devoted to large volumes though some small ones are noted in it. The Lanthony catalogue gives no indication of the press-mark, though it occasionally makes some comment on the condition of the book or whether it is bound or in a wrapper.[28] *Plate 5* The Titchfield catalogue is much more precise, and not only provides an invaluable introduction setting out the arrangement of the library, but gives a brief guide as to which cupboards contain what kind of book. The Titchfield library was apparently housed in a book room in four cupboards or *columpna* which were subdivided into *gradus*, or shelves. These shelves were given a letter, and, if the subject indicated by that letter extended to more than one shelf it was given a number as well. The books themselves

were also marked with a letter and a number, both on the outside
and on their first folio. The Titchfield catalogue, unlike the earlier
book lists, not only mentions the press-mark, but also gives all the
contents of the particular volume. This is indeed something of an
advance. The most marked advance is found in the rather earlier
catalogue of Dover Priory, a daughter house of Christ Church,
Canterbury, made in 1389.[29] This contains extremely important
additions to the information given in either the Titchfield or
Lanthony catalogues. It is in fact a much more complete affair.
It was made by John Whytefield, who was probably precentor,
and his introduction is well worth quoting from. He explains how
the catalogue is separated into three divisions: 'The object is that
the first part may supply information to the precentor of the house
concerning the number of the books and the complete knowledge
of them: that the second part may stir up studious brethren to
eager and frequent reading: and the third may point out the way
to the speedy finding of individual treatises by the scholars.' Part
one contains a list of volumes for each of which it gives its title,
the folio selected for quotation of the opening words for the purposes of identification, the number of leaves and the number of
tracts. Part two contains the shelf list but, if a book contained more
than one item each other item was mentioned as well, its incipit
given and the number and side of the leaf on which each tract
begins. Part three contains an alphabetical list of all the works in
the library. Dr James who edited it says 'In the elaborate, I might
say tender care which has been exercised in its compilation, it
stands alone among medieval catalogues.'[30] What is, however, so
significant is its modernity. You have everything—shelf list, list
of contents and finally the author catalogue. It is a great change
from the rather perfunctory book-lists of earlier days. The catalogue of the Bridgettines of Syon made early in the sixteenth century is somewhat similar to the first part of the Dover catalogue.
That is to say it gives the press-mark, the contents, the second
folio and also—something the Dover catalogue does not give—
the name of the donor.[31]

Where did they get their books from? It is a quite mistaken idea
that the monastic library was supplied with books from the
scriptorium alone. Throughout the history of the English libraries

there must have been a trickle of incoming books in the form of gifts and later on of purchases. As early as the seventh century Benedict Biscop bought books abroad and, with these and others which he had been given, enriched the libraries of the English monasteries. In the tenth century when the revival of monasticism came under Dunstan and Ethelwold, there must have been many books brought into England. One of these (B.M. Cotton MS Claudius B.v) is a copy of the acts of the sixth general council of 680 which was presented by King Æthelstan to the abbey of Bath. It was certainly written abroad and may well have been a present to the king by some foreigner. When an abbey was founded, or an episcopal see reformed, a nucleus of books was brought from outside. For instance, when in 1050, owing to damage wrought by pirates, Leofric, bishop of Crediton, removed his see into St Peter's church at Exeter and established canons there who were to live under the rule of Chrodegang of Metz, he endowed the canons with a library. We are fortunate in possessing not only the list of the books he gave, but a number of the books themselves, some of them containing a note recording Leofric's gift.[32] Certain of them were quite naturally for use at the church services and would thus supply the nucleus of the liturgical side of the library. Besides these there were a number of books which we might expect to find in the more general library including works of St Gregory, Prudentius, a Sedulius and, above all, the great collection of English poetry, the Exeter Book, which is one of the glories of Exeter Cathedral to this day. That there was need of such a benefaction is unquestionable, since in the note recording these gifts there is the following sentence: 'And he found no more books when he came to the minster but one capitulary, an old portable breviary, an epistle book and an old lectionary in poor condition.'[33] It will be noted that these are all liturgical books. There is no sign of a general library. Leofric's gifts in this direction were obviously meant to fill an important gap. What we know of the Leofric manuscripts indicates that for the most part they were older books and not written specially for the new library. For instance, the Leofric Missal, in the Bodleian is a continental sacramentary of the early tenth century brought probably to Glastonbury, where a calendar and some compotus tables had been added in about 970. An

Amalarius in Trinity College, Cambridge, was written in England about 970, but both the Exeter Book and the Bede on the Apocalypse now at Lambeth Palace, similar in script, are rather later, though still about fifty years earlier than the date of their donation to Exeter. These donations may well have come from different sources. It seems clear that the manuscripts given by William of Saint Carilef to his library at Durham were of very miscellaneous origin.[34] Some of them, amongst them the Carilef Bible, were Norman productions, but others seem equally certainly to have been made at Canterbury.[35] How the founders of libraries got hold of their books is not clear, but in some cases it looks as if a round-robin may have been circulated asking for contributions. There is in the British Museum (Add. MS 48984) a late twelfth-century copy of the homilies of St Gregory which has at the beginning the following inscription written in large letters: 'In the year of Our Lord 1248 the lord abbot and convent of Caerleon gave this book to the convent of Hailes at the urgent request [the word used is *instantia*] of the Lord Richard earl of Cornwall, the gracious founder of that house, and brother of King Henry III of England.' Hailes had been founded in 1246 and from the inscription it looks as if other Cistercian houses had been asked to contribute something to start off the library of the new abbey.

Plate 6a

Throughout the history of the monastic and cathedral libraries gifts of books were constantly being made and anyone who has looked at one of the surviving mediaeval catalogues will have noticed how often the names of benefactors are mentioned. This fact has already been referred to in connection with the Syon catalogue, but Eastry's catalogue of the Christ Church, Canterbury, books has a very considerable portion of it arranged under donors, beginning with no less a person than Thomas Becket himself. Sometimes an entry excites our curiosity. For instance, it would be interesting to know something of Ralph, priest of Whitchurch, who presented to Reading Abbey the *Bucolics* and *Georgics* of Virgil, the *Odes*, *Art of Poetry*, *Sermones* and *Epistolae* of Horace and a Juvenal.[36]

It is less easy to discover much about the purchases of manuscripts in the later Middle Ages, but a good deal of buying must have gone on, since in some cases moneys were set aside for the library. Sometimes the monastic accounts of a house give us some indication. In the fourteenth-century accounts of Bolton Abbey there are references to purchases of books, including amongst other things the purchase of a *Liber Chronicorum* in York.[37] Manuscripts themselves sometimes contain their prices, but what these notations represent cannot always be determined. Exchanges too between houses may well have been frequent, particularly when the system of pledging came into full operation.

NOTES TO CHAPTER II

1. *S. Benedicti Regula Monachorum*, c. xlviii (ed. P. Schmitz and C. Mohrmann, Maredsous, 1955, p. 109).

2. See chapters v and vii.

3. For reading at church offices see *S. Benedicti Regula Monachorum*, cc. viii–xx, for the refectory c. xxxviii. Service books were probably set aside for sick monks, see amongst the Bury St Edmunds books 'Breuiarium ad infirmos'; M. R. James, *On the Abbey of Bury St. Edmunds* (Cambridge Antiq. Soc. Octavo Publications no. xxviii, Cambridge, 1895), p. 33.

4. At Trinity Hall, Cambridge.

5. Reproduced in Dugdale, *Monasticon Anglicanum*, ed. J. Cayley, H. Ellis and B. Bandinel, i, 1846, betw. pp. 120, 121.

6. See B.M. Cotton MS Titus D. vii, f. 9b.

7. See the Reading book-list, 'Item IIII cathenata, duo in ecclesia, duo in infirmaria', see *Eng. Hist. Rev.*, iii (1888), p. 122.

8. B.M. Egerton MS 2782, and Wisbech Museum.

9. M. R. James, op. cit., pp. 111, 112. Cambridge, St John's College, MS B. 13, St Gregory, *In Ezechielem*, is noted 'de refectorio monachorum sancti edmundi'. New York, Pierpont Morgan Library MS 823, is part of a bible which once stood in the refectory of the Augustinians of Taunton.

10. See *The Rites and Monuments of the Cathedral Church of Durham* (ed. J. Raine, Surtees Soc., xv, 1842), pp. 70, 71. It is clear that the books in Durham were kept in a number of places. The main collections were in the cloister and in the spendement, and after the 15th century in Prior Wessyngton's library which was upstairs between the south transept and the chapter house, see H. D. Hughes, *A History of Durham Cathedral Library*, Durham, 1925, pp. 1–6.

11. See *The Customary of the Benedictine Monasteries of St Augustine's Canterbury and St Peter Westminster* (ed. E. Maude Thompson, Hen. Bradshaw Soc., xxiii, 1902), ii, pp. 202, 203.

12. See J. W. Clark, *The Care of Books*, Cambridge, 1901, pp. 92, 93. The bookcupboards at Lanercost Priory and Tintern Abbey were in the same position.

13. See M. R. James, 'MSS. from Essex Monastic Libraries', *Trans. Essex Arch. Soc.*, n.s., xxi (1933), pp. 38–41; also N. R. Ker, 'More MSS. from Essex Monastic Libraries', *Trans. Essex Arch. Soc.*, n.s., xxiii (1945), pp. 299, 300.

14. *Chronica Monasterii de Melsa* (ed. E. A. Bond, Rolls Ser., 43, London, 1868), iii, pp. lxxxiii–c. The Meaux catalogue has the following divisions: (1) 'Pro magno altari'; (2) 'in choro'; (3) 'in capella infirmitorii'; (4) 'in communi almario

in ecclesia'; (5) 'in aliis almariis officii cantoris in ecclesia'; and finally (6) the main collection 'in communi almario claustri'.

15. See Clark, *The Care of Books*, p. 107.

16. *The Ordinale and Customary of the Benedictine Nuns of Barking Abbey* (ed. J. B. L. Tolhurst, Hen. Bradshaw Soc., lxv, 1927), i, pp. 67, 68.

17. For an interesting account of the origin of this practice see A. Mundó, 'Bibliotheca: Bible et Lecture du Carême d'après Saint Benoit', *Revue Bénédictine*, lx (1950), pp. 65–92.

18. Barking Ordinale, loc. cit.

19. *The Observances in use at the Augustinian Priory of Barnwell, Cambridgeshire*, ed. J. W. Clark, Cambridge, 1897, pp. 62, 63.

20. A very early, 7th-century, example from Bobbio may be seen in Milan, Ambrosiana s. 45. sup., see E. A. Lowe, *Codices Latini Antiquiores*, iii, Oxford, 1938, no. 365 with a reproduction.

21. For Æthelstan's gifts see J. Armitage Robinson, *The Times of St. Dunstan*, Oxford, 1923, pp. 51–71.

22. e.g. St Albans, see Oxford, Bodleian Library, Bodl. MS 752, f. iib and B.M. Harley MS 865.

23. Cambridge, University Library, MS Ii. 3. 12; see M. R. James, *The Ancient Libraries of Canterbury and Dover*, Cambridge, 1903, pp. xxxi–xxxv. The fragment of the catalogue with symbols is reproduced on pp. 3–6.

24. For valuable cautions see particularly N. R. Ker, *Medieval Libraries of Great Britain*, London, 1941, pp. xviii, xix. For facsimiles of some English monastic press-marks, see New Palaeog. Soc., *Facsimiles of Ancient MSS, etc.* 1st ser., pls. 17, 147.

25. For the Textus Roffensis list see *Archaeologia Cantiana*, vi (1866), pp. 120–8. The Reading list in B.M. Egerton MS 3031 is printed in *Eng. Hist. Rev.*, iii (1888), pp. 117–25.

26. The most reliable indication of the surviving catalogues and book-lists is to be found under the various houses in N. R. Ker, ibid., passim.

27. The Lanthony catalogue dating from the 14th century is in B.M. Harley MS 460. The Titchfield catalogue, made in 1400, is preserved in a MS (I. A. 1) belonging to the duke of Portland. It has been admirably edited by R. M. Wilson, 'The Medieval Library of Titchfield Abbey', *Proc. Leeds Philos. Lit. Soc.*, v (1940), pp. 150–77, 252–76. Pages are reproduced in the New Paleog. Soc., op. cit., pl. 18, and *A Catalogue of Letters, etc., Exhibited in the Library at Welbeck*, ed. S. A. Strong, London, 1903, opp. p. 2.

28. The notes in the Lanthony catalogue are in some ways confusing. Some books are called 'ligatus'; one 'cum rubeo pelle' (f. 6b); another 'coopertus cum rubeo pelle' (f. 6b). Many entries have the word 'quaternus' written after them. This presumably distinguishes them from those labelled 'ligatus', and may indicate some kind of loose wrapper or limp vellum cover. That it refers to some kind of cover seems clear, see f. 4b, 'Quaternus rubeus', f. 4b, 'quaternus niger'; f. 6b, 'quaternus simplex'; f. 7, 'utilis quaternus'; f. 11, 'quaternus parvus'. On the other hand on f. 8 is 'quaternus ligatus'. On f. 9 the entry 'Glose super preciani de constructione quaterni duo' presumably indicates just two unbound gatherings.

29. James, *The Ancient Libraries of Canterbury and Dover*, pp. 406–95. The original MS is in Oxford, Bodleian Library, Bodl. MS 920.

30. ibid., p. xci.

31. Mary Bateson, *Catalogue of the Library of Syon Monastery, Isleworth*, Cambridge, 1898.

32. See Max Foerster, *The Exeter Book of Old English Poetry*, London, 1933, pp. 28, 29.

33. loc. cit., p. 28 and n. 89 on pp. 26, 27.

34. See Otto Pächt, 'Hugo Pictor', *Bodl. Lib. Rec.*, iii (1950), pp. 96–103.

35. For the Norman relations of the Carilef Bible, see H. Swarzenski, 'Der Stil der Bibel Carilefs von Durham', *Form und Inhalt: Festschrift für Otto Schmidt*, Stuttgart, 1950, pp. 89–95. Durham Cathedral MSS B. 11, 10 and B. 11, 22 are on the other hand quite certainly English, see R. A. B. Mynors, *Durham Cathedral Manuscripts to the End of the Twelfth Century*, Oxford, 1939, pls. 22, 26. MS B. 11. 10 has great likenesses to Canterbury MSS.

36. B.M. Egerton MS 3031, f. 10b, see *Eng. Hist. Rev.*, iii (1888), p. 123.

37. Chatsworth, Collection of the duke of Devonshire, Bolton Abbey Accounts, f. 119b 'Pro constitucionibus scribendis, iiii^s' [1306]; f. 206b 'Pro uno libro qui vocatur veritates theologie, vi^s' [1310]; f. 294b 'Pro Croniclis apud Eboracum scribendis, ii^s' [1312–1313].

III

The Bibliography of the Manuscript-Book

G. S. IVY

THIS is an attempt to give a general account, so far as that is possible, of how the mediaeval manuscript-book was produced and of those features which distinguish it from a book in print. Neither *manuscript*, meaning only a text or document written by hand, nor *book*, derived from a Germanic word of uncertain connotation, are terms of precise definition. Until towards the close of the Middle Ages, all texts and documents were written by hand and the Middle English word, *boke*, was applied to almost any one of them without considering format. The manuscript-format, which will be discussed here, is that represented by the *codex*, in earlier classical times denoting wooden tablets, covered with wax and normally used for short ephemeral records. *Liber*, meaning literally the bark of a tree, originally denoted a roll, as did *volumen* or volume.[1] Rolls, made of membrane or papyrus, were used in classical times for permanent records, including literary texts. However, before the advent of monasticism in the sixth century A.D., the codex-format, now constituted of membrane, was being used for certain types of text previously monopolised by the roll.[2] But the ancient descriptive terms were retained, despite the changes which had occurred in the objects they designated: throughout the mediaeval period, *liber* and *volumen* were frequently applied to books of membrane in codex-form and *rotulus*, a relatively late coinage, became the word for a roll.[3] The Patent Rolls and King's Remembrancer Memoranda Rolls are still kept, today, in roll-form,[4] as were the majority of private, as well as public, records in England during the Middle Ages. We sometimes find mediaeval rolls containing literary texts, including English verse.[5] But the mediaeval roll is not suited to texts of any considerable length, since the writing is usually parallel to its breadth and a reader would therefore find a long roll difficult to manipulate. In ancient rolls, before the codex became fashionable, the writing ran parallel to the length of the roll, in columns the breadth of which was a matter of taste. The reader held the roll upright, unrolled it with his right hand and rolled it up in the reverse direction with his left.[6] Hence the word *explicit* with which mediaeval scribes sometimes conclude their texts, even though they happen to be writing in codices. The roll, besides containing half as much as a codex since its text was written on only one side of the material, had the additional disadvantage that it had to be re-rolled before it could be read a second time.

In the Middle Ages, anyone who had extensive dealings with books would have been familiar with the several processes involved in their manufacture. These processes varied according to locality and date. But their general outlines remained constant from the time of the gradual adoption of book-making by monks, in the sixth and seventh centuries, until the superseding of the manuscript by the printed book. In the early sixth-century Rule of St Benedict, the brethren are merely enjoined to read holy books, when not otherwise occupied.[7] But the reformed Benedictines of the tenth to the twelfth centuries manifest a fervent attitude to books, and from these later times we obtain explicit statements about book-production, delivered in a manner that shows how closely this occupation had become identified with the monastic ideal itself. Such statements are sometimes in the form of an extended metaphor and offer concise information, not only about the processes of book-production, but also about the order in which they were undertaken. The following is a translation by R. A. B. Mynors from a Latin sermon added, in a twelfth-century hand, to Durham Cathedral MS B. IV. 12, f. 37 sqq.:

Let us consider then how we may become scribes of the Lord. The parchment on which we write for him is a pure conscience, whereon all our good works are noted by the pen of memory, and make us acceptable to God. The knife wherewith it is scraped is the fear of God, which removes from our conscience by repentance all the roughness and unevenness of sin and vice. The pumice wherewith it is made smooth is

the discipline of heavenly desires . . . The chalk with whose fine particles
it is whitened indicates the unbroken meditation of holy thoughts.
The ruler [regula] by which the line is drawn that we may write straight,
is the will of God . . . The tool [instrumentum] that is drawn along the
ruler to make the line, is our devotion to our holy task . . . The pen
[penna], divided in two that it may be fit for writing, is the love of God
and our neighbour . . . The ink with which we write is humility itself
. . . The diverse colours wherewith the book is illuminated, not un-
worthily represent the grace of heavenly Wisdom . . . The desk [scrip-
torium] whereon we write is tranquillity of heart . . . The copy
[exemplar] by which we write is the life of our Redeemer . . . The
place where we write is contempt of worldly things.[8]

The stages of book-production may be grouped under three main
heads: first, the materials of mediaeval books; secondly, the quire,
its construction and peculiarities; lastly, the manner of filling
the pages. Binding will not be dealt with directly because, as will
be shown, mediaeval books were normally written unbound. It is
not surprising that the above-quoted metaphor makes no mention
of the covers of books, since binding was neither an integral part,
nor a necessary consequence, of mediaeval book-production.

Before 1400, the leaves of manuscripts made in England were
almost invariably different types of membrane, chiefly sheep-skin
or calf-skin. At one time it was fashionable for cataloguers to distinguish sheep-skin, or parchment, from calf-skin, or vellum, and
they were sometimes distinguished in mediaeval times, but an
experiment with skins from British Museum manuscripts has
shown that scientific accuracy on this point is not usually attain-
able.[9] A skin consists of several layers: the *epidermis*, or thin outer
layer, and then the *dermis*, which is constituted of grain membrane,
papillary layer and reticular layer, in that order. To know with
relative certainty what type of animal any particular skin is derived from, at least the papillary layer, containing glands and fat
cells characteristic of the several animal species, must be intact. But
the leaves of mediaeval membrane books were usually so tho-
roughly scraped when they were being converted from skins, particularly in the thirteenth century, that only the reticular layer
remains.[10] Identification of the animal species must therefore be
made by other means, such as the size and type of book and the

locality and manner in which its leaves were prepared. Vellum was more expensive than sheep-skin, could be obtained in larger sizes and stood up to more severe handling; it was used for fine productions of large books. Uterine vellum was the skin of still-born calves and was regarded as the finest writing-material that could be obtained. The very small bibles of the thirteenth century, written on exceedingly thin leaves, are thought to have been made of this material.[11] In Southern Europe, particularly in Italy, goat-skins were frequently used. The preparation of these and of sheep-skin differed, in one respect, from that of calf-skin. Leo Santifaller asserts that, in Northern Europe, writing-material was most frequently made out of calf-skin, which was shaved and smoothed on both sides, so that all the pages look almost alike: in Southern Europe, sheep-skin and goat-skin were employed and the inner or flesh-side of a skin was more carefully prepared than the outer or hair-side.[12] Recipes, or receipts as they are called, for making sheets of writing-material out of skins are numerous in later mediaeval manuscripts.[13] The following has not, to my knowledge, been printed before. It occurs in Trinity College, Cambridge, MS R. 14. 45, part V, f. 30, in a hand of the fifteenth century. It distinguishes between parchment and vellum and emphasises the above-mentioned difference in their preparation:

Forto make Parchemyne

Forto make *parchemyne* gode and ffyne Take þe a schepis skynne ⁊ caste hit inne lyme & wat*er* & late hit ligge ix dayes þer inne þanne take hit vp ⁊ streyne hit a brode on a harowe made for þe nonys þanne take suche a fleyssyng knyf as þis *parchemyners* vse & chaufe a wey þe flesshe on þe flesshe side ⁊ euermore loke þat þov have pouder of chalk inne þi handys forto casten on þe skyn so þat hit mowe alle wey ren*n*en a dovne be forne þe knyfe þan set houte þy*n* skynne on þe harowe forto drye þan*n*e whan*n*e hit is drye schave hit efte sonys on þe flesch*e* syde vntil hit be al smothe & þanne take þy*n* knyfe & kit hit of ⁊ rolle hit to geders

To make Velyme

And if þov wille make velyme Take þe a kalwes skynne and do þer with inne þe same maner as þov dedist wiþ þi schepis skynne save for þe her þat is on þe kalwes skynne þe nedis most schave hit on bothe sydys ⁊ a schepis skynne schal be shaven but on þe flesshe syde and alle wey loke þat wolle of þi*n* skynne be offe or hit come in þe lyme

From these and other receipts, it appears that the suppleness of the best mediaeval writing-material was due to a prolonged soaking in water and lime, the lime making the skins easier to pluck. Its thinness was partly due to stretching on a special type of frame, partly to scraping. For the latter, a semi-circular knife called a *lunellarium* was used, the blade pressing the skin into a small arc at each stroke and squeezing out the moisture. Unevenness was removed by scouring the flesh-side with pumice, after an additional light moistening, which was sometimes obtained by squirting the skin with a mouthful of good ale.[14] Whiteness would be imparted to the skin, if necessary, by rubbing it liberally with powdered chalk; a process known as pouncing.

Paper was introduced into England from France and Italy before 1300, but, so far as is known, its first use for writing in England was for the Red-Book of Bishop's Lynn, now King's Lynn, in Norfolk, which was begun in 1307–8 and contains copies of wills approved in the hustings court, etc.[15] Another early paper book, a register of the hustings court of Lyme Regis, Dorset, was begun in 1309.[16] But paper was not manufactured in this country until 1494, when John Tate set up a mill at Steyenage in Hertfordshire, and imported paper was not widely used for manuscript-books before 1400. Out of a group of eighty-two manuscripts, made in England, but of varying provenance and written between 1175 and about 1525, 63·5 per cent are membrane, 24·5 per cent are paper and 12 per cent are membrane and paper mixed; those manuscripts formed of paper wholly or in part are all later than 1400. Even after 1400, paper is not common in mediaeval English manuscripts. Of the eighty-three *Canterbury Tales* manuscripts, all written after 1400, 61 per cent are membrane, 34 per cent are paper, and 5 per cent are mixed.[17] Mixed manuscripts are of two kinds. The first kind is not strictly a single manuscript, but a collection of several manuscripts bound in one cover, the membrane and paper portions being segregated from one another and containing different texts, sometimes of different centuries. The second type of mixed manuscript consists of alternating leaves of membrane and paper, or sometimes of paper leaves enclosed at intervals by a membrane sheet.[18]

The use of paper, followed as it was by the introduction of printing, had consequences far beyond the narrow field of bibliography.

As early as the seventh century, the writing of letters by hand on skins was regarded by monks, with literal propriety, as manual labour. It was extolled as a comprehensive means of subjugating the body for the future benefit of the soul. Both English and Latin scribes and authors will often comment, in the text or in a colophon, on the labours of copying. Their comments usually follow a traditional pattern, of which the following, from a Gospel manuscript of the eighth century, is a fair example:

Ignorant people think the scribe's profession an easy one. Three fingers are engaged in writing, the two eyes in looking; your tongue pronounces the words and the whole body toils. But all labour comes to an end, though its reward shall have no end.[19]

To this provident occupation the printing-press delivered a mortal blow. In 1492, by which time print had become well established, Johann von Trittenheim, abbot of Sponheim, who was naturally a partisan of the old school, awoke to the dangers of this secular innovation and denounced it in an epistolary tract entitled *De Laude Scriptorum*. 'Our writing,' he says 'if it is on skin, may last a thousand years: but how long will a printed paper thing last? It will be doing well if it lasts two hundred years.'[20] With zealous logic, the abbot exhorted scribes to copy out printed books.

Paper is less suitable than membrane for historical as well as for aesthetic communication. It will not take and retain the same variety of inks and colours as properly prepared skins. Paper also will tear, easily gets dog-eared at the corners and, in a bound volume, after use over several centuries, will be cut through by the binder's strings. In addition, paper is injured, without much provocation, by the two worst enemies of books, damp and heat, whereas membrane, unless exposed to extremes of either, will shrivel and discolour, without its writing being consumed.[21] But mediaeval paper had qualities that to a certain extent counteracted these disadvantages. It was mostly tougher and thicker than modern paper, certainly than commercial paper since the first world war, and some fifteenth-century manufacturers discovered a pleasure in it for its own sake, treating as of subordinate interest the fact that it was to be written on.[22] Moreover, paper made books much cheaper to buy. Its availability was not dependent on

D

fluctuations in the numbers of local cattle; it was easier to store than skins and required no further treatment after its initial manufacture. For these reasons, it encouraged the making of books by people who were not professionals.[23] Paper was indispensable for the economic welfare of the printing-press, though books were occasionally printed on membrane and several libraries, which contain incunabula, are able to show more than one example. Such books were luxury productions. It has been estimated that to produce a single copy of the Gutenberg Bible in this manner required the skins of three hundred sheep.[24] The practice of printing on skins was mainly continental and was diminishing by the year 1500.[25]

MAKE-UP

The mediaeval scribe did not usually write on single, unattached leaves, but out of the sheets he received, he formed self-contained booklets or quires. Quires can be formed in two different ways. The first method may be called the bifolium method. A bifolium is a single sheet folded once down the middle to give two leaves. Four bifolia, placed one inside the other to give eight leaves, is a normal mediaeval quire. Secondly, there is the multi-folded method. Two large sheets are placed one on top of the other and then folded, once parallel to the longer side and once more parallel to the shorter side. When the leaves have been cut, this gives a quire of exactly the same appearance and number of leaves as a quire made out of bifolia. Evidence of this second method could at one time be observed in a twelfth-century manuscript from Durham Cathedral, MS A. IV. 34, which was recorded in the Durham catalogue of 1391 as being preserved unbound. In 1935 it was discovered, still unbound, in a drawer in the cathedral *Plate* 7   library. It was written by three scribes. The second and third scribes formed their quires of bifolia, but the first scribe used the multi-folded method. All the quires are alike in size and appearance, but when the book was removed from its drawer, leaves 1 and 4, also 2 and 3, of the first quire written by Scribe I, were still attached to one another by a thin strip of membrane at the top of the spine of the quire, betraying the method he had used.[26] Since quires formed by both of these two methods are the same in appearance, it is not possible, in most cases, to assert definitely that one or other of the methods was used. Graham Pollard discusses the multi-folded method in relation to the writing-material used and the size and shape of the book ultimately produced.[27] Of course, a larger book can be made out of cow- or calf-skin than out of sheep-skin. But we do not know for certain that mediaeval vellum and parchment sheets were always produced in standard sizes and it seems unlikely that they would have been, in view of the discrepancies between different beasts. Moreover, many of our extant manuscripts have been reduced in size owing to successive re-bindings. We cannot, therefore, safely conclude, from the size of extant manuscripts, that the multi-folded method was, or was not, often used. If the sheet was going to be folded several times to form an octavo or duo-decimo, two different shaped books could be obtained from it, according to whether the sheet was folded along a line parallel to its shorter or longer side. In this respect, university practices are said to have differed. Pollard states that at Paris the sheet was usually folded parallel to the shorter side, which gives a square-shaped book; whereas at Oxford, it was folded the other way, giving books which are tall and narrow.[28] But once again, these variations could be produced with the bifolium, as well as with the multi-folded sheet.

The mediaeval word for the booklets of which volumes were composed was *quaternio*,[29] denoting originally four sheets. But the word soon became synonymous with the French word, *cahier*, which means a gathering without reference to the number of its leaves. The number of leaves in a quire varies, both from one manuscript to another and often within any given manuscript. It has been said that, up to the twelfth century, manuscripts written in England and on the continent of Europe, also Greek and Coptic manuscripts, were usually quired in eights (*quaternios*), whereas Irish and Hebrew manuscripts were usually in tens.[30] From the twelfth century onwards, practice became more varied. Undoubtedly there were local traditions about the make-up of quires, but, with the exception of manuscripts produced under the supervision of universities, one cannot assign a manuscript to any particular locality on the length of its quires alone. For membrane manuscripts made in England, the favourite method of quiring was in eights and next in popularity were twelves. Out of a group of forty-four English manuscripts of varying provenance, written between the twelfth and sixteenth centuries, and now contained in the library of Trinity College, Cambridge,[31] it has not been possible to ascertain the quiring of six. Of the remaining thirty-eight, 63 per cent are quired throughout mainly in eights, 21 per cent in twelves, 3 per cent in tens, and of 13 per cent the quiring varies. Of the manuscripts quired in eights, twenty are membrane, three are paper and one is mixed; of the twelves, five are membrane, one is paper and two are mixed; the single manuscript quired in tens is mixed; of the manuscripts with 'various' quires, two are membrane, two are paper and one is mixed. The predominant tendency to quire in eights is borne out as well by the membrane manuscripts of the *Canterbury Tales*.[32] In this connection, Trinity College, Cambridge, MS B. 14. 52, written in the thirteenth century, is of interest. Part one, containing *Poema Morale*, consists of a quire of ten leaves: part two, containing *English Homilies*, is quired almost throughout in eights. *Poema Morale* begins on the second leaf of part one and ends on the ninth. It therefore occupies only eight leaves, which makes it very probable, to my mind, that after being written on a quaternio, it was inserted into a bifolium sheet, thus converting the first quire of the book into a ten.[33]

Paper is a more convenient material for quiring than membrane. It is not surprising that among the manuscripts quired in twelves, the proportion of paper or mixed manuscripts is much higher than among those quired in eights. In addition, one also finds paper manuscripts of sixteen, eighteen, twenty and sometimes of twenty-four leaves.[34]

In manuscript times, the quire was the basic unit of the book. Most books were probably written by their authors in quires. They were copied in the same fashion and scribes were usually paid by the quire. Miscellaneous manuscripts were compiled by the quire. Unless you know where the quires of a manuscript begin and end, you cannot know how the book was planned and made. But if you know the 'collation', as it is called, of the quires, you can discover things which are not apparent from a

survey or list of the book's contents. Often a scribe, to accommodate some variation of his text, will lengthen or shorten a quire.
Owing to alterations in the quires, both accidental and deliberate,
the character of a surviving manuscript is very often quite different
from what it was originally. One quire may have been lost, so
that the juxtaposition of two items, which would appear from a
list of contents to be purposeful, may turn out to be purely accidental. Some quires may have been wrongly bound; others may
have been added at a later date. These alterations have diminished
since the introduction of printing, but until then, and for more
than fifty years afterwards, manuscripts were subject to all kinds
of alterations and additions; a feature which makes them commonly and strikingly different from printed books. Particularly
noticeable is the scribes' tendency to shorten their quires when
little of their text remained to be copied and when they were not
going to include more texts in the same volume. When this
feature occurs within a volume and not at the end, it should
awaken us to the possibility that the remaining texts, even if they
are in the same hand and similarly decorated, were not part of the
volume as originally planned.

The addition of a leaf to a manuscript otherwise written in
regular quires may give us an insight, obtainable in no other way,
into the history of the book's production. For example, Trinity
College, Cambridge, MS R. 3. 2. contains Gower's *Confessio
Amantis*, which was here copied from a text distributed between
five scribes. It is quired in eights, except for quires *d* and *t*, which
have nine leaves each. Scribe II wrote quire *d*, except for its final
leaf, f. 33, the latter being in the hand of scribe III, who also wrote
the following quire, *e*. What seems to have happened is that
scribe III, owing to his own error or that of the distributor of the
exemplar, began his portion a number of lines too late. When
quires *d* and *e* came to be united, the error was observed and the
scribe supplied the missing text on an additional leaf, which was
later sewn to the end of quire *d* by the binder. That f. 33 was thus
written after quires *d* and *e* had already been filled, is proved by
the fact that the omitted portion of text was not sufficient to fill
both sides of the leaf, so scribe III has spaced out his writing, leaving
extensive blanks.

Another manuscript at Trinity College, Cambridge, MS R. 14. 45, exhibits a different type of quire augmentation. The volume consists of six booklets of various dates and sizes bound together. Booklet VI, written in the fifteenth century, contains thirty-eight leaves, but the only quire of which it has been possible to determine the collation is quire 1, a twelve. The first two leaves of quire 1 look, at first sight, as if they were separate from the remainder.[35] But closer investigation shows that they are joined at the back to ff. 11 and 12, the two final leaves of quire 1. One is misled for two reasons. First, there are signatures running a. 1, on f. 3, to a. 4, on f. 6. Secondly, there is a catchword, in the hand of the text, on f. 10b, as if the quire concluded with this page.[36] An English alchemical text begins at the top of f. 3. The scribe evidently began this text in a quire of eight, starting with present f. 3 as f. 1. When he reached present f. 10b and had written his catchword, he inserted his written eight into a blank quire of four, left the first two leaves blank and continued his text on the last two leaves, i.e. on present ff. 11 and 12. After the conclusion of quire 1 in its present form, his text fills thirteen more pages and the remainder of the booklet is occupied by miscellaneous receipts. Except for f. 1, the pages at the beginning did not remain blank, but received texts in three different hands. The first writes numerals at the top of f. 1b and a Latin paragraph towards the middle. The second writes, towards the bottom of f. 1b: 'Inquer*e* ffor john stone off Tychefelde besyde hamyll off the hoke for bak akyin(?)'. The third hand writes, on ff. 2–2b, a list of 'the namys of the meyerys & schryvys in the tyme of kynge henry the vte beryyd at Westmestr*e*'; also, towards the bottom of f. 1b, an English prose charm to protect a house against thieves. The probability, in view of their desultory placing on the pages, that these items were written later is confirmed by investigating the make-up of quire 1.[37]

When a scribe had folded his sheets and arranged them in the form of a quire, he usually ruled them before writing. Falconer Madan has given a clear general description of the method of ruling:

Down each side of the page, holes were pricked at proper intervals with an awl, and a hard, dry, metal stilus used to draw the lines from hole to hole, with others perpendicular to mark the margins; space was also left for illuminations when the place could be judged beforehand. The stilus made a furrow on one side of the parchment and raised a ridge on the other side, and was carried right across a sheet of parchment. This ruling was not such a simple matter as it might seem . . . First, it must be noted that the two sides of a piece of parchment are seldom alike; one is usually smoother and whiter (the original flesh-side), and the other rougher and yellowish (the hair-side). Now a quaternion was almost always so arranged that wherever the book was opened, the two pages presented to the eye were *both* hair-side or *both* flesh-side. Dr. Maunde Thompson lays down as a general rule that in Greek MSS. the first page of a section generally exhibited a flesh-side, and in Latin MSS. a hair-side. Secondly,—although the point has not been fully investigated,—at any rate in Greek MSS. of the ninth, tenth and eleventh centuries, the first page of a quaternion usually exhibited a set of *ridges*, and consequently the second page a set of furrows, when ruled.[38]

Madan's general description requires several qualifications. First, a dry point or stilus was used for ruling up to the twelfth century. From the twelfth century onwards, a solid piece of lead, known as a plummet, was used and by the fifteenth century, we find lines ruled with ink. Secondly, holes were pricked in the parchment *Plate 9* sometimes with an awl, but also with a pair of compasses and sometimes, it is thought, with a spiked wheel.[39] The advantage of pricking over any other method is that several leaves can be done at the same time and, if done well, the mark that remains can only be seen if you are looking for it, and therefore does not spoil the appearance of the page. Thirdly, as has been seen, in vellum manuscripts it is sometimes difficult to distinguish the hair-side of a leaf from the flesh-side, since both received equal care in preparation. Fourthly, the arrangement of hair-side and flesh-side, to which Madan refers, was not established as a system until the end of the eighth century.[40] In the scriptorium at Tours, at any rate, a strict method of arranging the leaves and ruling was not observed until after Alcuin's appointment as director in 782. Subsequently, sheets were usually ruled two, sometimes four at a time, the lower sheets being ruled by pressure on the top one, and in Latin manuscripts, this top sheet was always a hair-side. When the sheets were folded down the middle to make a quire, the outer page, f. 1, would be a hair-side showing grooves from the ruling; its verso, f. 1b, would be a flesh-side with ridges; f. 2 would be a flesh-side with grooves, f. 2b would be a hair-side with ridges. A further change took place about 820, when scribes at Tours devised a method whereby all the flesh-sides received ridges and all the hair-sides grooves. That is to say, they now stacked their sheets for ruling with all the hair-sides uppermost. To form a quire, the sheets were rearranged, after being ruled, in the customary manner, so that all the flesh-sides with ridges faced one another, as consequently did the hair-sides with grooves. Towards the end of the eleventh century, they began to rule each leaf separately; this coincided with the substitution of a plummet for the stilus. Palaeographically, we know that the influence of Tours was considerable. Whether due to its influence or not, it so happens that all the manuscripts of the ninth to the twelfth centuries, which I have come across, show grooves on the hair-sides and ridges on the flesh-sides, in those instances where it is possible to distinguish clearly one side of the leaf from the other.

The normal method of writing, if the scribe was using a quire of double-leaves or bifolia, was straight through the quire. That is to say, the scribe wrote his pages in the order in which they were to be read, thus writing only half a sheet at a time, except for the middle sheet of the quire, of which the second half would be written immediately after the first. This was the usual procedure. But it has been noticed that Durham scribes often cramp their writing at the foot of a page, as if they were trying to keep exactly level, page for page, with their exemplars. For this reason, it has been suggested that perhaps manuscripts at Durham were written a whole sheet at a time. Thus, the sheet written first, if the quire were an eight, would receive pages 1 and 2, 15 and 16. At the end of the sheet written next, when completing page 14, the scribe might have to cramp his handwriting, or enlarge it, to make the text join properly with the page already written.[41] For bifolia, undoubtedly the normal method was best. For the multi-folded sheet, the method of the printed book would have been used. After pricking and ruling several sheets, the scribe took one of them and folded it to the shape of the book he was writing, obtaining by this means a clear demarcation of the pages. Finally, the sheet was unfolded and the scribe copied out his text on the pages in their proper order.[42]

A point that has been generally overlooked is that, under the normal system of writing, the scribe must have had to pause, after writing each recto, to let the ink dry before turning the sheet to write the verso. So far as I can discover, it was not customary to blot wet ink in the Middle Ages, even with sand or powdered chalk. In mediaeval descriptions of book-making, which are often detailed, there is no mention of blotting-paper, although it was known to Horman in the early sixteenth century.[43] There is a further consideration. Judging by mediaeval receipts for making ink, what the scribes aimed at for their normal writing was a good, fast black. Many receipts emphasise *nigrum optimum*, which was best achieved by the use of a charcoal basis made from the young shoots of a grape-vine.[44] Trinity College, Cambridge, MS R. 14. 45, besides containing receipts for parchment and vellum, has also the following, normal receipt for ink, which has not been printed before, in part v, f. 18:

Forto make hynke of lombardie

Forto make gode lombardye hynke Take 1 lb of gallez and stampe hem in a morter al to pouder / þan put hit in a galonn of water and sette hit over the ffire and lette hit sethen welle þer'inne / þanne take a povnde of grene coporose and grynde hit to povder and put þerto and stere hem welle to geders and lete hem sethen a while / þanne take a povnde of gumme of Arabye & put þerto and stere wele alle to gedir / þanne lete hit sethe a while to geders til hit torne blak I nowe þanne take hit adovne and lete hit kelyn & þanne clense hit thorowe a canuas in to a wessel and lette hit stonden and þov schalt have gode hynke and fyne for to write with

Blotting of ink would have absorbed the top surface and left it pale instead of black. On indifferent paper, this blackness is not so easy to achieve. The ink, if there is insufficient gum in its composition, sinks in and lightens in colour. On membrane, which is more impervious than paper, if the gum solution is too strong, the opposite may occur. The writing stays on the surface and, the gum becoming brittle after a while, flakes away. This is often the cause of the semi-obliteration that one finds on the pages of certain manuscripts. We do frequently find pale or brown ink in membrane manuscripts, but this is more probably due to oxidisation than to blotting, and occasionally it is an intentional decorative feature.[45]

Writing well by hand with a quill pen must have been a slow and tedious business. If a scribe had to pause after writing every recto and could never write more than two pages without interruption, the time taken for writing a book would have been considerably protracted. Might a hasty copyist have attempted to speed up his task by writing all the rectos of his quire in sequence and subsequently all the versos? The answer is that scribes could have done this, but probably did not. It is reasonable to suppose that they would have been glad of a regular pause, in which, moreover, they could occupy themselves with subsidiary essentials such as mixing ink, sharpening pens, pricking and ruling quires, cleaning their pages and giving them a final preparation by sewing up small holes and smoothing roughnesses. If they were writing in open cloisters in the winter, it would have been a matter of sheer necessity to stand up and take exercise at intervals. Osbern Bokenham, the friar and versifier of Saints' Legends, provides a realistic fifteenth-century counterpart to the classical scribal complaints of the labour of writing. During the course of his *Vita S. Margaretae*, he compares himself to a tired pilgrim, travelling on his way and thinking of his lodging and a good meal:

> Ryht so, as I seyde, it faryth be me;
> For sykyr myn handys gynne to feynte,
> My wyt to dullyn, and myn eyne bleynte
> Shuld be, ner helpe of a spectacle;
> My penne also gynnyth make obstacle,
> And lyst no lengere on paper to renne,
> For I so ofte haue maad to grenne
> Hys snowte vp-on my thombys ende,
> That he ful ny is waxyn vnthende;[46]
> For euere as he goth he doth blot,
> And in my book makyth many a spot,
> Menyng therby that for the beste
> Were for vs bothe a whyle to reste,
> Til that my wyt and also he
> Myht be sum craft reparyd be.[47]

At the foot of a page of a manuscript, the writing is sometimes cramped and shaky. This is usually attributed to the scribe's having to stoop over his sloping desk, whereas, when writing the top lines of a page, his hand would be almost on eye-level. But I question whether bad writing is not occasionally a symptom of the weariness described by Bokenham and of the bluntness of the scribe's pen.

Under the normal system, the scribe wrote, as has been emphasised, on separate sheets and only half a sheet at a time. As a guide to reassembling the sheets in the form of a quire, the scribe would often write, in the right-hand bottom margin of his rectos, a small letter of the alphabet, or some other distinguishing mark, followed by a small roman numeral. These are called signatures. Arabic numeration in signatures is late, usually fifteenth century.[48] Sometimes the first quire of a manuscript is signed with a cross followed by a numeral, instead of with a letter of the alphabet. Scribes always used the roman alphabet of twenty-three letters: this treats *i* and *j* (also *u* and *v*) as the same and omits *w*. When all the letters of the alphabet had been used up, ways of continuing the signatures varied, but frequently scribes began the alphabet over again, using capital letters instead of small ones. Normally only the first half of a quire is signed. In a quire of eight, formed of bifolia, if the first four leaves are arranged in their correct order, the remaining four will naturally be in the correct order too. Signatures, being written low in the bottom margins, were often lost when the book was trimmed for binding. Possibly scribes wrote signatures low down with the intention that they should be cut off. Before a book was stripped for binding and stitching a second time, the signatures might be again inserted to ensure that the sheets, when lying about in the workshop, would be kept in their correct order.

There is often found a system of quire numeration, which should be mentioned here. E. A. Lowe formulates the general rule that the more modest and simple the quire-mark, the older is the manuscript in which it occurs.

Its position in the oldest Latin manuscripts is regularly in the lower right-hand corner of the last page of each quire. It is only exceptionally that the quire-mark appears on the first page of the quire. When it does, it may be taken that there has been Greek influence. Gradually quire-marks are moved towards the centre of the lower margin, gain in size and are embellished. This does not happen before the seventh century.[49]

Originally, quire-marks consisted of the letter 'q' followed by a numeral. But later the 'q' is discarded and the numerals, most often large roman, appear by themselves. In Trinity College, Cambridge, MS B. 3. 29, a late twelfth-century 'Isaias Glosatus', originally belonging to Christ Church, Canterbury, and very probably written there, the numerals, which appear at the end of almost every quire, were first inserted in plummet, subsequently erased and then re-written alongside in ink. In B.M. Royal MS 15 A. xxxiii, dating from the beginning of the tenth century, originally owned by Worcester Cathedral Priory, the numerals that remain begin at the end of the third quire in small roman, in ink, and are continued after the fifth quire in plummet. A late eleventh-century manuscript, originally from Gloucester Abbey, B.M. Royal MS 13 C. v, shows the numerals on the first leaf of each quire, written in the middle of the bottom margins in large roman, between two coloured dots. Another Christ Church, Canterbury, book, B.M. Royal MS 1 A. xiv, also probably written there, has examples of both final and initial numeration on ff. 40b and 41 respectively, though on the latter, the numeral is written in the top margin instead of the bottom.

SCRIBAL PRACTICE

The system of writing which has been described is identical, so far as the order of the leaves is concerned, with that which would be used when writing in a bound volume. If there are no signatures in a volume, and in very many manuscripts the signatures have disappeared wholly or in part, or are later insertions, it might well be asked, how do we know that the manuscript was not bound before it was written? This question derives some apparent support from the frequent illuminations in mediaeval manuscripts, *Plate 6b* which represent a scribe at work. In later manuscripts, the scene is often depicted in great detail.[50] We see the study or carrell with books, bound and clasped, lying upon shelves or chained fore-edge outwards, behind partly drawn curtains. In the centre stands a

desk, often designed more to excite the admiration of the observer
or to balance the picture, than to serve the purpose of writing.[51]
Scattered around are ink-bottles, pens, knives, paper-weights and
magnifying-glasses and amid them is seated the scribe, with an eye
of strenuous concentration, writing in a bound volume. It will be
shown presently why this last feature can most probably be regarded as a misrepresentation. It occurs, perhaps, because the
illuminator usually wanted to show the scribe writing, not just
anything, but a book; sometimes the very book in which the
illumination appears.

A good example of this last point could be found until recently
in B.M. Royal MS 10 A. xiii containing 'Expositio super regulam
beati Benedicti noua'.[52] It is a medium-sized membrane manuscript, at one time the property of Christ Church, Canterbury, and
dating from the late twelfth or early thirteenth centuries. It is very
well written and decorated with plain initials of red, blue or
green. Folio 2 has now been extracted from the volume and is
preserved apart in a box. On f. 2b is a fine full-page miniature,[53]
enclosed in a five-fold frame, with the superscription 'SCS
DUNSTANVS'. St Dunstan, wearing a mitre and nimbed, sits in an
arched throne. In his right hand he holds a quill pen; in his left, a
large-handled lunellarium.[54] Before him, an open book rests on a
linen cloth, the cloth being draped on top of a desk and enfolding
an ink-pot, in shape like the large end of a horn, which projects at
a convenient point. The pedestal of the desk is totally unrepresen-
tational and its top is tilted unrealistically towards the observer, so
that one can see the pages of the book clearly. The pages are ruled
and contain the following words in red and blue capitals, which
stop half-down the recto of the right-hand leaf: OBSCVLTA:
O FILI PRECEPTA: MAGISTRI. These words occur in the text of
B.M. Royal MS 10 A. xiii itself, where they constitute the opening
rubrics on ff. 3 and 3b. Plainly the intention is to show St Dunstan
writing this particular commentary, though in actual fact he had
nothing to do with its composition.

Possibly a more authentic author-portrait is that contained in
B.M. Royal MS 14 E. i, a late fifteenth-century copy of Vincent de
Beauvais' *Speculum Historiale*, executed, with miniatures in the
Bruges style, for Edward IV, whose arms appear three times in the

border of the first miniature. This last shows a writer with a quill in his right hand, which rests firmly on the page, and a knife in his left. He is writing in a book, not on a single leaf, the blue edge of its final board being clearly visible beneath the leaves. The picture is said to be intended to represent Vincent de Beauvais himself.[55]

Records of all kinds, chronicles and other books, which were augmented yearly or at more frequent intervals, would sometimes have been written bound. In 1313, it would appear that William de Southflete, a London stationer, sold blank membrane books, in which the annual accounts of the royal wardrobe were to be kept. A record in *Exchequer Accounts* 375-8, f. 8, says:

Willelmo de Southflete, stacionario Londinensi, pro factura et ligatura quatuor librorum de nouo factorum per ipsum pro expensis hospicii infra scribendis et contrarotulandis de anno sexto (E.II) x.s.[56]

The author of the Winchester-Hyde chronicle, used at Waverley and Worcester, recommends the following method for keeping a book up to date:

You will have to see to it that in this book there should at all times be a blank sheet on which you can note with a pencil such matters as the decease of well-known men or anything memorable about affairs of state if you chance to hear of it, and at the end of the year, one of you (not just anyone, but whoever should be appointed to the task) should write out briefly in the body of the book itself, whatever he considers to be reliable and best worth preserving for the knowledge of posterity; and then the old notesheet should be removed and a new one put in.[57]

The opinion that the practice of writing in bound volumes was infrequent in the Middle Ages is based on several further features of manuscript-production, about each of which a little must be said. First, there is the question of off-sets. As has been seen, the scribe must have had to pause, after writing every recto, to let his ink dry before turning the leaf to write its verso. In a bound volume, if he turned the leaf too soon, the wet ink would set-off, in looking-glass writing, on the previous page. Such off-sets do not occur in manuscripts from this cause, even when the books have other appearances of having been made in haste. An eighth-century Gospel manuscript at Durham has such marked off-sets in

looking-glass writing, which shows through the right way round
on the opposite side of the page, that it was at one time thought
to be a palimpsest. But instead of indicating that the book was
written bound, these off-sets prove the opposite. Each bifolium,
after it was written, was laid on a pile and left long enough to set-
off on its neighbour. For example, ff. 36 and 42, 37 and 41 form
two bifolia. On f. 42 is set-off the writing on f. 36b; on f. 42b is
set-off the writing on f. 37.[58]

Secondly, there is the practice of inserting catchwords. On the
final page of a quire, the scribe would often write at the foot of
the text the first words of the quire which was to follow. To
arrange his completed quires in the correct order, it would merely
be necessary to determine that the catchwords corresponded with
the subsequent text. The majority of professional manuscripts
must have been written with catchwords. Their insertion would
have been an obvious first rule for a well regulated scriptorium, lay
as well as monastic. They have often been cut off when a book was
rebound, but not so frequently as signatures, because catchwords
were usually written higher up the page. If books had been written bound, there would have been no need for catchwords, signatures or quire numeration; their presence, often in the hands of the
original scribes, shows us that books were most often written in
quires.

The third reason for supposing that books were written unbound is the occurrence, in the books which I have examined, of
blank leaves at the beginnings and ends of texts. Professor
Wormald has pointed out, elsewhere in this book,[59] that a great
number of manuscripts are composite in character. There are
many mediaeval works, both Latin and English, which are inordi-
nately long, but it is surprising how few manuscripts contain one
work only. To a certain extent this can be attributed to the practice in later centuries of binding manuscripts together for the sake
of convenience. But such combinations existed in mediaeval times
also, as can be seen from almost any list or inventory of mediaeval
books. Chaucer's Wife of Bath's fifth husband, Jankyn the clerk,
owned a manuscript containing sayings and stories, made by a
number of different people, about the frailty of women. The
Wife says in her *Prologue*:

> He hadde a book, that gladly, nyght and day
> For his desport he wolde rede alway;
> He cleped it Valerie and Theofraste,
> At which book he lough alwey ful faste.
> And eek ther was somtyme a clerk at Rome,
> A cardinal, that highte Seint Jerome,
> That made a book agayn Jovinian;
> In which book eek ther was Tertulan,
> Crisippus, Trotula, and Helowys,
> That was abbesse nat fer fro Parys;
> And eek the Parables of Salamon,
> Ovides Art, and bookes many on,
> And alle thise were bounden in o volume.[60]

Such a combination would not have surprised a mediaeval reader.
Of the forty-four manuscripts at Trinity College, Cambridge,
referred to above, only seven are definitely non-miscellaneous. Of
these seven, only three can strictly be considered to contain, or to
have always contained, one text and no more: they are B. 15. 32,
containing Nicholas Love's English translation of *Meditationes
Vitae Christi*, R. 3. 8, containing *Cursor Mundi*, and R. 3. 13, containing the English verse *Speculum Vitae* attributed to William of
Nassyngton. Of the remaining four non-miscellaneous manuscripts, R. 3. 3 and R. 3. 23 are imperfect and therefore may have
had additional texts on their missing leaves. B. 3. 29 of the twelfth
century has early texts, admittedly very short, added on the flyleaves. R. 3. 14, apparently complete and containing only *Piers
Plowman*, turns out, on examination of an old foliation sequence,
to be lacking twenty-three leaves at the beginning; so undoubtedly, like the other *Piers Plowman* manuscript at Trinity,
B. 15. 17, it at one time had additional texts.

If the blank leaves, which have been mentioned, occurred only
at the beginnings and ends of volumes containing a single long
text, one might argue that they were intended to function as flyleaves. One purpose of a fly-leaf is to prevent the boards of a book
from rubbing against the first and last leaves of the text. When
the boards are heavy, as they necessarily are in large manuscripts,
this rubbing might seriously disfigure the pages and any illuminations which they happened to contain. Mediaeval binders inserted

as guards, at the beginnings and ends of their books, scraps of vellum, parts of old deeds and leaves from unfashionable texts or from worn-out liturgical books. But the blanks, which are being referred to, are not inserted leaves. Those at the beginning are formed by starting a text, not on the recto of the first folio of a quire, but at some subsequent point, sometimes as late as folio 3.[61] Moreover, these works are not always at the beginning of a volume; sometimes they are in the middle or at the end. Blank leaves at the ends of texts are far more frequent than those at the beginning.[62] With long works, this is natural. It must have been difficult to calculate exactly on what leaf a hand-written work would end, although an attempt to do so was very often made. A manuscript, which has a uniform length of quires throughout, will frequently end with an abnormally short one. Sometimes the final quire is not short enough. The text is completed and the last leaf or two have to remain blank. But it is surprising to find that short works, wherever they may occur in a manuscript, and even if they are all written by a single scribe, so frequently end with blank leaves. Or, if the leaves are not blank, they exhibit the further peculiarity that they are filled with subsidiary or irrelevant matter.[63]

As editors of mediaeval texts have not given much attention to the position, in the quire, of subsidiary matter, this point may be illustrated from Trinity College, Cambridge, MS B. 1. 45. It was written in the thirteenth century and contains now eighty-six folios, though at one time it had eighty-eight. The first two sections are written in a single hand, except for two very short additions. Section 1 consists of three quires with eight, six and ten leaves respectively. ff. 1–18b contain the Latin prose *Sigillum S. Marie super Cantica* by Honorius of Autun. f. 18 is the fourth leaf of quire 3, which ends with f. 24. The *Sigillum* is followed immediately by a Latin prose *Sermo S. Anselmi Ep. de Conceptu Uirginali* and by some French prose paragraphs containing rules for the government of some religious house.[64] These end on the last leaf of the section, f. 24, where there begin at once English verse lines on flirtation, followed by a passage of metrical English prose on the pride that women take in clothes. The latter turns into an English sermon on our sinful forgetfulness of the sufferings of

E

Christ, which ends at the bottom of f. 24b. At the very foot, another hand has added a Latin tag in blacker ink.

Section II, ff. 25–42, consists of two quires containing Latin sermons, which end at the top of f. 41b. Nearly three pages of the section remain. As in the previous section, the final pages of the last quire contain short items. They are: an English prose sermon, taking for its text the first two lines of a secular English song; the Ten Commandments in English verse, and a note, in the blacker ink, 'de elemosina'. The texts end at the bottom of f. 42; f. 42b is blank.

Section III, ff. 43–74, consisting of four quires, is mainly occupied by 'Regula S. Augustini exposita', which is written in another hand and ends towards the bottom of f. 72. The scribe of this section likewise filled his remaining pages with subsidiary matter, namely miscellaneous paragraphs of Latin prose, but between these, on f. 73b, come the popular English verse lines, 'Proprietates Mortis', inserted in the hand and blacker ink that also made additions to sections I and II.

The final two quires of the volume, ff. 75–86, written in a different thirteenth-century hand, contain Augustine, *De Trinitate*, followed by four theological items in Latin prose, which end imperfectly at the bottom of the final page.

This description illustrates how, in a Latin manuscript, a scribe will sometimes drop into English to fill the final leaves of a section. Often he writes mnemonics or Latin tags, which he turns into English. Or he inserts an English lyric, many of our best being preserved on initial or final leaves of a section. If the leaves were not filled by the original scribe, a later owner might insert texts of his own, usually receipts or memoranda.[65] As often as not the blanks are cut out, leaving only the stubs to tell the tale.

This has led some way from the original theme. The cost of mediaeval binding forbids us to believe that these short texts and tracts could ever have been bound separately, with their blanks, when they occur both at the beginning and the end, acting as flyleaves. They must originally have been written unbound and destined to be bound with other works or not at all. While awaiting this fate, they would have been protected by these blank leaves and surely this was the purpose of the latter.[66]

The final reason for saying that books were written unbound is simply this: we meet with a relatively large number of references, in mediaeval catalogues and book-lists, to books that were kept unbound. Such books are usually referred to as being 'in quaternis', or 'in quaterno', or 'tout en cayers'. In a catalogue of the Louvre library, made in 1373, twenty-seven books are described as unbound.[67] Unbound books are quite frequently referred to in the ancient catalogues of Durham,[68] in the catalogue of Titchfield Abbey, begun in 1400,[69] and also in the fourteenth-century catalogue, now in the British Museum, of the library of Lanthony Priory near Gloucester. Private owners as well as institutions seem to have kept some of their books in quires. In a list, drawn up before 1474, of eleven books thought to have belonged to John Paston the younger, five are described as unbound.[70] Trinity College, Cambridge, MS O. 9. 38, a fifteenth-century commonplace-book, made and owned by a Glastonbury monk, is now in a modern binding, but at the beginning is the first half of the membrane wrapper in which it was originally preserved.[71]

CORRECTION AND DECORATION

There remain two processes which, though they have been left to the last, where they properly belong, taken together constitute the whole aim of mediaeval book-making. They are, correcting and illuminating; or, to translate them into terms of motivation, the intention to produce an accurate record and the intention of giving aesthetic pleasure.

When a copyist had finished a quire, the writing was often compared with the original by another person. The ideal corrector would compare the copy carefully with the exemplar and insert words or lines that the scribe had omitted. Mistakes would be lined through and the corrections written over the top, or scraped out with a knife and written correctly. It is this last type of correcting that Chaucer is referring to when he complains of having 'to rubbe and scrape' the copies of his Boethius and Troilus written by a scribe called Adam.[72] But, as might be expected, correcting varies according to the individual and to the amount of time at his disposal. Some correctors merely glanced through the copy, placed a mark against anything doubtful and afterwards consulted the exemplar for the marked passages only. Signs for omissions, insertions and the like vary. There were local traditions, some of which, mainly continental, have been described by W. M. Lindsay.[73] But there is an outstanding need for a concerted attempt to collect and compare the different signs used at English writing-centres, since it would provide a valuable aid to tracing the provenance of books.[74] As a rule, monasteries and universities were careful about the correctness of the books issued under their auspices, and Manly and Rickert would have us assume that the same is true of the commercial scriptoria, which undoubtedly were responsible for the production of many vernacular books in the fourteenth and fifteenth centuries.[75] For *Canterbury Tales* manuscripts, when other evidence is lacking, Manly and Rickert usually assert that a carefully corrected copy comes from a commercial scriptorium. As several of these manuscripts may have been written in religious houses,[76] this seems to me an unsafe assumption to make, although it does seem probable that a commercial scriptorium would have had an overseer, who would have corrected the daily copying of the scribes. More certain, perhaps, is the converse of Manly and Rickert's assumption. When we find a *Canterbury Tales* manuscript that has few or no traces of correction, we may not be far wrong in supposing, other things being equal, that it was made by a private scribe or an amateur.[77]

It is a matter of common observation that mediaeval manuscripts aim to communicate by aesthetic means as well as by intellectual. In addition to the type of illumination or decoration, which is usually displayed in show-cases in libraries, there is the less ostentatious kind known generally, and often inaccurately, as rubricating. Very few mediaeval manuscripts are without some touches of colour on their pages. In a carefully produced manuscript, the illuminator would write in titles and chapter-headings in red and would supply coloured capital letters, in spaces left by the scribe at the beginning of each division of the work. If the capitals had already been written, the illuminator might touch or flourish them with colour, or add to them a decorative border in the margin. Directions as to what titles or letters he should supply were written by the scribe, or sometimes by the corrector, which shows that illuminating was the last of the processes which have been discussed here. These directions were not always obliterated when they had served their turn. Often if you look carefully at an illuminated initial, you will see, underneath the coloured pigments, traces of the letter, usually written very small, which told the illuminator what initial he was to insert. Sometimes these guide-letters, or lengthier directions for a picture, are written towards the edges of the outer and inner margins, with the intention that the outer should be trimmed away and the inner concealed by the binding.[78] In this connection, the illustrated manuscripts of *Plate 8a* *La Somme le Roy*, compiled in 1279, are interesting. Extant manuscripts show that there was in existence, by 1294, a fixed cycle of fifteen pictures illustrating the text.[79] Two later manuscripts, now in the Bibliothèque Nationale, Paris (MSS français 14939, dated 1373, and français 958, dated 1464), contain, in addition to the pictures, detailed descriptions of them 'written in red by the scribe of the text'.[80] Millar admits the possibility that the descriptions were merely drawn up by a reader from the pictures in front of him; but in his opinion, they were, in the first instance, directions to an illuminator, as their detail and syntax suggest, later incorporated by a scribe into a copy of the text.[81] Like scribes, some illuminators, or their apprentices, were dull-witted, even perhaps illiterate. They not infrequently inserted the wrong initial, despite the use of guide-letters and the help that could be obtained by reading the text itself.[82]

There would seem to be a practical reason for the insertion of rubrics. A mediaeval manuscript is not an easy type of book to use for the purpose of reference. It is not invariably paginated or foliated and when you do find an old foliation sequence, it is often incomplete, sometimes mutilated by the binder and nearly always wrong. If you want to refer to an item in a manuscript, you have to count the leaves yourself. Even if you are familiar with the handwriting, it is not easy to skim through a manuscript to find the passage you want. Hence the mediaeval practice of drawing a finger or a hand in the margin, pointing to something in the text which the owner might want to turn up later; often we find 'nota' or 'nota bene' alongside the text. In this situation, rubrics help to a certain extent, since they act as signposts in the text, to tell you where you are. But in many cases the subsidiary work of the illuminator seems to have no practical value at all. Often paragraph-marks, in blue and red alternately, are inserted on each page, at random as it appears. Verse texts sometimes have the first letter of each line touched with red.

It may be added that all the activities described above were not only major factors in the production of the manuscript-book, but were, many of them, capable of being performed with a high degree of art. Practical motives will not suffice to account for all these activities or for the manner in which they were sometimes performed. The selection of skins for writing-material and the care with which they were prepared, could have a marked effect on the ultimate appearance of a book. The arrangement of hair-side and flesh-side would seem to serve no practical purpose and, as has been noted, the custom of using prick-holes, as guides for ruling, must be attributed partly to a desire not to spoil the appearance of the page. Ruling by stilus could be similarly unobtrusive: when ink is used for ruling, it is sometimes coloured various shades of red or violet and, if the text is written in double columns with glosses, the ruling-lines can be made to form a complex contribution to the design of the page. It is not necessary to remark here on the decorative features of mediaeval handwriting. But it may be observed that the same feeling for balance and elaboration can be seen uniformly in other features of a well-made book. Trouble was not usually expended on signatures, since they were destined to be trimmed off by the binder, but quire numeration is often written boldly and with touches of colour. The same is true of catchwords, which are sometimes enclosed in elaborate scrolls. It is the care and sensitivity with which each of the processes of book-production was performed, that, in combination, accounts for the finest mediaeval manuscript-books.

To sum up: to the fourteenth century, the leaves of codices made in England were membrane, which was challenged in the fifteenth century, and later superseded, by paper; the latter event coinciding with the adoption of print. Throughout this period, the stages in the production of a manuscript-codex, and the order in which they were undertaken, did not change, although the diversity of book-producing centres and the necessity of performing every process by hand rendered a standardized performance unthinkable. Transcription, which was slow, on to unbound quires, kept in proper sequence by signatures, quire-numeration and catchwords; and the inclusion of subsidiary matter on initial and final leaves of sections, accustomed people to the notion of a book as a leisurely accumulation of heterogeneous texts. The book produced by the human hand is the most natural embodiment for the productions of the mind. Though lacking the uniformity and accuracy of printed books, despite the precautions taken by mediaeval book-producers, a manuscript-codex is capable of drawing from its reader, by personal and aesthetic means, a wider response than can be achieved by the productions of a machine.

NOTES TO CHAPTER III

1. For forms of books and their nomenclature in classical times and earlier, see Leo Santifaller, *Beiträge zur Geschichte der Beschreibstoffe im Mittelalter*, i, Graz, 1953, ch. iv; Sir E. Maunde Thompson, *An Introduction to Greek and Latin Palaeography*, Oxford, 1912, ch. v, and Falconer Madan, *Books in Manuscript*, London, 1893, ch. ii.

2. C. H. Roberts, 'The Codex', *Proc. Brit. Acad.*, London, 1954, pp. 169–204, shows that, for pagan literature, the final victory of codex over roll took place in the fourth century A.D., which he regards (p. 201) as the beginning of the Middle Ages in this respect as in others. But there is the strange anomaly that Christians, in the second century and probably earlier, used the codex for biblical texts, although until the fourth century their non-biblical writings were usually on rolls, ibid., pp. 185 ff.

3. See Santifaller, op. cit., pp. 156–8; also W. Wattenbach, *Das Schriftwesen im Mittelalter*, 3rd edn., Leipzig, 1896, pp. 175 ff.

4. My thanks are due to Dr J. C. Davies for this information; also for courteously reading through this paper and suggesting a number of improvements.

5. A fourteenth-century English manorial roll is described by A. H. Smith, 'The Middle English Lyrics in Additional MS 45896', *London Medieval Studies*, ii (1951), pp. 33–49. This MS cannot now be traced. Cambridge, Trinity College MS O. 3. 58 is a fifteenth-century membrane roll, about six feet long, containing twelve carols and a song, all with music. For another fifteenth-century 'literary' roll, see the description of William Billyng's MS by W. Bateman, *The Five Wounds of Christ*, Manchester, 1814, preface. For verse-prayers on rolls, see R. H. Robbins, 'The Arma Christi Rolls', *Mod. Lang. Rev.*, xxxiv (1939), pp. 415–21.

6. For this and other matters connected with rolls, see E. M. Thompson, op. cit., pp. 46 ff.

7. See 'Of daily manual labour', the forty-eighth chapter of the Rule, cited by J. W. Clark, *The Care of Books*, Cambridge, 1901, p. 66. But Cassiodorus, the foundation of whose monastery at Vivarium shortly preceded that of St Benedict, considered the transcription of books to be, in some instances, more meritorious than other types of labour because, by studying the scriptures, the monks improved

their minds and by transcribing them, they disseminated Christianity far and wide:

> Ego tamen fateor votum meum, quod inter vos quaecunque possunt corporeo labore compleri, antiquariorum mihi studia, si tamen veraciter scribant, non inmerito forsitan plus placere, quod et mentem suam relegendo Scripturas divinas salutariter instruunt, et Domini praecepta scribendo longe lateque disseminant.

Cassiodori Senatoris Institutiones, lib. i cap. xxx. 1, ed. R. A. B. Mynors, Oxford, 1937, p. 75.

8. R. A. B. Mynors, *Durham Cathedral Manuscripts*, Oxford, 1939, p. 9. I am indebted to Professor Wormald for drawing my attention to this passage. In the MS it occurs on f. 38. For other extended metaphors, comparing books and the stages of their production to the lives of Christ and of the Virgin Mary, see W. Wattenbach, op. cit., pp. 208–9.

9. For this statement and for what follows, see Hedwig Saxl, 'Histology of Parchment', *Technical Studies in the Field of Fine Arts*, William Hayes Fogg Art Museum, Harvard, July 1939, pp. 3–9.

10. ibid., p. 7.

11. G. Pollard, 'Notes on the Size of the Sheet', *The Library*, 4th ser., xxii (1941), pp. 108 ff., discusses the material of mediaeval manuscripts in relation to their size. In view of the difficulty of obtaining large quantities of uterine vellum, D. V. Thompson suggests that books, sometimes said to be of this material, were really made out of rabbit-skins, *The Materials of Medieval Painting*, London, 1936, pp. 27, 28. Uterine lamb was also used, see E. M. Thompson, op. cit., p. 29.

12. op. cit., p. 80.

13. Several are quoted by D. V. Thompson, 'Medieval Parchment-Making', *The Library*, 4th ser., xvi (1935), pp. 113–17.

14. See D. V. Thompson, 'Medieval Parchment-Making', p. 117 n. i. For smoothing the skin, there is also evidence of the use of an iron plane (plana), see Wattenbach, op. cit., pp. 211–12.

15. *New Palaeographical Soc.*, 2nd ser., London, 1913–30, i, pl. 90. The paper, of which the whole volume is composed, is described here as 'of very coarse quality, without water-marks and abounding in imperfectly pulped rag fibres'.

16. B.M. Add. MS 31223. The leaves, long and narrow, are now mounted. There are fourteen folios; ff. 1 and 14 being membrane and blank, except for a later inscription on f. 1, 'Hustins Book'. The membrane leaves look like remains of the document's original wrapper, but the *Catalogue of Additions to the Manuscripts in the British Museum* MDCCCLXXVI–MDCCCLXXXI, London, 1887, p. 165, describes the material of this manuscript merely as paper and says it has only eleven folios. The paper leaves are uneven and fibrous.

17. See the descriptions by J. M. Manly and E. Rickert, *The Text of the Canterbury Tales*, Chicago, 1940, i.

18. For the first type, see the following MSS at Trinity College, Cambridge: B. 2. 18, B. 14. 19, R. 14. 32, R. 14. 51 (a 15th-century membrane book, which has a 16th-century paper index). Item 181 in M. R. James, *A Descriptive Catalogue of the Western Manuscripts in the Library of Trinity College, Cambridge*, Cambridge, 1900–4, i, 233 ff. contains, in a modern binding four separate manuscripts: one early 15th-century membrane booklet, one 16th-century and two 17th-century paper booklets. Similar combinations of booklets occurred in mediaeval times, as I shall show. MS R. 3. 20, dated in the second quarter of the 15th century, from the London commercial scriptorium of John Shirley, is paper, except

for a final quire of membrane. But the opening text of the latter is a continuation from the previous paper quire.

The second type is rarer; G. Pollard cites only one example, Shrewsbury School MS 15 of the early 15th century, op. cit., p. 117. For examples at Trinity College, Cambridge, see B. 11. 24 and R. 14. 26; the latter has many leaves missing, but the outer and inner sheets of each quire seem to have been membrane, the rest are paper. Both are 15th-century books and neither is particularly well made.

19. Qui scribere nescit nullum putat esse laborem. Tres digiti scribunt, duo oculi vident. Una lingua loquitur. totum corpus laborat, Et omnis labor finem habet. et praemium ejus non habet finem.

Quoted by Wattenbach, op. cit., pp. 495–6. The various elements of this particular scribal comment can be traced through succeeding centuries in examples cited ibid., pp. 279 ff. and pp. 433 ff.

20. Scriptura enim si membranis imponitur, ad mille annos poterit perdurare: impressura autem cum res papirea sit, quamdiu subsistet? Si in volumine papireo ad ducentos annos perdurare potuerit, magnum est.

Quoted by Wattenbach, op. cit., p. 452.

21. See, for example, some of the British Museum Cotton MSS, relics of the Ashburnham House fire of 1731, consisting now of single, mounted leaves, e.g. Tiberius A. ii, Tiberius B. xi, Otho B. xi and Vitellius E. xviii.

22. See Marjorie Plant, *The English Book-Trade*, London, 1939, p. 60. For a brief comparison of the qualities of oriental and occidental papers, see Santifaller, op. cit., p. 119.

23. See p. 56.

24. Dard Hunter, *Papermaking*, London, 1947, p. 16.

25. ibid.

26. See Mynors, op. cit., p. 57 n. In the manuscript, which is still unbound, there is no trace left of the membrane strip.

27. 'Notes on the Size of the Sheet', pp. 110 ff.

28. op. cit., p. 113. His information about university books comes from Jean Destrez, *La Pecia dans les manuscrits universitaires du XIIIe et du XIVe siècle*, Paris, 1935, p. 46.

29. In the early days of universities, the quires of their books, which are dealt with in chapter iv of this volume and are therefore excluded from the present chapter, were called *peciae*, see Destrez, op. cit., *passim*.

30. See G. Pollard, op. cit., p. 108.

31. W. W. Greg says of the Trinity MSS in his introduction to *Facsimiles o, Twelve Early English Manuscripts in the Library of Trinity College, Cambridge*, Oxford, 1913: 'The hundred or so English manuscripts written before 1501 form a very representative as well as important collection in which every period from the 11th century onwards is fairly illustrated.' His statement seems equally true if limited to the English verse MSS, which are the only ones that I have examined in detail. My thanks are due to the Master and Fellows of Trinity, and to the Librarian and his assistants, for providing me with every facility for examining these books.

32. See Manly and Rickert, op. cit., p. 13.

33. f. 1 was originally blank, except for an imperfect 'Litany of the Virgin' on the recto, which stretches for half a column only. f. 10 is now mostly cut away; it was probably also blank, but now has traces of writing on the verso. That these two leaves were in the volume before it received its present binding is evinced by

an inscription at the top of f. 1b: 'Rithmus anglicus cum omiliis anglicis in hoc volumine continentur', described by M. R. James, op. cit., p. 460, as 'a xvth cent. monastic title'. The present binding looks old, being leather over compressed paper boards, with traces of clasps along the fore-edges, and is stamped with the arms of Whitgift, who resigned the mastership of Trinity in 1577 and died in 1604.

34. It was recognised in the early 16th century that the mediaeval quire, with its variable number of leaves, differed from the modern: 'There shulde be foure or fyve and twenty sheetes in a queyre: and twenty queryis in a reme: though the olde waye were other.' W. Horman, *Vulgaria* (Roxburghe Club, 1926), p. 124.

35. M. R. James, op. cit., ii, p. 332, treats them as if they formed the end of booklet v.

36. For information about signatures and catchwords, see pp. 47, 51.

37. Among the *Canterbury Tales* MSS are many which give insights into scribes' difficulties, some of the latter deserving to be called 'crises' of book-production. They can only be detected by observing the collations of the quires. For two particularly interesting ones, see Hengwrt MS (National Library of Wales, Peniarth MS 392 D.) and B.M. Royal MS 18 C. ii, described by Manly and Rickert, op. cit., pp. 266–83 and 485–93.

38. *Books in Manuscript*, pp. 37–8.

39. See L. W. Jones, 'Pricking Manuscripts: the Instruments and their Significance', *Speculum*, xxi (1946), pp. 389–403.

40. For this statement and for what follows, see E. K. Rand, *A Survey of the Manuscripts at Tours*, Cambridge, Mass., i, 1929, pp. 10–18.

41. See Mynors, op. cit., p. 19 n.: but he admits that such a practice would be peculiar.

42. This method is described by G. Pollard, op. cit., p. 107.

43. See *Vulgaria*, p. 123. Dard Hunter refers to mention of it in English in 1465, but says that blotting-paper did not 'come into general use until the beginning of the nineteenth century' (op. cit., pp. 523–4).

44. See D. V. Thompson, *The Materials of Medieval Painting*, pp. 80–8.

45. A good example of flaking, leaving the outlines of letters visible, is to be seen in the Lydgate portion of Cambridge, Trinity College MS R. 4. 20, particularly on ff. 101 and 102b.

46. unprosperous, i.e. 'has almost ceased to work'.

47. *Legendys of Hooly Wummen* (ed. M. S. Serjeantson, E.E.T.S., O.S. 206, 1938), p. 25, ll. 894–908. Cf. with this and with the general tradition of complaints by book-producers, Caxton's excuses, in the Epilogue to Bk. III of *The Recuyell of the Historyes of Troye*, for having learned the art of printing:

And for as moche as in the wrytyng of the same my penne is worn/ myn hande wery & not stedfast myn eyen dimmed with ouermoche lokyng on the whit paper / and my corage not so prone and redy to laboure as hit hath ben . . . Therfore I haue practysed & lerned at my grete charge and dispense to ordeyne this said book in prynte after the maner & forme as ye may here see.

The Prologues and Epilogues of William Caxton (ed. W. J. B. Crotch, E.E.T.S., O.S. 176, 1928), p. 6.

48. For an example, see above, p. 42, ref. to Cambridge, Trinity College MS R. 14. 45, booklet vi, ff. 3 and 6.

49. E. A. Lowe, *Codices Latini Antiquiores*, vi, Oxford, 1953, p. vii.

50. The subject is found in manuscript-illuminations of the sixth century, but not usually with so much detail as later. What I proceed to describe is a conflation

of a number of later portraits. Examples are listed by Wattenbach, op. cit., pp. 275–8. Two are reproduced by A. W. Pollard, 'Some Pictorial and Heraldic Initials', *Bibliographica*, iii (1897), pp. 234 and 236; see also F. Madan, op. cit., pls. ii and iv, and E. A. Savage, *Old English Libraries*, London, 1911, pls. xiv, xxx and xxxii. In some of these the scribes are shown writing, as I think they must usually have done, on loose sheets.

51. The impracticability of writing-desks in mediaeval illuminations is discussed by E. M. Thompson, 'Calligraphy in the Middle Ages', *Bibliographica*, iii (1897), pp. 286 ff.

52. Described as 'the commentary ascribed to Smaragdus, Abbot of S. Mihiel (809), written after the Council of Aachen in 817', G. F. Warner and J. P. Gilson, *Catalogue of Western MSS. in the Old Royal and King's Collections*, i, London, 1921, 309. My attention was drawn to this manuscript by Dr C. E. Wright.

53. Reproduced by E. G. Millar, *English Illuminated Manuscripts from the Xth to the XIIIth Century*, Paris, 1926, pl. 59a.

54. Scribes are almost invariably depicted holding a lunellarium as well as a pen. The knife was used, at this stage, for sharpening the quill, smoothing rough-nesses in the writing-surface, scraping out mistakes and holding down firmly the springy membrane while writing. In B.M. Royal MS I A. xiv and Cotton MS Tiberius A. ii occur frequent small slits at the ends of writing-lines, which are definitely additional to the ruling-pricks and may be attributed, I suggest, very probably to the pointed end of the lunellarium used to immobilise the writing-surface.

55. G. F. Warner and J. P. Gilson, op. cit., ii, 139; they also identify the coats of arms.

56. Quoted by T. F. Tout, *Chapters in the Administrative History of Mediaeval England*, Manchester, 1920, p. 47. The use of 'ligatura' would suggest that they were codices, not rolls. *Contrarotulum* is a counter-roll, meaning a copy of a roll or document kept for the purpose of controlling (i.e. counter-rolling) or checking. To this end, current wardrobe accounts would have been transferred at intervals to the ready-made volumes sold by de Southflete. He is mentioned in 1311, in connection with the sale of similar books, in Oxford, Bodleian MS Tanner 197, ibid.

57. See *Annales Monastici* (ed. H. R. Luard, Rolls Series 36, London, 1869), iv, p. 355. Quoted, in translation, by E. P. Goldschmidt, *Medieval Texts and their First Appearance in Print*, Bibl. Soc. Trans. Supp. 16 (London, 1943), pp. 100–1.

58. The MS is Durham A. II. 16, see Mynors, op. cit., p. 19 and pls. v–vii. G. Pollard, 'Notes on the Size of the Sheet', p. 106, takes this MS as an example of the normal method of writing, but it rather suggests the other method, in which the whole of a bifolium was written at once.

59. See p. 22.

60. *The Complete Works of Geoffrey Chaucer*, ed. F. N. Robinson, Cambridge, Mass., 1933, p. 99, ll. 669–81. Incidentally, this is a good example of the loose use of bibliographical terminology in the mediaeval period.

61. Among the Cambridge, Trinity College MSS examples occur in: B. 15. 40 (16th century), B. 11. 24, B. 14. 19, B. 14. 39, B. 14. 52, B. 15. 31, R. 3. 19, R. 14. 45 (three examples), O. 2. 13. It has to be remembered that sometimes these initial leaves, though originally left blank, have received later texts or been cut out.

62. Among the Trinity MSS, examples occur in: B. 2. 18, B. 10. 12, B. 11. 24,

B. 14. 19, B. 15. 31, B. 15. 40, B. 15. 42, R. 3. 14, R. 3. 19, R. 3. 22, R. 4. 20, R. 14. 32, R. 14. 45, O. 2. 13, O. 2. 53, O. 5. 6.

63. Such matter, however, is sometimes unique and may be of more importance to a modern editor than longer texts.

64. Carleton Brown, 'Texts and the Man', *Bull. Mod. Hum. Res. Ass.*, ii (1928), pp. 107 ff., puts a strong case for thinking that this MS was compiled in a convent of itinerant friars. The book could have been carried about the countryside by them, since it measures only $5\frac{3}{4}$ by $3\frac{7}{8}$ inches.

65. e.g. see additions to Cambridge, Trinity College MS R. 14. 45, ff. 1b–2b, listed above, p. 42.

66. They are to be distinguished from the blank leaves recommended by Quintilian to students taking notes in parchment codices: 'scribi optime ceris, in quibus facillima est ratio delendi, nisi forte visus infirmior membranarum potius usum exiget . . . relinquendae autem in utrolibet genere vacuae tabellae . . .', quoted by C. H. Roberts, op. cit., pp. 174–5.

67. See G. D. Hobson, *English Binding Before 1500*, Cambridge, 1929, Appendix K.

68. *Catalogi Veteres Librorum Ecclesiae Cathedralis Dunelm* (ed. B. Botfield, Surtees Soc., vii, 1838).

69. Printed by R. M. Wilson, 'The Medieval Library of Titchfield Abbey', *Proc. Leeds Philos. Lit. Soc.*, v (1940), pp. 150–77, 252–76. The Titchfield phrase for unbound books was 'in quaterno'.

70. See *The Paston Letters*, ed. James Gairdner, iii, London, 1875, pp. 300–1.

71. The book measures $11\frac{7}{8}$ by $4\frac{3}{8}$ inches and is therefore of a suitable shape for carrying in a holster. We sometimes find account-books of this shape, but 'literary' holster-books are rare. B.M. Harley MS 1239, containing Chaucer's *Troilus* and five of the *Canterbury Tales*, measures $15\frac{1}{2}$ by $5\frac{1}{2}$ inches. Oxford, Balliol College MS 354, the commonplace-book of Richard Hill, paper, dating from the first half of the sixteenth century and containing much English verse, measures $11\frac{1}{2}$ by $4\frac{1}{4}$ inches; its items appear to have been entered over a period of more than thirty years, see R. L. Greene, *The Early English Carols*, Oxford, 1935, pp. 339–40. Prof. G. Kane has drawn my attention to a *Piers Plowman* holster-book: B.M. Harley MS. 3954, containing also Mandeville's *Travels* and other Middle English texts, measures $11\frac{1}{2}$ by $5\frac{3}{4}$ inches. B.M. Egerton MS 3323, acquired by the British Museum in 1946, consists of fragments of a number of MSS: ff. 19–31, containing extracts from St Anselm and other texts, measure 25·7 by 13·5 cm., belong to the first part of the 12th century and are probably North French in origin; see F. Wormald, 'A Medieval Description of Two Illuminated Psalters', *Scriptorium*, vi (1952), pp. 18–25.

72. 'Chaucer's Words unto Adam', *Works*, ed. Robinson, p. 628.

73. 'Collectanea Varia', *Palaeographia Latina*, xvi, 1923, pp. 10–14. See also E. A. Lowe, 'The Oldest Omission Signs in Latin MSS.' in *Miscellanea Giovanni Mercati*, vi (Studi e Testi, 126, Vatican City, 1946), pp. 36–79.

74. Though, with a monastic book, the fact that it was corrected at a particular centre would not prove absolutely that it was produced there. In the second half of the 14th century, William le Stiphel, of Brittany, was employed, both at Durham and Finchale, for transcribing new copies of books and rendering existing copies more serviceable. He wrote and signed B.M. Burney MS 310, a Finchale book, and wrote Durham Cathedral MS A. I. 3, dated 1386, see J. Raine, *The Priory of Finchale* (Surtees Soc., vi, 1837), p. xxiii n. In Cambridge, Trinity

College MS B. 15. 30, he wrote and signed section II, a table of contents of the *Summa* of Thomas de Chabham, the text of which occurs, in a late 13th-century hand, in section III. The Trinity MS is assigned to Durham, with a query, by N. R. Ker, *Medieval Libraries of Great Britain*, London, 1941, p. 39.

75. Stationers, non-monastic book-producers and corporations of people connected with book-production are to be met with in the 13th century and earlier; see below, chapter IV. But for England in the later 14th and 15th centuries, only one large-scale, commercial, book-producing house is known for certain, that of the Londoner, John Shirley, for whom see E. P. Hammond, *English Verse between Chaucer and Surrey*, London, 1927, pp. 192 ff., and A. Brusendorff, *The Chaucer Tradition*, Copenhagen, 1925, pp. 207–12. However, continental houses existed and the general opinion is that there must have been other English ones, see Brusendorff, op. cit., p. 55; L. H. Loomis, 'The Auchinleck Manuscript and a Possible London Bookshop of 1330–1340', *P.M.L.A.*, lvii (1942), p. 596; H. J. Chaytor, *From Script to Print*, Cambridge, 1945, p. 107; E. P. Goldschmidt, 'Preserved for Posterity', *The New Colophon*, viii (1950), pp. 329–30.

The Trinity College, Cambridge, Gower MS R. 3. 2, mentioned above, was produced by five scribes, who, if non-monastic, could only have been employed by a commercial house, as perhaps were the scribes of at least three other Gower MSS: Cambridge, University Library MS Mm. 2. 21 (described by G. C. Macaulay, *The Complete Works of John Gower*, ii, Oxford, 1899–1902, pp. cxl–cxli); the Keswick Hall MS (described ibid., pp. clxi–clxii), and Oxford, Bodley MS 902 (described ibid., pp. cxxxviii–cxxxix).

76. For example, B.M. Harley MS 7333, a large vernacular MS, begun in the mid-15th century, which includes texts showing the influence of John Shirley, was written in a house of Augustinian canons at Leicester, see Manly and Rickert, op. cit., pp. 207–18. For other Chaucer MSS ascribed to religious houses, see their descriptions of Manchester, Chetham MS 6709, Longleat MS 257 and MS 144 in the Huntington Library, California.

77. See Oxford, Christ Church MS CLII and Cambridge, University Library MS Dd. 4. 24, described by Manly and Rickert, op. cit., pp. 85–91 and pp. 100–7. With these contrast B.M. Sloane MS 1686 (described ibid., pp. 510–14). Although made cheaply and of paper, it is very carefully corrected, first in the ink of the text and then again in red ink, which makes more corrections and emphasises those already made. These facts, together with evidence that the MS remained long unbound, suggest to Manly and Rickert that it was used as an exemplar, to be distributed among the scribes of a commercial house.

78. Guide-letters underneath initials can be observed on the final fly-leaf of B.M. Royal MS 13 C. v. Marginal guide-letters are occasionally visible in B.M. Harley MS 447. Longer marginal directions, or their remains, occur in Royal MS 6 C. vii on ff. 94b, 95b, and 134 (verge of top margin).

79. See E. G. Millar, *An Illuminated Manuscript of 'La Somme le Roy' Attributed to the Parisian Miniaturist Honoré*, Roxburghe Club, 1953, p. 13.

80. ibid., p. 19. Millar says here that the descriptions occur also in a manuscript which he has not seen, namely Valencia University library MS 863, dated about 1325.

81. The descriptions are printed, from the two Paris MSS, ibid., pp. 49–51.

82. Several examples occur in B.M. Royal MS 1 A. xiv.

IV

The Universities and the Mediaeval Library

C. H. TALBOT

THE movement away from the monasteries and towards the new university centres which is characteristic of the thirteenth century brought in its train many and great changes in the social and cultural sphere. Not least among these changes was that brought about in the production and the distribution of books.

In the monasteries of the preceding centuries manuscripts had been written in the tranquillity of the scriptorium by monks working *sub specie aeternitatis*, and the leisurely manner in which their toil was carried out was not disturbed by the clamour for more and more books by avid and impatient readers. The monk received one book at the beginning of Lent of each year, which he read, according to the prescription of St Benedict *in ordine, ex integro*, until Lent of the following year came round.[1] It was fairly easy, therefore, to cater for the needs and tastes of even a large community.

But with the influx of students from all parts of Europe to the university towns the need for more and more books dealing with the subjects treated in the scholastic curriculum became acute. It was imperative to multiply certain texts without which the lectures of the masters could not be followed, and to produce them within a short space of time. Quiet leisure, unhurried writing, artistic adornment, fine binding were out of the question. What was needed in the new circumstances was something immediately useful, practical, convenient for carrying about, relatively inexpensive and without frills and flourishes. So began industrial book-making.

Too much emphasis cannot be placed upon the effect produced by the rise of the universities. It had repercussions not only on the size of the manuscripts, but also on the quality of the parchment, the style of script, the disposition of the text on the page, the type of ornamentation, the use of colours and the method of book-binding.

In the twelfth century the size of the manuscripts, particularly those of the Bible and the works of the Fathers, was very large, though this differed from abbey to abbey according to its economic position. The writing, even in small texts, was comparatively large and round, easily legible, amply spaced and artistically set. The parchment was thick, the binding of oak boards covered with stout leather, often elaborately decorated, on which sometimes five large-headed nails were placed, one at each corner and one in the middle, to preserve it from becoming worn as it rested on the desks in the cloister or the choir.[2]

University book production to a large extent put an end to all this. The need for a rapid multiplication of texts made simplification in every branch of book making a necessity and, in consequence, a new form of script was adopted, abbreviations were used in number, ornament was almost completely abandoned (leading to the disappearance of the colours yellow and green), and a more pliable and easily portable binding was introduced. The parchment employed was also much thinner, almost transparent in some cases, the number of folios in each gathering was increased, the writing was frequently placed in two columns on the page and in general the format of books became much smaller.[3]

The method adopted for the rapid multiplication of texts was that which had been familiar in monasteries since the ninth century. When a work was urgently required, perhaps because the model had to be returned to its owner within a short space of time, the monks separated the gatherings of the manuscript and distributed them among the members of the scriptorium, who were thus enabled to copy different but complementary parts of the text at the same time.[4] This method was taken over by the university scribes and brought to perfection. The unit of their work was the *pecia*, a technical term (borrowed no doubt from the tanners and parchment makers) designating a sheep-skin which could be treated for writing on.[5] The parchment was folded in the middle, which gave four pages in folio, or, if folded again, gave eight pages quarto with a total of sixteen columns. The work to be produced was copied on to as many *peciae* as were necessary and these were numbered, verified, and corrected, and bound together to form what was called the *exemplar*. This *exemplar* was then deposited with the stationer, where students or scribes could borrow it for a certain fixed sum and copy it *pecia* by *pecia*. Thus one *exemplar* could be reproduced by seven, eight or even more scholars at the same time, and, if they in turn lent their copies to others, the rapid multiplication of texts was easily achieved.

It is commonly held that the invention of the *pecia* belongs to the thirteenth century, but if we are to believe an inscription which occurs in a manuscript of Trinity College, Cambridge, it must have been current between 1150 and 1180.[6] The *pecia* was certainly in use in the book trade at Oxford and Cambridge in the thirteenth century and there are several manuscripts in which the divisions are easily observable.[7] We can even see which *peciae* have been loaned out by the owner to other masters or students (for their names are scribbled in the margins), and what was the price they paid.[8] The size of the *pecia* appears to have differed somewhat in the manuscripts we know, but the general conclusion seems to be that it was a sextern. A manuscript now at Peterhouse, Cambridge, and which has been considered to be by the hand of Roger Bacon, contains no less than seven different manuscripts bound together, of varying number of lines and columns, but all marked with the *peciae*.[9] In some of the latter we find the highest point of accuracy reached by the scribes: not only are all the columns numbered, but between the columns the lines are marked off in fives and on each side of the page the *distinctio* and the *quaestio* are indicated.[10] One peculiarity of English manuscripts of the thirteenth century from Oxford is that not only are the *peciae* numbered, but each leaf of the sextern is marked from one to six so that the leaves may not be misplaced, and to distinguish the gatherings horizontal or perpendicular strokes or other combinations are employed.[11]

Though the statutes which regulated the process of book production and book selling did not appear until some time after the

Plate 9

establishment of the universities, it is quite certain that, almost from the beginning, the monopoly of the book trade was in the hands of the university authorities.[12] The control which they assumed, especially on the continent, extended to every detail of book production and book distribution. It applied to sellers of parchment (and later of paper), as well as to copyists and their employees, illuminators and even to bookbinders.

At Paris, for instance, the parchment was brought by merchants each year to the Lendit Fair and submitted to the rector of the university, who selected what was needed for the various faculties and fixed in advance the price of all the rest. This measure was introduced to ensure that materials for writing would be available to both masters and students at a fair price, free from fluctuation caused either by unforeseen economic difficulties or the rapacity of the tradesmen.[13]

When an author had written out his manuscript and handed it over to the bedel of the university, for transmission to the stationer, the latter was bound to make an *exemplar* of it within twenty days and display it in a conspicuous place in his shop for publication. This *exemplar* was bound to conform to a pre-determined format: there must be so many letters to the line and so many lines to the page.[14] If we reflect that the scribes were paid according to the number of *peciae* they copied, and that the enlarging of the letters and the wider spacing of the words would enable them to cover much parchment in a short time and thus to earn more whilst working less, this curious regulation becomes intelligible.

Before the *exemplar* was allowed to be loaned out for copying, it was handed over to the *peciarii*, officials appointed by the university to examine texts to see that they conformed in all particulars with the original.[15] Incorrect work was followed by a fine, sometimes rather heavy according to our standards, and in an effort to eliminate it, all masters and students were obliged, under pain of fine also, to denounce to the authorities any mistakes which they detected in books offered to them for sale or loan.[16]

At Paris the *exemplars* had to be displayed in the houses of the Franciscans and Dominicans on the four occasions of the year when the university sermons were preached, the purpose being to

F

bring to the notice of all members of the university what books were available. This was the counterpart of our modern publisher's advertisement.

The *exemplars*, however, could not be disposed of by the stationers without due licence from the assembled congregation of the university,[17] nor could such a book be allowed to pass out of the city to another university without permission.[18] In a place like Oxford, where all the booksellers were not sworn members of the university, such a regulation could not be enforced, with the result that many valuable manuscripts were sold overseas.[19] But a way was found of circumventing this difficulty by enacting that no one except the official stationers or their deputies could sell books worth more than half a mark.[20]

A continual supply of fresh literature was ensured by the regulation that after holding a disputation every doctor should, on pain of a fine of ten ducats, write out his argument and deliver it to the bedel of the university, by whom it was transmitted to the stationer for publication.

The stationers could not refuse to hire out or sell to the students any of their wares. This measure was enforced in order to prevent them from selling books to people who did not belong to the university; for, since they carried on their trade on a percentage basis and were allowed $2\frac{1}{2}$ per cent if they sold to an outsider, but only $1\frac{1}{2}$ if they sold to a master or student, they were inclined to consider their own interests rather than those of the university.[21] And in order to prevent new writers from being squeezed off the market, old texts were not allowed to be written in a smaller hand than those of the current writers. The encouragement to get more for one's money might otherwise have been too strong for the impecunious student.

Some of these trade regulations which the stationers swore strictly to observe, but of which we have little evidence in England, may appear to our eyes curious, if not unreasonable. But the main idea of the university authorities was to protect the interests of the students and to provide books for them at the cheapest possible rate. It must be remembered that most of the members of the book trade were as much members of the university as the professors, masters and scholars. They enjoyed certain privileges, such as exemption from the civil courts, from royal and municipal taxes, from taking their turn on the city night watches.[22]

It must not be supposed that the book trade was entirely the creation of the universities. The universities simply absorbed the trade as soon as it came within their jurisdiction. We know from other sources that the making and selling of manuscripts had been carried on throughout the Middle Ages,[23] but the first reference to a public dealer in books is provided by a letter of Peter of Blois,[24] archdeacon of Bath, about 1170, and is not entirely creditable to the book trade. Peter tells us of a shabby trick played upon him by a *mango* of Paris. The archdeacon, who was an avid collector of books, found upon the stalls there a number of valuable legal texts which he much coveted. When the price was agreed upon, he paid out his money, and, intending to pick them up later on, foolishly left the books at the shop. In the meantime, his friend, the provost of Saxeburgh, came along, saw the parcel of books and offered the dealer a higher price than Peter had paid for them. After some discussion, the provost won the day, and when Peter returned for his purchase, he found that the books had disappeared.

We know some of the places where these booksellers sold their wares. In Oxford at the beginning of the thirteenth century, parchment makers, scribes and illuminators were to be found in Catte Street:[25] later on they had their shops near the north gate of the town.[26] In Paris, so John of Garland tells us, it was in the Parvis Notre Dame.[27] But the booksellers had other premises as well. A regulation issued by the university of Paris forbade any stationer or bookseller to engage in any mean occupation, but since the authorities felt perhaps that the taverns would be more respectable if kept by their own officers, parchment makers, bookbinders and stationers often kept these as well. It is certain that Nicholas, the Englishman, was taverner whilst carrying on his business as bookseller. One must admit that it was a fascinating combination, and it must have solaced many an anxious student worrying whether he could afford the *Summa* of Thomas Aquinas to be able to solve his problems over a bottle of *Vinum Theologorum* (whatever that may have been) and a couple of Jacobin tarts, much favoured, we are told, by the Dominican Friars.

It would be erroneous to conclude that because the multiplication of manuscripts had become much more rapid and straightforward, the price of books was within the reach of every student. We know too little of the price of materials at that time to be able to assess with certainty the possibility of students ever acquiring a library, and what we do know does not lead to the assumption that the buying of books was an easy matter. It may help us a little to consider for a moment the comparative prices of other things at that period. If we bear in mind that a single room could be rented for about a pound a year and that the total expenses for a student were about five pounds a year, we shall be in a position to compare the cost of manuscripts. Parchment cost from a halfpenny to twopence a skin. The normal price of copying a *pecia*, that is eight pages or sixteen columns, was threepence or fourpence: gold letters were threepence apiece, common paragraphs sixpence a hundred. The bill actually paid for a folio volume of two hundred pages, called *The Romance of the Four States*, which was presented by John of Limoges to his library, and which is still to be seen at Paris, runs as follows:

Parchment		8s	8d
Script	£1	9s	4d
Correction		2s	10d
Illumination		1s	1d
Binding		1s	5d
Total	£2	3s	4d

This, however, was a better book than the ordinary texts sought after by the students. In the flyleaves of manuscripts we meet other indications of prices, but it is not until the fourteenth century that the individual items are noted down.[28] For instance, for a thirteenth-century book, measuring $9\frac{1}{4}$ by $7\frac{1}{4}$ inches and composed of 76 folios of thirty-nine lines to the page, the price was 8 shillings; for another, measuring 11 by $7\frac{1}{2}$ inches with 249 folios, the price was 13 shillings and 4 pence. In a copy of St Augustine's *De Trinitate*, 85 folios of forty-seven lines, measuring 11 by $7\frac{3}{4}$ inches we find the note: 'Emptus per fratrem Rogerum de Norwyc precium 12*s*.';[29] whilst a book, 'emptus apud Avinionem' containing two glosses and two different texts of the decretals cost thirty florins.[30] On the whole, the prices, as far as students were concerned, must have been prohibitive, and we can well understand that when a book changed hands there was as much ceremony about it as when a house or property was transferred. In the flyleaf of a manuscript, now at Gonville and Caius College, we find the following note: 'Memo that I bought this book from John Haclay on the Vigil of the Apostles Saints Simon and Jude in the house of William de Nessfylde, stationer, before the following witnesses'; then are mentioned the names of about eight people, 'cum multis aliis'.[31] This took place in 1309–10, the earliest record I have come across of a stationer at Cambridge.[32]

The people who bought books were usually in comfortable financial positions, sometimes officials of the king or the ecclesiastical authorities, who had the opportunity to travel and indulge their tastes in the markets abroad. How otherwise, can one explain the manuscripts whose flyleaves tell us that they were bought in Paris, Avignon, Constance, Bologna and so on?[33] Some of these people acquired quite considerable libraries: Geoffrey de Lawath, for example, rector of the church of St Magnus in London, who entered a list of forty-eight of his books, dealing with canon law, grammar, dialectic, medicine and theology.[34] But the inventories of goods of graduates at the universities contain hardly any books, and leave us with the impression that they could not afford to buy them.[35] The pledges left with the keepers of the university chests tell us the same tale: large numbers of books were constantly changing hands, good perhaps for the second-hand book trade, but not favourable to the building up of private collections.[36]

We have already remarked that the universities in England were not able to exercise the same control over the book trade as was exercised elsewhere on the continent. As time went on the freedom to write and sell books almost anywhere becomes more and more apparent, and it was not merely the stationers who dealt in books and book materials, but bankers, merchants and even grocers. In the housekeeping accounts of King John of France, covering the years of his captivity in England, 1359–60, the following entries occur:[37]

Pierre le Parcheminnier, pour une douzainne de parchemin achetée de li, 3s. 4d.

Jehan Huistasse, pour une main de papier et 1 peau de parchemin,
. . . 10d.

Berthélemi Mine, 3 quaiers de papier, 27d.

We find books sold at all the principal fairs: at Stourbridge, at
St Giles, Oxford, at London, and it is quite evident that other
places as well, far distant from the universities, had a good book
trade.[38] One man, with an eye to securing future business, no
doubt, put his name at the end of a manuscript now at Gonville
and Caius College, Cambridge: 'Johannes Carl–w scriptor de
Anglie Lyn in Norfolckia'.[39] We find another made at Lincoln,
another at York, another bought at Uttoxeter. It would be weari-
some to list all the places where writing was carried on as a profession and where books could be bought.

The coming of the friars greatly stimulated this trade in books.
Their motto 'Nihil habentes et omnia possidentes' became a source
of criticism when their libraries were mentioned, for they had an
insatiable thirst for books. Richard de Bury said of them: 'These
men are like ants, ever preparing their meat in summer or like
bees continually building their cells of honey.' '. . . although they
were late in entering the Lord's vineyard, they have added more
in this brief hour to the stock of sacred books than all others.'[40]
Entering as they did into the very centre of university life, and in
some cases actually founding the theological faculty,[41] their need
for texts was acute. As teachers, students, preachers, and at an early
stage, as unwilling controversialists, they found themselves in need
of a whole armoury of books.

There was nothing in the Constitutions of the Friars to regulate
what, up till that time, had been an essential element in every
religious order: the scriptorium. They did not produce their own
books for the simple reason that this would have involved them
in manual rather than in intellectual work.[42] For them it was of far
more importance to be able to think and argue than to write well.[43]
As a result, if we examine the books of the friars, we frequently
find that they have been bought:[44] only the *reportationes* of lectures
followed at the university are written out by their own hands.
The early thirteenth-century bibles which belonged to them, now
in the Royal Collection in the British Museum,[45] were the work
of professional scribes: the numbers of small initials and large

capitals are jotted down on the last page, and there is a note in one volume, for there are eight volumes to complete one bible, that the copyist was lacking one quaternion. Roger Bacon tells us the same story. When he wished to have a fair copy made of his *Opus Maius* for presentation to the pope, he complained that none of his brethren was capable of making it: on the other hand, he dared not entrust the work to the stationers lest, without his consent, they might publish it.[46] It is exceptional to find a book written out completely by a friar, and since the alms and gifts of money which they received were often expended on buying books, it is understandable that they felt no compulsion to do so.[47]

It was through the friars' connection with the universities that their libraries, in comparison with the older monastic libraries, took on a completely new aspect. No longer were they content with the works of the Fathers, some copies of the classics, one or two books on the natural sciences and a sprinkling of writings on systematic theology. The curriculum of the schools was far wider in scope, the theological training was becoming more intense, and the methods of teaching impregnated with Aristotelian logic were completely different from anything envisaged by the monastic legislators. Consequently, a whole host of new texts made their appearance.

The *Constitutions* of Humbert of Romans affords us some idea of the scope of their studies.[48] He lays it down as a rule that all the houses of Dominican friars shall have the following types of books: there are to be bibles, complete and in parts, bibles with glosses, also partial and complete; then there are to be concordances, commentaries, interpretations of Greek and Hebrew words, Summae of theology and canon law, Quaestiones, ecclesiastical decrees, the Decretals, Distinctiones morales (that is, lists of theological terms in alphabetical order), sermons for Sundays and feasts of the year, biblical and secular histories, systematic *Sentences* like that of Peter Lombard, chronicles, lives of the Saints and Martyrs, 'and many other books of a like nature, in order that the brethren may find ready to hand whatever they need'.

The further subjects of study mentioned by Roger Bacon show that even this imposing list did not satisfy the curiosity of some of the early friars. They soon found that the study of the Bible involved a knowledge of the ancient languages, Greek and Hebrew[49] (and in Spain, of Arabic), that *correctoria* were needed to deal with the mistakes made by scribes in the transcription of the scriptures,[50] and that a knowledge of natural history, alchemy, astronomy and other physical sciences was needed to interpret the text. All this had repercussions on the kinds of libraries that they assembled.

But this was not all. The appearance of scores of new writers,[51] all concerned with the fundamental problems of philosophy, theology and law, stimulated the production of books and the growth and reorganisation of their libraries. Within a century of their establishment, the Dominican friars alone had produced more than 120 new writers of considerable importance, some of whose works were voluminous, and the same may be said of the Franciscans and Augustinians. One has only to refer to Albert the Great, Thomas Aquinas, Alexander of Hales, Duns Scotus and others of the same rank for this fact to be recognised. Each friary was anxious to have not only the works produced by the masters of its own school, but, when controversies arose, such as that on the plurality of forms, the writings of the opposite school as well. Moreover, the friars did not remain teaching in one place. Part of their works would be produced in one university centre, part in another. Thomas Aquinas wrote both in Paris and Naples, Duns Scotus in Oxford, Paris and Cologne. In each place, their colleagues and disciples would endeavour to procure the whole corpus of their writings, no matter where they had been composed. Hence, there was a continual exchange of books and on such a scale as had not been known before.

To meet this new demand, the scribes increased in numbers, and Roger Bacon tells us that the number of professional scribes was infinite: 'Nam circa quadraginta annos sunt multi theologi, infiniti et stationarii Parisiis.'[52]

This movement of masters and students from place to place affected the size of books. When we read that Fishacre, a friend of Roger Bacon, always carried about with him a copy of the works of Aristotle, we can understand that it must have been a small copy. Indeed, the tremendous trade in small books that is evident at this period is undoubtedly attributable to the friars. Unlike those students who had servants to carry their books to and from the schools and who were taxed according to the space they took up on the desks, the friars had to carry their own books,[53] sometimes over great distances. Hence, the tiny bibles and books of sermons, 6 inches by 5 inches, fifty or more lines to the page with 500 or more folios, of which a great number survive.

The monastic houses, meanwhile, were also being affected by the new trends in education. Their recruits were falling off, mainly owing to the popularity of the new orders, and in an effort to counteract this attraction and meet the friars on their own ground, they began to found colleges of their own in the university towns.[54] The students who frequented the lectures on Aristotle acquired tastes that were foreign to the normal tradition of monastic culture and gradually introduced into their libraries books that belonged to the scholastic field. These books were not produced in the monastic scriptoria but were bought from the stationers.[55] Slowly, in spite of the fact that the general chapters of the Benedictines counselled the writing and illumination of manuscripts instead of manual labour,[56] the scriptoria became less active. The accounts for Abingdon and Norwich are revealing on this score. Over a period of fifty years, the annual expenses for parchment average not more than fourpence, which in the event was used for drawing up the accounts, whilst the accounts themselves were written by a professional scribe. If we compare this with the 3s 8d paid for tankards, the 10d spent on buckets or the 1s 2d spent on three crates for carrying fish, perhaps we shall understand how little writing was being done.[57] In Durham, there seems to have been a fair amount of copying carried out, but the type of book produced shows that the early study of the Fathers had given place to the compilation of indexes and *tabulae* containing snippets which would be useful for quoting as authorities. On the whole, the catalogues show that creative activity was lessened rather than stimulated by the growth in the book trade.

Something new, however, did happen even in the monasteries, and this lay in the field of library organisation. This change was mainly the result of the activity of the friars. With the increase of books, which were not placed exclusively in the library, but were often scattered about all over the house in the various rooms of the brethren, it became imperative to have detailed lists of what was owned, not merely to prevent losses through negligence, borrowing, selling and so on, but also in order that the masters and students should have at hand whatever was needed for their studies. Hence the great strides in cataloguing at this time.

The *Constitutions* of Humbert of Romans, general of the Dominicans, drawn up about 1260, go into great detail on the obligations of the librarian and the care of books.[58]

The old method of listing merely the first work in any one volume was, perhaps, sufficient in the monastic houses where systematic study was not pursued as it was in the new orders. But now the friars, following perhaps the lead given by the Sorbonne and the various Synodal decrees, not only divided up all their books into the various faculties of theology, law, medicine, philosophy and so on, but also listed every treatise contained in any one single volume. By a system of letters which corresponded not only to the various disciplines, but also to the books contained in that section and to the smaller treatises found within the book, it became an easy matter to lay one's hand on whatever was needed at a moment's notice. The leading example of this was to be found at the Sorbonne; but the same fundamental conception was applied also at Canterbury, where Prior Eastry's catalogue shows that the library was divided up into nine sections,[59] each section into so many shelves numbered with a roman numeral, and each volume on the shelf having its contents listed with the requisite page number.

We have also about this time, the inter-library catalogue. Savigny seems to have been the first to have added to its own list of books the catalogues of those libraries which existed in the same province. This system was followed by the colleges in Paris, and finally we have as the fullest development of it the *Registrum* of the English friars. The alphabetical catalogue[60] as such was still rare and reduced to an index of the normal register according to classes. We find for instance the catalogue of St Mary's, Leicester, preceded by a 'tabula de nominibus omnium doctorum, auctorum seu compilatorum quorum libri . . . notantur in isto registro'.[61]

Of greater importance was the division of books according to their place. This method had been known already in the eleventh century, when we hear of the *bibliotheca, schola interior et exterior, commune et minus armarium*. It was now adopted by the friars and the college libraries, and, at the Sorbonne, for instance, there was the *libraria communis*, open to all the fellows, which contained the books exclusively for their use, the *libri cathenati*, and the *parva bibliotheca* with its *libri vagantes*, which, either because they were not in good condition or were duplicates, could be sent out on loan.[62]

This question of the lending of books had not been in favour with the communities.[63] Indeed, to judge by a decree issued by the council of Rouen in 1212, it would appear that some religious had been in the habit of taking an oath that they would not lend out the books of the monasteries.[64] The decree, however, points out that it was a work of mercy and piety to lend books to poor scholars, and as time went on it became an accepted principle that books, which could be borrowed by brethren within the house, could also be borrowed by outsiders provided they left sufficient pledge.[65] Within the friaries a book was kept for the purpose of entering all loans, but to make sure that a less valuable book was not substituted for the one taken away, the second folio entry, or sometimes the beginning word of the penultimate folio, had to be mentioned after the title of the book.[66] Soon this became usual even when describing a book in the catalogue, and thanks to this custom we are able today to identify certain manuscripts which formerly belonged to monasteries or friaries.

The knowledge that books bequeathed to religious houses would also be lent to private individuals encouraged the gifts of whole libraries to these institutions, and the number of wills in which we find the proviso that such gifts should be accepted on the understanding that others could borrow them led to the widespread acceptance of the idea of the public library.[67]

A further change, exemplified by the Vatican, of the religious into the princely library need not detain us now. But if we try to summarise what has already been said, we notice the following steps.

The evolution of the mediaeval library was favoured and determined by three new circumstances: cultural factors, such as the rise of the universities with their numerous clientele, new educational system and particular needs; economic factors, leading to specialised methods of book production and book distribution and the growth of a professional class to deal with them; and historical factors, such as the rise of the new religious orders.

This evolution profoundly modified the mediaeval library as regards content, organisation and diffusion. The books produced by the mendicant orders changed the character of the old conventual libraries not only by placing less emphasis on elegance and more on accurate transcription and serviceability of content, but also by neglecting the *originalia* of works of the Fathers for summaries and indexes, and creating a completely new type of biblical, theological and scientific literature. Their care regarding the good order of the books, the accuracy of the catalogues, and the putting aside of funds for the acquisition of new works became a prime factor in the later development of library administration, whilst the system of loans previously neglected, led first to the acceptance in principle, later to the practical institution of public libraries.

NOTES TO CHAPTER IV

1. *Regula S. Benedicti*, c. xlviii; cf. *The Monastic Constitutions of Lanfranc*, ed. M. D. Knowles, London, 1951, p. 19. See also p. 151.

2. B. Van Regemorter, 'Évolution de la technique de la réliure du viiie au xiie siècle', *Scriptorium*, ii (1948), pp. 275–85.

3. J. Destrez, *La Pecia, dans les manuscrits universitaires du* xiiie *et du* xive *siècle*, Paris, 1935, pp. 42 ff.

4. Cambridge, Pembroke College MS 308; 'Exordium Parvum Cisterciensis Cenobii' in Ph. Guignard, *Monuments Primitifs de la Règle Cistercienne*, Dijon, 1878, p. 68.

5. R. Steele, 'The Pecia', *The Library*, 4th ser., xi (1931), pp. 230–4.

6. Cambridge, Trinity College MS O. 7. 40, fol. 71: 'In hoc libello continentur xxv pecie different.' The script is of the second half of the 12th century, between 1150 and 1180.

7. A. G. Little and F. Pelster, *Oxford Theology and Theologians* (Oxford Hist. Soc. xcvi, 1934), pp. 56 ff., quote as examples Oxford, Bodl. MS 200 (with indications on ff. 25, 37, 193), Oxford, Balliol College MSS 133, 193, 212.

8. Assisi MS 158, f. 105b: 'Henricus Ibericus peciam habet sequentem'; f. 156b: 'Peciam precedentem habet Cancellarius; Oxoniensis.' Oxford, Balliol College MS 62, fol. 5b: 'Memorandum accomodasse tres pecias super librum Topicorum Laurencium Cornubiensem.'

9. Cambridge, Peterhouse MS 262, fol. 1: 'Tabula Augustini . . . in 5 peciis'; fol. 68: 'Tabula suhampton . . . in duabus peciis'; fol. 80: 'Tabula super Antissiodorensem duarum peciarum'; fol. 104: 'Capitula . . . in 5 peciis'; fol. 198: 'Tabula super Arismeticam . . . in duabus peciis'. See M. R. James, *A Descriptive Catalogue*

of the MSS. in Peterhouse, Cambridge, 1899, pp. 332, 333. Here the *pecia* is generally of twelve leaves.

10. Oxford, Balliol College MS 62; cf. also B.M. Royal MS 10 B. vii; Oxford, Oriel College MS B. 4. 3 (Coxe 43); Bologna, Univ. Lib. Cod. 1546; Vatican, Ottobon. 294. This practice is not found in any other university centre.

11. Oxford, Bodl. MS 200; Balliol College MSS 133 and 193. As time went on the *pecia* as a unit does not appear to have survived. It is always the *quaternio*, particularly in the 14th and 15th centuries: cf. the price lists mentioned later in the chapter.

12. *Munimenta Academica Oxon.* (ed. H. Anstey, Rolls Ser. 50, London, 1868), i, p. 150.

13. What follows is based on various statutes to be found in H. Denifle and A. Chatelain, *Chartularium Universitatis Parisiensis*, Paris, 1889, i. no. 462, pp. 532–3, ii, no. 1064, pp. 530–2 and Anstey, op. cit., ii, pp. 383–7.

14. H. Denifle, *Archiv. f. Literatur- und Kirchen-Geschichte*, iii (1887), p. 295, no. 25, prints the Bolognese statute, *Ex quot litteris et columnis constituatur pecia*: 'Statuimus quod pecia constituatur ex sexdecim columnis, quarum quelibet contineat sexaginta lineas, et quelibet linea literas triginta duas secundum taxationem studii Bononiensis.'

15. L. Frati, 'Gli Stazionari Bolognesi nel Medio Evo', *Archivio Storico Italiano*, 5th ser., xlv (1910), pp. 380–5.

16. Strickland Gibson, *Statuta antiqua Vniversitatis Oxoniensis*, Oxford, 1931, p. 186: 'Item quod stationarii et alii quicumque qui exemplaria librorum locant, teneantur sub pena amissionis eorumdem aut sub pena aliqua graviori per universitatem taxanda, integra, completa, correcta, ac fidelia exemplaria exhibere.'

17. cf. Wilkins, *Concilia*, iii, London, 1737, p. 317: 'per nos seu successores nostros expresse approbetur et universitatis nomine ac auctoritate stationariis tradatur, ut copietur; et facta collatione fideli, petentibus vendatur justo pretio sive detur, originali in cista aliqua universitatis extunc perpetua remanente.'

18. Denifle and Chatelain, op. cit., ii, no. 733, pp. 190–2: 'et universitas exemplaris usu non defraudetur.'

19. Strickland Gibson, op. cit., pp. 183–7.

20. Anstey, op. cit., i, pp. 233, 234.

21. At Paris a distinction was made between 'stationarius' and 'librarius'. The latter took commission on sale, but could not sell without permission of the university authorities and so his business was carried on within prescribed limits: P. Delalain, *Le Libraire parisien du xiiie au xve siècle*, Paris, 1891, and Savigny, *Geschichte des römischen Rechts im Mittelalter*, iii, p. 591.

22. Anstey, op. cit., ii, p. 52; Denifle and Chatelain, op. cit., ii, no. 661, p. 123.

23. W. Wattenbach, *Das Schriftwesen im Mittelalter*, 3rd edn., Leipzig, 1896, pp. 545 ff.

24. Epist. 71, Migne, *Pat. Lat.*, ccvii, 219, 220.

25. H. E. Salter, *The Medieval Archives of the University of Oxford* (Oxford Hist. Soc., lxx, 1920), i, pp. 291, 292. Among the witnesses who transfer property in Catte Street are one binder, three illuminators, one writer and two parchmenters, all evidently residing close to School Street of later times. The deed is probably not earlier than 1205, though T. E. Holland, *The University of Oxford in the 12th century* (Collectanea, Oxford Hist. Soc. xvi, 1890), pp. 178, 179, dates it 1180–1200.

26. Anstey, op. cit., ii, p. 174. cf. *Memorandum Rolls*, 45 & 46 Hen. III, m. 96 (A.D. 1262): 'Mandatum est vicecomiti quod venire (faciat) . . . Reginaldum

stacionarium Oxoniensem ad respondendum Ricardo Brun de Rowell, clerico de scaccario, de 1 codice precii xx s. quem ei debet et iniuste detinet, ut dicit.'

27. 'Paravisus est locus ubi libri scolarium venduntur', quoted in Wattenbach, op. cit., pp. 558, 559.

28. For other prices see Cambridge, Peterhouse MSS 88, 114, 142, 154, 193, 198, etc. Peterhouse MS 42 of the 13th century has reference to *pecia* and on the flyleaf (f. 2) the following account, written in the 14th century, occurs: 'Et pro scriptura et alumpnura et aliis custubus (?) factis pro parte (?) unius primur per dominum dat' domine regine Castelle de nova facta et scripta lxiii s. vi d.' To judge by the prices, the usual cost was 3d a quaternion for parchment, 16d for writing, 6d for illumination, and two shillings for binding.

29. Cambridge, Peterhouse MS 199, flyleaf.

30. Cambridge, Gonville and Caius MS 253.

31. Cambridge, Gonville and Caius MS 17.

32. Oxford, New College MS 100, see H. O. Coxe, *Cat. Cod. MSS. Coll. Novi*, Oxford, 1852, p. 37, records an early Oxford stationer in 1358.

33. Cambridge, Pembroke College MS 161: 'Istum librum emi in Messana pro 8 ducatis venitis'; Cambridge, Gonville and Caius College MS 299: 'Iste liber est . . . quem emit in civitate avinionis a.d. M^oCCC^o XXXIII'; Cambridge, Gonville and Caius MS 510: 'M.Joh. Loppham dedit hunc librum . . . in consilio generali apud Constanciam.'

34. Cambridge, Pembroke College MS 162, Printed in M. R. James, *A Descriptive Catalogue of the MSS. in the Library of Pembroke College Cambridge*, Cambridge, 1905, pp. 158, 159.

35. Anstey, op. cit., i, p. lxxvii: cf. Cambridge, Gonville and Caius MSS 161, 414, and others for evidence of pawning, selling, etc.

36. We have a list of these secondhand books with some prices on the flyleaf of Cambridge, Peterhouse MS 203: cf. Strickland Gibson, op. cit., p. 162 and pp. 183-7.Wattenbach, op. cit., p. 550, quotes the following lines which are pertinent:

> A Gandelus lez la Ferté
> La lessai-je mon A. B. C.
> Et ma patenostre à Soisson,
> Et mon Credo à Monloon
> Et mes set siaumes à Tornai,
> Mes quinze siaumes à Cambrai,
> Et mon sautier à Besençon,
> Et mon kalendier à Dijon.
> Puis m'en revint par Pontarlie,
> Ileuc vendi ma litanie,
> Et si bui au vin mon messel
> A la ville où l'en fet le sel.

37. L. Douët-D'Arcq, *Comptes de l'Argenterie des Rois de France au XIVe siècle*, Paris, 1851, pp. 247, 236, 256.

38. W. H. Harrison, *Description of England*, part i, bk ii, c. xviii, ed. F. J. Furnivall, 1877. On the beginnings of English bookselling see A. Kirchoff, *Die Handschriftenhändler des Mittelalters*, Leipzig, 1853, pp. 132-41.

39. Cambridge, Gonville and Caius College MS 339.

40. *Philobiblon* cap. viii. 136 (ed. E. C. Thomas, London, 1888, pp. 76, 77).

41. A. G. Little, 'The Friars and the Foundation of the Faculty of Theology at the University of Cambridge', *Mélanges Mandonnet*, Paris, 1930, pp. 389-401.

42. There are examples, however, of friars writing books: *Monumenta Franciscana* (ed. J. S. Brewer, Rolls Ser. 4, London, 1858), i, pp. 355, 391; cf. Cambridge, Gonville and Caius MSS 388, f. 125; 464, f. 67.

43. Acta Capituli generalis Valencenis celebrati 1259 in Martène and Durand, *Novus Thesaurus Anecdotorum*, Paris, 1717, iv, col. 1725: 'Qui scribunt magistro vel provincialibus vel capitulo scribant de littera grossa et legibili et breviter, aliter non habeant pro malo si nihil eis rescribatur.'

44. e.g. Cambridge, St John's College MS 147; Cambridge, Emmanuel College MS 20; Cambridge, Pembroke College MS 269.

45. B.M. Royal MSS. 3E. i–v.

46. *Scripta Inedita* (ed. J. Brewer, Rolls. Ser. 15, London, 1859), i. p. 13: 'Sed scribi non posset littera bona nisi per scriptores alienos a statu nostro, et illi tunc transcriberent pro se, vel aliis, vellem nollem, sicut saepissime scripta per fraudes scriptorum Parisius divulgantur.' This reflects on the bad script caused by lack of training, haste and the need to economise as much as on the untrustworthiness of the professional scribes who pirated original works.

47. cf. Cambridge, Peterhouse MS 89: 'quem dictus frater W scribi fecit et de amicorum suorum elemosinis pro scriptura satisfieri procuravit et nihilominus manu sua a principio usque finem diligenter correxit et notabilia specialia in marginibus titulavit et per decursum alphabeti in separatis quaternis per modum tabule designavit . . .'

48. *Opera de Vita Regulari*, ed. J. J. Berthier, Rome, 1888–89, ii, p. 265; W. A. Hinnebusch, *The Early English Friars Preachers*, Rome, 1951, pp. 180–6.

49. Denifle and Chatelain, op. cit., i, no. 279, pp. 317–19; cf. Cambridge, St John's College MS 169.

50. Martène and Durand, op. cit., iv, col. 1676, no. 34.

51. It may be asked where the scribes came from. The answer is that the number of clerics increased more rapidly than the foundations by which they were supported, consequently they were employed as scribes and secretaries at courts and elsewhere. They eagerly accepted the work because the remuneration was larger than for any other class of artisan or official. E. Dümmler, *Anselm der Peripatetiker*, p. 32, quotes a Lombard cleric named Anselm as saying, c. A.D. 1050: 'Multos oportet libros scribere, ut inde precium sumeres, qui a tuis lenonibus te redimeres.' Abbot Faritius of Abingdon (1101–15) appears to have employed some of them: 'Abbas Faritius instituit . . . scriptores praeter claustrales qui missalia, gradalia, antiphonaria, troparia, lectionaria et ceteros libros ecclesiasticos sibi scribebant. *Chronicon Monasterii de Abingdon* (ed. J. Stevenson, Rolls Ser. 2, London, 1858), ii, p. 289. Thomas of Chabham has an interesting passage about them in his *Summa Paenitentiae*, B.M. Royal MS 8 A. xv, f. 59.

52. *Opus Minus* (ed. Brewer, in *Opera Inedita*, Rolls Ser. 15, p. 333). Bacon goes on to say: 'qui [stationarii] cum illiterati fuerint et uxorati, non curantes nec scientes curare de veritate textus sacri proposuerunt exemplaria vitiosissima, et scriptores infiniti addiderunt ad corruptionem multas mutationes.'

53. Martène and Durand, op. cit., iv, col. 1727, no. 35: 'Item quod fratres portent ad scholas libros qui leguntur in schola, si habent, et non alios.'

54. cf. J-M. Canivez, *Statuta capitulorum generalium Ord. Cist.*, Louvain, 1934, 1935, ii, p. 253, iii, pp. 37, 38, 142.

55. e.g. Cambridge, Pembroke Coll. MS 5; Cambridge, St John's Coll. MSS 142, 170; Worcester Cathedral Q. 20: see S. G. Hamilton, *Catalogue of MSS. preserved in the Chapter Library of Worcester Cathedral*, Oxford, 1906, p. 119;

H. W. Saunders, *An Introduction to the Obedientiary and Manor Rolls of Norwich Priory*, Norwich, 1930, p. 180.

56. *Chapters of English Black Monks, 1215-1540* (ed. W. Pantin, Camden Soc., 3rd ser. xiv, London, 1931), i, p. 74, repeated ibid., ii (xlvii, 1933), p. 51.

57. *Accounts of Obedientiaries of Abingdon Abbey* (ed. R. E. G. Kirk, Camden Soc. N.S. 51, London, 1892), pp. 75, 81, 88, 106, 108, 130.

58. *Opera de Vita Regulari*, ii, 263: 'Officium librarii est, habere curam ut potest, quod habeatur bonus locus pro libraria et securus, et bene aptus contra pluviam et intemperiem, et copiam habens boni aeris pro libris custodiendis. Armarium autem in quo libri reponuntur debet esse de lignea materia, ut melius custodiantur a putrefactione vel nimia humectatione et habere multa intermedia et distinctiones, in quibus reponantur libri, et scripta diversarum facultatum, et diversi libri et huiusmodi eiusdem facultatis separatim, et non confuse, cum signationibus debitis factis per scripturam, quae applicanda est unicuique interstitio, ut sciatur ubi inveniatur quod queritur . . .' cf. H. W. Garrod, 'The Library Regulations of a Medieval College', *The Library*, 4th ser. viii (1928), pp. 312-35; C. R. L. Fletcher, 'A Catalogue of the Library of Oriel College in the year 1375', in *Collectanea* (Oxford Hist. Soc., v, 1885), i, p. 63. The Customs of the Augustinian Priory of Barnwell are practically identical with those of Humbert.

59. M. R. James, *The Ancient Libraries of Canterbury and Dover*, Cambridge, 1903, pp. xxxv–xliv; C. R. Haines, 'The Library of Dover Priory', *The Library*, 4th ser. viii (1927), pp. 73–118; cf. A. L. A. Franklin, *Les Anciens Bibliothèques de Paris*, ii, Paris, 1867, p. 352; L. Holstenius, *Codex Regularum*, ed. M. Brockie, iv, p. 338.

60. The oldest example is that of Corbie. L. Delisle, *Recherches sur l'ancienne Bibliothèque de Corbie*, Paris, 1860, pp. 49 ff. cf. L. Holstenius op. cit., iii, pp. 360-1, especially c. xi, 5: 'Habeat insuper Bibliothecarius omnium librorum qui in Bibliotheca custodiuntur, inventarium seu repertorium alphabetico ordine.'

61. M. R. James and A. Hamilton Thompson, 'Catalogue of the Library of Leicester Abbey', *Trans. Leic. Arch. Soc.*, xx (1938), xxi (1939-40).

62. Franklin, op. cit., i, pp. 237-8, note 10; L. Delisle, *Le Cabinet des Manuscrits*, ii, Paris, 1874, pp. 185-96.

63. *Statuta, constitutiones et decreta generalia congregationis Gallicanae fratrum et sororum tertii ord. S. Francisci de Penitentia*, c. xxv, p. 75: 'Nulli extraneo, etiam religioso vel sacerdoti saeculari, concedetur liber ullus extra monasterium asportandus, ne libri perdantur'; College of Bernardines in Paris: 'Nullus cuiuscumque status, officii vel gradus fuerit, librum extra librariam, pro se vel pro altero, in collegio aut extra, quacumque causa, nisi forte causa reparationis sub poena gravissima extrahere praesumat.' Franklin, op. cit., i, p. 210.

64. G. Bessin, *Concilia Rotomagensis Provinciae*, Rouen, 1717, pp. 118-19: 'Interdicimus inter alia viris religiosis ne emittant iuramenta de non commodandis libris indigentibus, cum commodare inter praecipua opera reputetur misericordiae.'

65. L. Holstenius, op. cit., iv, pp. 338 ff.

66. Franklin, op. cit., i, p. 238: 'Non sufficit scribere; talis habet talem librum vi librarum vel huius, nisi scribat etiam sic in registro: incipit secundo folio sic vel sic; ne fiat fraus in commutando librum maioris precii in librum eiusdem speciei, minoris tamen pretii, vel si perderet unus non restitueretur pejor.'

67. See Cambridge, Gonville and Caius College MS 129, ivb: 'ad utilitatem studencium ut sit in communi libraria eiusdem collegio (*sic*) non quovismodo inter libros distributivos sociorum evocandus sub pena deperdicionis eiusdem.'

1. Press in the Pepysian Library, Magdalene College, Cambridge
(*see page* 12)

2. Pepys's Library in York Buildings (*see page* 12)

3. Carrells in the cloister of Gloucester Cathedral (*see page* 18)

4b. Spendement Grill at Durham Cathedral
(*see page* 22)

4a. Book cupboard at Lanercost Priory
(*see page* 20)

liber·xl· omeliar̃ de eccliastice· offic̃· quatũ?
Templũ dñi ⁊ salutatõnes b̃ marie Tã̃no nigro·
Sermones· ꝟ· Hefoꝛd epi·cũ qbꝛoꝛ̃ alijs·albꝛ qũi?
Lamẽtatõnes Jeremie Glosate quatũ?
Jeronĩ? de catalogo viroꝛ illustium q̃ũ niger·
Lib̃ de mtꝑretatõmbꝫ noĩm eb̃icoꝛ quatũ?
Sũ ꝓsitũ sup sentencias petri lũbardi·
Sũma theologie·quatũus rubeus·
de matĩnoꝛ̃ v̄l̃ gingio·
De re militari quatũus simplꝛ·
Libellꝰ Huẽudoꝛ quatũ? rubeus·
Expõnes sup quqi libꝛos moysi q̃ũ sũꝑ·
Smones in dñicis ꝑ āñũ q̃ũ? albꝛ·
tẽ sermones in fest· scõꝛ q̃ũ? simplꝛ·   ⁊ aliꝰ ꝼp oꝛꝺno
Glose sup epl̃as pauli impr̃fce·
tem libellus qui sic meipit liber guomis Jhũ x̃·
Lib̃ sermonũ q̃ incip au oꝛe festi·
(Tabula sup libꝛ̃ moralĩ Gregory oꝛꝺ̃)

Prĩ? Gradus Scdi Armarij·
Labꝛi Clemẽtis poꝛ· ũj· volũ̃· magñ de gaoꝛꝺ noj. Livuglutaꝛ·
Libell̃s qui inticulat̃ vnũ ex quatoꝛ·
Alms libellus qui in trlut̃ vnũ ex q̃tioꝛ·
Sũ Clemtis de dialetica ⁊ theologia ꝑ̃ libell̃·
Dialetica Clemtis paruis libellus·
Gramatica Clementis puis libellus·
Clemẽs sup actus apl̃oꝛ hter mediocꝛs·
Clemẽs sup epl̃as canõicis liber mediocꝛs·
Clemẽs super apocalipsim q̃ũ? mediocꝛs·
Psaltari? de trinitate magnũ volũme·
Prĩa pars sũme fr̃is Thome de Alquo·

5. Library catalogue of Lanthony Priory (*see page* 25)

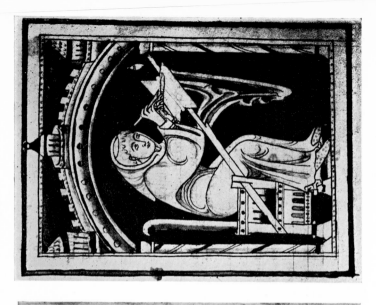

6a. Memorandum recording the gift of the MS
(see page 28)

6b. Laurence, monk of Durham, writing
(see page 48)

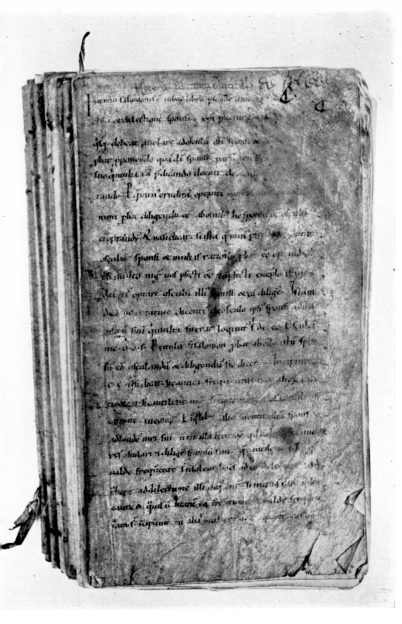

7. An unbound MS (*see page* 38)

8b. John Tiptoft's MS of Tacitus (see page 123)

8a. Directions from the scribe to the illuminator (see page 57)

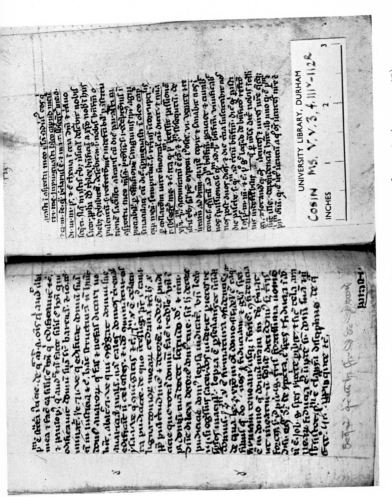

9. Memorandum relating to the borrowing of a pecia (*see page* 68)

diuino p annū glosat anglice
Gesta pontificū anglie
Cresepco bibliue frā a genuldo Combrensi.
In b̄ uohue ornex
Vetnenal hystoꝛ eusd.
Vita sci thome mīe.
ꝉ vita sci thome mīe.
Eple de tempe Baldewin.
In b̄ uohue ornex
Penitentiale magdalene.
Sīnoꝺ quidam.
Radlf de diceto.
Libꝛ Anglie.
Genelis anglie depicta.
Lib passionū a smoꝛe anglie.
Dialoḡ bi Gꝛ.
Boeciꝰ de consolōne.
Herbari anglice depictus.
Lib sīmonū catholicoꝛ anglie
Lib .z. bi Auḡ .a.
Cronica venustissa. a
Lib de ozdie mostico .a.
Cronica sedm Bedam .a.
Text̄ nij. Euāgel anglice
Actus apsoꝛ anglice.
Lib sīmonū anglice.
Regula Canonicoꝛ .a.
Cronica latine ꝛ anglice.
Lib Edwyn̄. a.
Excepcōes de plciano. a.
Lib de armanolo daustu
Bibla bipita in insirmaria
in duobꝰ volūib̄z.
Bibla Edwīn.
Tpetal salteū Edwīn.
Pma pꝑs Auḡ sꝑ ꝓoꝛ.
Sꝺa pꝑs.
tria pars.
pma pꝑs oꝛcaltū.
Sꝺa pꝑs.
pma pꝑs plinij.
Sꝺa pꝑs.
pima pꝑs baymoꝛ.
Secūda pꝑs.
tria pꝑs.
Quarta pꝑs.

Auḡ sꝑ Johm.
pma pꝑs cassiodoꝛ sꝓ pꝑs.
Sꝺa pꝑs. tria pars.

Pma pꝑs Josephi.
Sꝺa pars.
Raban̄ sꝑ evathim.
Raban̄ de nātie rey.
Isidoꝛ ethimologiaꝛ.
Papias liuꝛ de wynchelese
hungunto vivine de leycestꝛ.
Eirculphus.
Paciuꝰ.
Sinie longobardi.
S. Elineri poꝛe.
Weaven . W. Bꝛtonis.
Weaven Juanis.
Corp̄ cānonū.
Cronica variaꝛ.
Musica Boecī.
vitaꝛ patrum.
hystoꝛ Anglor̄ noua.
Cōuracta sci thom . W. froncard.
Epla sci thom Mainpoꝛe
Passionalia.
Vita sci silvestꝛ orne ꝛ vitaꝛ
ꝛ passiones scoꝛ quoꝛ festa ce
lebrant a die sci silvestꝛ vsq̄
ad fin sci Jgnaci.
Passionale sca Jgnaci. pmū.
Passione sci Jgnaci. sedm.
Vita sce Marie Egiptiace.
Passionale aplor̄ Petꝛ ꝛ pauli
quarti.
Inuentio sci Stephi . V̄.
Passionale sci Marci. vj̄.
Vita sci Martini. vij̄.
Passionale aplor̄ vetꝰ.
Omeliaꝛ Lanfsū.
ꝉ Omeliaꝛ.
Marminanuꝰ.
Lectionalia.
Lectionale . pmū.
Lectionale . sedm.
Lectionale . trium.
Lectionale . quium.
Lectonale . quintū.
Lectonale . sextū.
Lectonale . vuū froncard.
Genesis.
Liber Regum.

Job.
Ronale . R. de Elbū.
Serdeciū sphere.
Loui testamentū.
Quintuꝉ Eūgelia.
Lib sompnioꝛ.
Lib rachionis.
Correctoꝛ . h̄ . de dephni
Aucenna.
Libri de gramaticis.
Piscian̄ magn̄ Lanfsca trepi.
Lib . xbj.
Piscian̄ magn̄ . W. poꝛcel . l . rbj.
Piscian̄ Abel nign̄ . l . rbj.
Piscian̄ iij̄ magn̄ . l . rbj.
Piscian̄ v magn̄ . l . rbj.
Piscian̄ vj̄ nign̄ . l . rbj.
Piscian̄ vij̄ nign̄ . l . rbj.
Piscian̄ ostructonū . b . j.
In b̄ uohue ornex
Libꝛ ꝓnorū aristotol̄.
Piscian̄ ostruttonū . W. Bꝛtonis.
In b̄ uohue ornex
Sompn̄ sapiencie.
Macrobiuꝰ sꝑ eundē.
Remigī sꝑ donatū.
In b̄ uohue ornex
Beda de arte metrica . l . j.
Jom de seruanis. ꝛ tropis. l̄ j.
Exemplaria vitsice de ꝓductoꝛ.
ꝛ correptoꝛib̄. vbaꝛ.
Lib cassiodoꝛ de oꝛtogꝑphia.
In b̄ uohue ornex
Litell̄ de Gerundinꝰ.
triphonia Galie.
Abcedariū.
Wechmacoes ꝓnom.
Regle piores ꝛ supioꝛ albe
niatre.
Regle vocaliū ꝛ conantiū.
Wechmacoes nom.
Regle Regumnū.
Sin de octo ꝓib̄ conantis.
titiae de affirmacoe ꝛec sillab̄z.
Libri de Rethorica.
Rethorica pma.
Rethorica sꝺa.

V

The Contents of
the Mediaeval Library[1]

R. M. WILSON

THERE is little satisfactory evidence available for the contents of the average mediaeval library. The number of extant copies of any particular work can take no account of the manuscripts worn to shreds by the hands of generations of eager readers,[2] while frequency of reference to a particular work may only be due to the presence of a short extract from it in some popular anthology. On the whole it seems possible that the best evidence is that afforded by the extant catalogues of the libraries. *Plate* 10

Altogether some eighty such catalogues have survived, representing nearly sixty different libraries,[3] and not counting lists of a dozen books or so—which may or may not include the whole library of the place—from about a score of others. This may seem only a small proportion of the total number of mediaeval libraries, but coming as the catalogues do from libraries of different types formed for different purposes, it seems likely that, taken together, we may derive from them some knowledge of the contents of the average library.

Most of the monastic catalogues are naturally from Benedictine houses,[4] four are from houses of Augustinian canons,[5] three are Cistercian—an unduly small proportion[6]—, the same number Premonstratensian,[7] two Cluniac,[8] and one from the Bridgettines of Syon. The friars are represented only by the Ipswich Franciscans, the York Austin friars, and the Carmelites of Hulne. In addition, there are catalogues from seven cathedral chapter libraries,[9] from four collegiate establishments of different kinds,[10] and from three hospitals.[11] The universities are represented by catalogues from the Cambridge University Library, from nine Cambridge colleges,[12]

G

and seven colleges at Oxford.[13] There are, of course, some very obvious gaps here: no catalogue of a nunnery library has survived, none from the Gilbertines, or from a Charterhouse, while the friars are almost as poorly represented. No Dominican house appears, the Franciscans are represented only by a single small house, and some of the smaller groups, the Crutched friars, friars of the Sack, etc., are again completely absent.

The difficulty of using the evidence provided by these catalogues is obvious enough. The majority of them date from the fourteenth and fifteenth centuries; they are late from the point of view of the general history of mediaeval libraries, and can therefore give only the end of the story. They can tell us nothing of the contents of the libraries before the twelfth century, and little before the fourteenth. Even then they can give only a glimpse of the library at one particular time taken at random, so that later accessions or losses must remain unknown. It is unfortunate that so few of them are from the early sixteenth century, when the libraries of the religious houses may be assumed to have reached their maximum expansion. Moreover it is rarely possible to be certain that the extant catalogues are comprehensive. Some are certainly fragmentary, and even when they appear to be complete—as at St Augustine's, Canterbury—the omission of some particular class of books—in this case civil law—leads to the suspicion that the catalogue is in fact defective. Rarely is the cataloguer as frank as the one at Exeter, who notes the existence of 'multi alii libri vetustate consumpti Gallice, Anglice, et Latine scripti, qui non appreciantur, que nullius valoris reputantur', and which consequently he fails to enter. Similarly a sixteenth-century cataloguer of the same library mentions forty or more 'libri antiqui' in the Old Treasury which he declines to describe in detail,[14] while the library at Bermondsey contained 'libri id est quaterni numero 54 exceptis non ligatis quorum numerum penitus ignoro', of which the cataloguer gives no further details.[15]

Moreover the method of cataloguing often leaves much to be desired. In the early period few details of the contents of the different manuscripts are given, only the first or the most important treatise in the volume being mentioned. Even when fuller information is available we can never be certain that all the different works in the manuscript have been listed. In fact, on occasion, it is certain that the less important treatises are still being ignored since, after enumerating some items, the cataloguer is apt to conclude with a *cum aliis, et aliis*, or with other words which make it clear that he has given only a few items from the volume. Later the catalogues tend to become more detailed. All except the very briefest works are listed, and the opening words of the second folio may be given as a means of identifying the particular volume.

A further difficulty arises from the fact that the description of any particular treatise may be quite inadequate. On occasion we find merely some such general description as *Liber Diversorum Tractatuum, Multi Compilationes Simul, Plures Tractatus*, etc. Or an uninformative title may be all that is given, e.g. *Liber de Sacramentis, Tractatus de Confessione, Sermones Dominicales*, etc. In such cases it is impossible to say what particular work is intended. Alternatively, only the name of the author may be given, with no indication at all of which particular work is meant.

Nevertheless it seems possible that a cautious use of the evidence provided by the extant catalogues may give some indication of the normal contents of the average mediaeval library, though this, of course, is not necessarily any real indication of what was being read at the time when the catalogue was being drawn up. Consequently when, in what follows, any particular work is said to be popular, this merely means that it occurs frequently in the catalogues.

In the first place religious works would seem the obvious type of literature to deal with, since of their nature they should, and do, form the bulk of the mediaeval collections. It may be taken for granted that any library, according to size, will have in its possession one or more bibles, along with copies of the individual books in separate volumes, and usually provided with a gloss. With these will be the *Sentences* of Peter Lombard,[16] often abbreviated, versified or glossed, while the fourth book frequently appears separately. The glossed *Psalter* and *Epistles* of Gilbert de la Porrée are found in many libraries, along with the *Rule* of St Benedict, the latter often in more than one copy, and not only in Benedictine houses. There will also be a host of anonymous, and usually unidentifiable, treatises on common religious subjects.

It is unlikely that the library will possess a complete collection of the works of the Fathers of the Western Church. The *Hexaemeron*, *Exposicio secundum Lucam*, *De Officiis Ministrorum*, and *De Sacramentis* of Ambrose are likely to be present, but little else, particularly in the smaller libraries. Similarly with Jerome; the *Adversus Jovinianum*, *Epistolae*, and *Quaestiones Hebraicae in Genesim* are common to most libraries, while the *De Interpretatione Nominum Hebraicorum* is inevitable, often in more than one copy, though it is not always possible to be certain that the treatise so-named is that by Jerome rather than a later compilation. Most of the larger libraries have a useful selection of Jerome's works, but there is little in the smaller ones. A good many tracts are also ascribed to him which are not to be identified with any of the extant works, and no doubt represent mere guesses. As for Augustine, practically every library, whether large or small, had a good number of his works, and when they are completely absent, as at Bridlington, the catalogue is pretty certainly defective. The *Confessiones*, *De Civitate Dei*, *De Anima*, *De Doctrina Christiana*, and the *Enchiridion*, in that order, are those most frequently met with,[17] and of all his works the directly controversial are perhaps the least frequent, while a few others, notably *De Continentia*, appear to have been very rare indeed. A large number of spurious works are also ascribed to Augustine, some of them so regularly that the attribution has evidently become traditional. This is particularly the case with the *De Vera et Falsa Penitentia*, *De Spiritu et Anima*, *Contra Quinque Haereses*, *De Vera Innocencia*, and the *Rule*. All these are at least as frequent as the most popular of the authentic works, and would appear with them in the library.

But of all the Fathers Gregory was evidently far and away the most popular. Practically every library has a complete set of his works, often in more than one copy. Particularly noticeable is the fact that they are just as frequent in the small as in the larger libraries. Their inevitability is one of the most striking things about libraries of all kinds, as also the fact that so few works are wrongly ascribed to him. The canon of his works was evidently much more certainly known to the Middle Ages than that, for example, of Augustine. No doubt it was a good deal more straightforward; and it was certainly much easier to possess a

complete set of his works than those of Augustine. In any case
the evidence suggests that the influence of Gregory during the
Middle Ages may have been even more pervasive than that of
Augustine.

The Eastern Fathers, of course in translation, are perhaps rather
more common than might have been expected. Not infrequently
no indication of the particular work or works is given, but only
the name of the author. In such cases it is likely that only a single
work was in the library—presumably the commonest one. Bury
St Edmunds appears to have had a fair selection of the works of
Athanasius, but they are otherwise rare. The *Rule* of St Basil, in
the translation by Rufinus, is fairly frequent, as also the *Monita*, but
there is little else by him. The *Apologeticus* is the only work of St
Gregory Nazianzen mentioned by name, and is perhaps that intended when, as not infrequently, only the name of the author is
given. The *De Compunctione* and the *De Reparacione Lapsi* of
Chrysostom are common, and he is fairly well represented in most
libraries. The *Sententiae*[18] of Damascenus is the only work of his
at all frequent, and the works of Origen are rather rare.

Commoner than any of these are three works which are regularly but wrongly attributed. The *De Principio et Fine Mundi*,
ascribed to Methodius, is in many libraries; an incomplete series of
Homiliae super Matthaeum, attributed to Chrysostom is more frequent than any of his authentic works; and the Pseudo-Dionysius[19] also appears often in mediaeval libraries, though only the
De Celesti Hierarchia is named at all frequently.

Of the other religious writers only about a dozen can be said to
have been really common, i.e. with the odds in favour of their
more important works being present in any given library. The
Collationes of Cassian would be there, and the *Rule* ascribed to him
is also not uncommon. Naturally enough Boethius is particularly
popular; his *De Consolatione Philosophiae* will certainly appear,
perhaps in more than one copy,[20] and not infrequently glosses on
it are mentioned. But it should be noted that the *De Trinitate* and
the spurious *De Disciplina Scolarium* were almost as popular. The
Institutiones of Cassiodorus was another common work, along with
his *De Anima* and *Super Psalterium*, while the *Etymologiae*[21] and
Libri Sententiarum of Isidore are almost invariable whether the

library be large or small. The *De Officiis* of Amalarius is again in most libraries, and the *Disciplina Clericalis* of Petrus Alphonsi was also remarkably popular.

But undoubtedly the most popular of all the later religious writers was Hugh of St Victor. Most libraries contain a wide selection of his writings, though the less important works are distributed more irregularly. Those which appear most frequently are the *De Institutione Novitiorum, De Sacramentis Christianae Fidei, De Arca Noe,* and the *Didascalicon.* Two other popular writers were Hildebert of Le Mans and St Bernard. The *Epistolae* of the former was a favourite work, with his life of St Mary of Egypt and his *De Mysterio Missae* almost as common. As for St Bernard, again most libraries contain a good selection of his works; the spurious *Meditationes* is particularly frequent, but the *Sermones, De Diligendo Deo, De Praecepto,* and *De Gratia et Libero Arbitrio* are also common. The versification of the *Bible* by Peter of Riga,[22] which went under the title of *Aurora,* is not infrequent, and St Thomas Aquinas is well represented in the larger libraries, with the *Summa,* not always complete, as his most popular work, but with *Super Ethica* and *Super Sententias* not far behind. But few of the smaller libraries have anything by him, and the *Quodlibeta* of his contemporary and rival Henry of Ghent was almost as common.

Other works which might well appear are the *Epistolae* of Cyprian, along with the spurious *De xii Abusionibus Saeculi* often attributed to him; the *De Vita Contemplativa* of Julianus Pomerius,[23] the *Homiliae* of Caesarius of Arles, and the comment on the Pauline *Epistles* by Haymo of Auxerre. Of the works of Rabanus, only the *Super Matthaeum, De Naturis Rerum,* and *De Corpore et Sanguine Domini* are likely to be present, but Remigius' *De Celebratione Missae* was quite common, and so also were the *Epistolae* of Ivo of Chartres, and the *Cosmographia* of Bernard Sylvester, while the *Sermones* of Peter Comestor and the unpublished *Allegoriae* often ascribed to him[24] are not infrequent. The *Sermones* of Jacobus a Voragine were evidently fairly popular, and works by St Bonaventura appear in most of the larger libraries, though with no one of them particularly outstanding.

So far as the English religious writers are concerned, the significant fact is how few of them appear to have been known at all widely. Bede was naturally popular, and all libraries have something of his, with *De Arte Metrica*, *Historia Ecclesiastica*, and *De Temporibus* as the commonest. The *Cur Deus Homo*, *Meditationes*, *Proslogion*, and *Monologion* of Anselm were apparently favourites, but most libraries have a good selection of his works, with numerous treatises, including the *De Similitudinibus* of Eadmer, wrongly ascribed to him. More surprising is the popularity of John of Cornwall's *Eulogium*, written in 1176 against one of the heretical doctrines of Abelard, and addressed to Pope Alexander III by whom the doctrine had been condemned. The *Policraticus* of John of Salisbury is not uncommon, but is the only one of his works at all frequent. The *Epistolae* and *Compendium in Job* of Peter of Blois were apparently well known, and his *Remediarium Peccatorum*[25] is also fairly common. But the most influential of all the English religious writers appears to have been Robert Grosseteste. Easily the most popular of his works was the *Testamenta XII Patriarcharum*, a translation from the Greek of a forgery of the second century A.D., but in addition the *Sermones*, *De Cessacione Legalium*, *De Confessione*, and *De X Mandatis* were all fairly common.

However, these are the only English writers whose works appear to have been at all generally known. If we are to judge from the presence of their works in the catalogues most of the others enjoyed only a strictly localised favour. This would not perhaps be remarkable in the cases of Aldhelm and Alcuin, writers not of the first rank, who might well have fallen out of fashion by the twelfth century, but the same appears to have been true of most of the later writers, including such important figures as Lanfranc, Ailred, Alexander Hales, Kilwardby, Duns Scotus, and Ockham.[26]

None of this is perhaps very surprising. But one thing which the catalogues do show clearly is the popularity of certain writers or works which are not as a rule given any prominent position in the text books. Yet they appear the most frequently of all, especially in the monastic libraries, and were apparently much more popular than the works of any of the great writers, with the exception of Gregory. It may be significant that they are usually anonymous in the catalogues, so that they are evidently present on their own merits, and not because of attribution to some great writer esteemed on account of his other works.

The commonest of all these treatises was the *De Conflictu Viciorum et Virtutum*, a comparatively short tract ascribed to a certain Ambrosius Autpertus, an eighth-century abbot of the monastery of San Vincenzo al Volturno. By the twelfth century the name of the real author had been forgotten, and the esteem in which the treatise was held is reflected by the great names on which it is sometimes fathered. Often anonymous, it is almost as frequently ascribed to Augustine or Gregory, often to Leo or Ambrose of Milan, while St Bernard and Anselm are also on occasion credited with it. Certainly the work appears to have been remarkably popular during the Middle Ages, and no library seems to have been without copies of it.[27]

Almost equally popular was the *De Claustro Animae* of Hugo de Folieta,[28] of which the second of its four books, the *XII Abusiones Claustri* modelled on the pseudo-Cyprian *XII Abusiones Saeculi*, is often found separately. The popularity of the *Rationale Divinorum Officiorum* of William Durandus[29] is natural enough; it was the standard authority for the ritual of the thirteenth century, and for the symbolism of the rites and vestments. Another extremely popular work of the same century was the ascetic treatise of Pope Innocent III, *De Contemptu Mundi*, which is in practically every library. It is often anonymous, but appears occasionally under the name of Lothair, Innocent's style before his elevation to the papacy.[30]

Influential works from an earlier period include the *Formula Honestae Vitae* of St Martin of Braga, and the *Prognosticon Saeculi Futuri* of Julian, archbishop of Toledo. The first of these deals with the four cardinal virtues, the second with the question of the resurrection of the body. Both are found in practically every library, whether large or small, and along with them are the *Homiliae* of St Ephraem,[31] and the *Paradisus*, a collection of the lives of the eastern saints ascribed to the sixth-century hermit Heraclides.

But it was not only the older works which kept their popularity; some of the more recent ones appear quite as often, if not more so. So with the *Elucidarium*, an attempt to deal with the whole domain of theology in three books by a certain Honorius, 'presbyter et scholasticus', probably of Regensburg, who flourished during the first half of the twelfth century.[32] Other particularly popular compilations include the *Summa 'Qui Bene Presunt'*,[33] the *Summa Confessorum* of John of Friburg,[34] the *Dominus Vobiscum* of St Peter Damian, the *Distinctiones* of Maurice, apparently of Hibernia, and the allegorical treatise on Leviticus by a certain Radulphus, a monk of Flaix, of whom all that is known is that he lived during the twelfth century. In addition three popular anthologies of pious reading would appear in most libraries: the *Liber Scintillarum* of a certain Defensor,[35] the *Diadema Monachorum* of Smaragdus,[36] and the *Manipulus Florum*.[37]

From the catalogues, then, one gets the impression that an average library, and particularly an average monastic library, would possess a good selection of the works of Augustine, a complete set of those of Gregory, and a fair number of the works of Jerome and Ambrose. The Eastern Fathers would almost certainly be represented, though not perhaps to any great extent. Of later writers the most important works of some dozen or fifteen would pretty certainly be present, but apart from these it would be very much a matter of chance and the affiliation of the particular monastery as to which religious writers were present and which were not. But almost all the works mentioned in the last section would be present, though probably anonymous.

Most of the books included in the modern Apocrypha formed part of the mediaeval Bible, and are normally included in it. In addition there were a number of legendary stories which appear to have been popular during the Middle Ages. Most libraries would contain some form of the *Vita Adae et Evae*, including the legend of the Holy Rood; the *Libellus de Asenath*[38] might be present, Grosseteste's version of the *Testamenta XII Patriarcharum*, some form of the *Infancy Gospels*, and, most popular of all the apocryphal New Testament literature, the *Gospel of Nicodemus*. In addition, many of the catalogues contain a copy of the debate of the philosopher Secundus with the emperor Hadrian,[39] while the account of St Patrick's purgatory is frequent, with the *Visio Monachi Eynesham* a good deal less so.

A version of the *Vitae Patrum* appears in most libraries, along with a *Legenda Sanctorum* and a *Martyrology*,[40] the *Legenda Aurea* becoming fairly frequent in the later catalogues. A wide variety of individual lives of saints is naturally to be found, but comparatively few of them recur at all frequently. A notable exception is the almost invariable presence of some life of the Virgin, along with a collection of her miracles. The native saints are, as one would expect, those most frequently represented, and one or other of the accounts of the life and martyrdom of St Thomas of Canterbury would be particularly likely to be found. Cuthbert, Edward the Confessor, Brendan, Augustine of Canterbury, Dunstan, Edmund of Abingdon, Anselm, and Godric[41] were next in order of popularity it would seem, with the other native saints represented even less frequently. Of the foreign saints, the popularity of Katherine of Alexandria, Martin, Nicholas, and Gregory the Great, is natural enough, while others only slightly less favoured were St John the Almoner, Bernard, Brigid, Giles, and Jerome. More surprising is the comparative popularity of Silvester, Vincent, Laurence, Anthony, and Alexius, though the account of Barlaam and Josaphat probably owes something of its popularity to reasons other than the desire for pious reading.

Logic is well represented in most of the larger libraries. In the Middle Ages the chief texts were usually divided into the *Old* and the *New Logic*. The former comprised the *Isagoge* of Porphyry, the *Categories* (*predicamentorum*), and the *De Interpretatione* (*periarmaniarum*). With these were sometimes included the *Divisions* and *Topics* in the translation of Boethius, and the *Sex Principia* of Gilbert de la Porrée. Aristotle's *Topics*, *Prior* and *Posterior Analytics*, and the *Sophistical Refutations*, were translated and commented on by James of Venice during the twelfth century, and were known as the *New Logic* in opposition to the *Old*, the latter being the only part of the *Organon* known to the West before the twelfth century, though the Latin text of the *New Logic* is not infrequently ascribed to Boethius. In the catalogues the works are sometimes entered simply as *Logica vetus* and *Logica nova*, but more commonly the individual works are mentioned, and are sometimes present in considerable numbers.[42] Porphyry, the *Topics*, *Sophistical Refutations*, *Prior Analytics*, and the *Categories* are those most commonly met with, the *Sex Principia*, *Divisions*, and *Posterior Analytics*, being the least frequent, though even here the odds are in favour of their appearance in any of the larger libraries. In addition, the

Timaeus of Plato is very frequently met with, either under that title or simply as *Plato*.

There is a good deal of variation so far as the other works of Aristotle are concerned. Some are usual, some comparatively rare, and others completely absent. The first class would include the *Physics, De Coelo, Meteorology, De Anima, Metaphysics, Ethics,* along with some of the *Parva Naturalia.*[43] The *Historia Animalium* is fairly frequent, though not necessarily complete; the *Oeconomica, Politica,* and *Problemata,* are sometimes found, but the other Aristotelian works hardly at all, though on the other hand some spurious works are regularly included.[44]

Most of these standard texts will be found in all the larger libraries, though there is little in the smaller ones. But the commentaries on them will vary considerably according to the particular library; some are excellently equipped with the writings of later scholars on the subject, e.g. St Augustine's, Canterbury, York Austin Friars, and Leicester, but there are comparatively few authors whose work is at all widespread. The *Philosophia* of William of Conches is not uncommon, along with the *Sophismata* of William Heytesbury, a fellow of Merton during the fourteenth century, but apart from these, only works by Averroes,[45] Egidius,[46] and, to a lesser extent, some of those by Avicenna[47] and Burley[48] are common.

The standard texts of the *Corpus Juris Canonici* might be expected to be present in most mediaeval libraries. By the end of the fourteenth century they comprised: (*i*) the *Concordantia Discordantium Canonum* of Gratian (fl. 1140), usually appearing as the *Decreta*; (*ii*) decretals issued by the popes after the time of Gratian, and grouped together by subjects in the so-called *Five Compilations.* The arrangement began c. 1190 and was made permanent in the books of *Decretalia* issued by Gregory IX in 1234; (*iii*) decretals issued between 1234 and 1298 collected by Boniface VIII (d. 1303). Since five books of decretals had already been issued, the collection by Boniface was usually known as the *Liber Sextus*; (*iv*) a collection of papal decretals made by Clement V and promulgated in 1314 is usually called the *Liber Septimus* or *Clementinae*; (*v*) later, certain 'stray' decretals, not codified or collected in the works mentioned, were added, but retained the customary designation of *Extravagantes* in order to distinguish them from the older part of the collections.

The *Decreta* and the *Decretalia* are almost invariable in all libraries, large or small, often in considerable numbers; the *Liber Sextus* and *Liber Septimus* are regular but not invariable, especially in the smaller libraries, while the *Extravagantes* are comparatively rare, though this may be partly due to the fact that the lateness of its compilation means that fewer catalogues are available for purposes of comparison.

Similarly with the *Corpus Juris Civilis*. This consisted of: (*i*) the *Institutes*, the name given to an introductory part of Justinian's codification of Roman Law; (*ii*) the *Digest*, a summary of the writings of Roman jurists; (*iii*) the *Code*, a codification of imperial legislation; and (*iv*) the *Novellae*, the later legislation of Justinian. But in the mediaeval period the *Digest* is usually divided into the *Digestum Vetus* (i–xxiv, 2), the *Digestum Inforciatum* (xxiv, 3–xxxviii), and the *Digestum Novum* (xxxix–l), while the *Institutes*, the *Novellae*, and the last three books of the *Code*, are often included together in the *Parvum Volumen*. Here again the *Institutes*, *Digest*, and *Code*, are common to most libraries, whether large or small; the *Parvum Volumen* appears rather less frequently, while the *Novellae*, at any rate under that title, are rare.

But if the basic texts of both canon and civil law are alike common to most mediaeval libraries, a considerable difference appears in the commentaries. Few writers on civil law appear, and these are usually restricted to one or two libraries. On the other hand, some of the commentators on canon law are to be found almost as frequently as the basic texts. In a library of any size there would be included one or more of the works of Durandus,[49] Archidiaconus,[50] and Bernardus;[51] the *Summa Hostiensis*[52] would be likely to be present, along with Innocent[53] on the *Decretals*, the *Summa Raymundi*,[54] and the *Summa Tancredi*.[55] The *Decreta* of Ivo of Chartres is not infrequent, and there might also appear the *Penitential* of Thomas Chabham,[56] Mandagota *De Electionibus*,[57] Gelasius *De Recipiendis*,[58] and one or more of the works of John Andreas.[59] Most libraries will also have some of the *Constitutions*[60] of the various archbishops, bishops, and papal legates. They will vary in frequency according to the importance of the issuer, and the position of the library, with the *Constitutions* of the papal legates Otto and Octobonus amongst the more common. Similarly, most libraries will have a work with some such title as *Tractatus de Legibus Anglie*, and an occasional treatise on some aspect of common law.[61]

Most libraries have a fair selection of the classics, and of them all Virgil appears to have been the favourite. When the individual poems are mentioned it is the *Bucolics* that appears most frequently, but when, as is often the case, only the name of the author is given, this probably includes the *Aeneid*, whatever else there may have been in the volume. It seems likely that the *Aeneid* and the *Bucolics* were to be found in most of the larger libraries, with the *Georgics* not far behind, whereas in the smaller ones only the *Bucolics* were at all frequent. In addition, Virgil's popularity is indicated by the appearance of glosses to the various works, while the commentary of Servius, a fourth-century grammarian, is almost as frequent as the works themselves. The poems of Ovid are perhaps not quite so common as those of Virgil, but most of the larger libraries had a fair selection, with the *Fasti*, *Tristia*, and *De Remedio Amoris*, as the most frequent, but with little to choose between these and the others.[62] *Ovidius Magnus* is a not uncommon entry, which sometimes seems to refer to the *Metamorphoses* only, but on other occasions may well have included a number of works. In addition, some spurious works commonly attributed to Ovid are not infrequent.[63] The works of Horace were also evidently popular, though they are rarely particularised. When they are, the *Odes* are the most common, followed by the *Epistolae*, with the *Carmen Saeculare* and the *Satires* relatively rare.

Of the Silver Age poets, Lucan and Statius are likely to be present. Normally no title appears for the works of Lucan, only the name of the author, and in this case the entry presumably refers to the *Pharsalia*. Of the poems of Statius, the *Achilleis* is mentioned by name rather more frequently than the *Thebais*, but the *Silvae* was apparently not known—unless included in the not uncommon *Statius Magnus*. A good deal more popular than either of these were the satirists, of whom Persius is the most frequently found, in the smaller as in the larger libraries. Almost as common are the *Satires* of Juvenal, but the works of Martial seem to have been comparatively rare.

In opposition to the pagan poets of classical antiquity the Middle Ages were accustomed to place the early Christian poets, Arator, Juvencus, Prudentius, and Sedulius. Of these Sedulius was easily the most popular, though since the common entry is simply *Sedulius*, it may on occasion refer to the prose rather than the metrical version of the *Carmen Paschale*. The paraphrase of the *Acts* in Latin hexameters by the Ligurian Arator was also a fairly popular work, but Prudentius seems to have been rather less common than might be expected.[64] The other Latin poets, Juvencus, Claudian, Sidonius, and Ausonius, are comparatively rare, and the odds are decidedly against their appearance in any given library.

The works of Terence must have been as popular as those of any of the classical writers. They appear in most libraries, but are rarely itemised, so that it is impossible to say exactly which of the plays were current. Plautus, on the other hand, is rare, though not unknown to the English Middle Ages.

The only prose writers, apart from the historians, who can confidently be expected to appear in any given library are Cicero and Seneca. In the case of the former the works divide themselves pretty sharply between those that are common and those that are not. The *De Officiis*, *De Amicitia*, *De Senectute*, *Rhetorica*, and probably the *Paradoxae* and the *Tusculan Orations*, would be present, but anything else is unlikely. The *Somnium Scipionis* appears only occasionally, but the commentary on it by the fourth-century writer Macrobius is frequent, and was evidently a popular mediaeval work, as is shown also by references in the vernacular writers. The commonest of Seneca's works were the spurious *Letters of Paul and Seneca*,[65] but the *Epistolae* are almost as frequent, followed closely by the *De Beneficiis*, *Ad Lucillium*, *Proverbiae*, and with the *De Clemencia*, and *De Remediis Fortuitorum* not far behind.

Few of the other prose writers are likely to be represented. Pliny's *Natural History* is perhaps a possibility, but its place will more probably be taken by the *Collectanea Rerum Memorabilium* of the early third-century writer Solinus.[66] This work seems to have been one of the most popular of all such treatises in mediaeval times, but almost the whole of it is taken, without acknowledgement, from the *Natural History*. Mediaeval quotations from the *Natural History* are much more likely to come from Solinus than direct from Pliny. Here, too, mention may be made of three writers on practical subjects, any or all of whom might appear. The *De Re Militari* of Vegetius, an obscure writer of the early fifth century, seems to have been particularly popular, and the chances would be in favour of its appearance in any given library. The *De Architectura* of Vitruvius, and the *De Agricultura* of Palladius, though less common than Vegetius, might also be there.

So far as the historians are concerned, Sallust alone is really common. His works appear in most of the larger libraries, but usually with no precise identification. Only the *Bellum Catalinae* and the *Bellum Iugurthinum* are ever mentioned by name, so that when the entry is simply *Sallustius*, as it usually is, one or both of these is probably intended. Not infrequently the catalogues include also an *Invectiva in Tullium* which they attribute to Sallust, and an *Invectiva in Sallustium* attributed to Cicero. Modern scholars are apparently inclined to accept the first as genuine, but not the second. Apart from Sallust the only historians found at all frequently are Suetonius and Pompeius Trogus. The *Vitae Caesarum* of the former is not uncommon under different titles, and when only the name of the author is given it is certainly this work which is intended. Rather more popular was the work of the Augustan historian Pompeius Trogus, who wrote a universal history in forty-four books, the *Historiae Philippicae*. It is known to us, as it was to the Middle Ages, only in the epitome of it made, probably in the third century, by a certain Marcus Junianus Justinus. In the catalogues the work may appear under either name, but there can be no doubt that both refer to the epitome. These are the only historical works likely to appear. Livy, Caesar, Ammianus, Valerius Maximus, are all extremely rare, while Tacitus, naturally enough, does not appear at all.

In dealing with later historical works, it must be remembered that much which we regard as romance was accepted by the Middle Ages as authentic history. Consequently most libraries would include under this heading romances dealing with the siege of Troy, Alexander, and Charlemagne, but they are usually entered in the catalogues under such general titles that definite identifications are impossible. Of the historians proper Josephus is common in large and small libraries alike. When only the author's name is given, as not infrequently, it is impossible to be certain whether the *Jewish War* or the *Antiquities*, or both, is intended, the two being named about equally often. A free adaptation of the former, under the title *De Bello Judaico et Excidio Urbis Hierosolomytanae*, made during the fourth century, is in practically all the larger libraries, where it usually occurs under the name Hegesippus.[67]

A popular fourth-century historian was Eusebius of Caesarea, whose *Ecclesiastical History*, in the translation by Rufinus, was to be found—usually anonymously—in practically every library of any size, and in many of the smaller ones as well. From the fifth century the *Historia adversus Paganos* of the Spanish monk Paulus Orosius was also extremely popular, and almost equally so was the *Historia Tripartita* ascribed to Cassiodorus.[68] The *Historia Scholastica* of Peter Comestor would certainly be present, and its popularity in large and small libraries alike is further shown by the fact that it was often abbreviated, sometimes versified, and glosses were written on it.

These are the general historical works which would almost certainly be found in any library. Anything else is a good deal less likely. The *Breviarium Historiae Romanae* of Eutropius, a compendium of Roman history to the reign of Valens, is not uncommon, and the *Historia Langobardorum* of Paulus Diaconus perhaps more frequent than might have been expected. The *Chronicle* of Martinus Polonus and that of Hugh de Fleury[69] are reasonably common, and so is the *Speculum Historiale* of Vincent of Beauvais, though perhaps not often complete. In addition the universal history of Freculphus[70] is sometimes to be met with.

The works of the English chroniclers are comparatively rare. A good many historical works are included in the catalogues with general titles such as *Historia Britonum*, *Gesta Britonum*, *Historia Anglorum*, *Chronica Anglie*, etc., for which no identification is possible. The first two may on occasion conceal the work of Gildas or Nennius, or perhaps even of Geoffrey of Monmouth—and *Brutus Latine* is certainly used sometimes for the *Historia Regum Britanniae*. But it is highly probable that such titles usually represent a valueless epitome of the early history of the country. A copy of Bede's *Historia Ecclesiastica* would be present, and a work which the cataloguers ascribe to Gildas appears occasionally, but it is difficult to be certain that in every case it really is the *De Excidio Britanniae* and not the work of Nennius. In fact a *Gesta Britonum* is entered by the Durham cataloguer as 'composita a Gildo vel Nennio'. Most of the twelfth-century historians, however highly they may be esteemed today, appear to have enjoyed only a strictly limited circulation. The only ones found more than once or twice are William of Malmesbury, Henry of Huntingdon, and Geoffrey of Monmouth, along with the thirteenth-century *Polychronicon* of Ranulf Higden. Even so the odds would be against finding them in any particular library. Geoffrey of Monmouth's *Historia Regum Britanniae*, duly ascribed to its author, is rather less frequent than the others, but pretty certainly an anonymous *Historia Britonum* or *Brutus* is sometimes to be identified with this work. The *Topographia Hiberniae* of Giraldus Cambrensis appears to have been fairly popular, but it is the only one of his books at all common.

Of the grammarians Donatus and Priscian are inevitable. The former usually appears in the catalogues simply as *Donatus*, with no indication of which particular work is meant. No doubt in such cases it is the *Ars Minor*, a discussion of the eight parts of speech in the form of question and answer. The *Ars Maior* seems to have been a good deal less popular, and only the third part of it, the *Barbarismus*,[71] was read at all widely. The *Institutionum Grammaticarum Libri xviii* of Priscian was the standard mediaeval text-book of grammar, and was usually divided into the *Magnum Volumen*, and the *Parvum Volumen*. The former consisted of the first sixteen books dealing with the parts of speech, the latter of the last two dealing with syntax. Both appear regularly, in large and small libraries alike, as *Priscianus Magnus*, and *Priscianus Minor*, or, in the case of the second, as *Priscianus de Constructionibus*. In addition a work, *De Accentibus*, and another, *De Nomine, Pronomine, et Verbo ad Instructionem Puerorum*, also ascribed to him, are fairly frequent. A shorter catechetical work in which the first twelve lines of Virgil served as a subject for dissection, though less frequent than the others, is not uncommon under the title *Priscianus de xii Versibus*.

The later grammarians will also be well represented. The

H

Magnum Doctrinale[72] of Alexander de Villedieu is common, though usually anonymous, and so is the *Summa super Priscianum* of Petrus Helias.[73] Of the thirteenth-century grammarians, the works of Hugutio of Pisa, Everard de Béthune, John of Garland, Alexander Neckham, and William Brito, are likely to appear in any given library, along with the work of the eleventh-century Lombard Papias. The first of these was bishop of Ferrara, and died in 1210. In the catalogues no title is as a rule given to his work, but it is presumably the *Liber Derivationum*, one of the most popular of mediaeval dictionaries, that is intended. The *Grecismus* of Everard de Béthune is usually anonymous. It takes its title from the chapter in which Greek words in current use in the Vulgate and the Fathers are interpreted, though the author apparently knew no Greek. Some of the grammatical works of John of Garland are almost certain to appear, though it is more difficult to say which. His *Dictionarius* was one of his most popular works, and when the title appears without any ascription, as not infrequently, this may well be what is intended. The most frequent of the other works ascribed to him are perhaps the *Liber Equivocorum*, a treatise on homonyms, the *Distigium Cornuti*, a short collection of distichs full of Graeco-Latin and strange Latin words, and the *Liber Merarii*. Similarly with the works of Alexander Neckham; the *Corrogationes Promethei*, under various titles, is perhaps the most likely of his works to be present, but the *De Utensilibus*[74] is also not uncommon. The appearance of the grammatical work of William Brito[75] is virtually certain, usually under the name of the author only, but occasionally as *De Derivationibus*, while equally probable is the work of Papias, along with some anonymous treatise on accentuation, and the *Catholicon*.[76]

In belles lettres, the *Disticha Catonis* is almost invariable in large and small libraries alike. It became the regular mediaeval primer of Latin, having been written under the later Empire but gaining added authority from its popular association with Cato the Elder. A Latin version of the works of Aesop is not infrequent, and a later collection of fables ascribed to Avianus is also likely to appear. The *Eclogue* of Theodolus became a favourite mediaeval school-book, as also the collection of elegies written c. 600 which goes under the name of Maximianus. Of later works the *Anticlaudianus* of Alanus de Insulis,[77] the *Oratio de Utensilibus ad Domum Regendam* by Adam de Parvo Ponte,[78] the *Cartula*,[79] so-called from its opening word, the *Nova Poetria* of Geoffrey de Vinsauf, the *Thobias* of Matthew of Vendôme,[80] and the *Disuasio Valerii ad Rufinum*,[81] might all well appear.[82]

In science the position is a good deal less straightforward. As a rule only the monastic libraries have anything like an adequate scientific section, the existence of which seems to have depended on whether at any given time there was someone in authority who was interested in the subject. Normally, a mediaeval library will possess little beyond the popular anonymous pseudo-scientific works, and the more technical ones will be present only under special circumstances. So far as we can tell from the extant catalogues, the only libraries with sections on science which are at all adequate, were St Augustine's, Canterbury, St Mary's, Leicester, and the York Austin Friars.

Most libraries have an anonymous *Algorismus*,[83] which is probably the elementary tract on arithmetic by Alexander de Villedieu, and an anonymous *Arithmetica*, also not infrequent, may have been the same work. A *Bestiarium* and a *Lapidarius* are present in most libraries, but it is rarely possible to say which particular versions they represent. Similarly most libraries, whether large or small, have a *Compotus*, and when any name is mentioned in connexion with it it is usually that of Helperic.[84] An anonymous work on the sphere is common, and is no doubt normally that attributed to John de Sacro Bosco.[85] The *De Proprietatibus Rerum* of Bartholomæus Anglicus is far and away the commonest of such compilations, and anonymous works with this title are no doubt often to be identified with it. In addition we could be fairly certain of finding the *Musica* and *Arithmetica* of Boethius, and the *Musica* of Guido.[86] The *Geometria* of Euclid, probably in the translation by Adelard of Bath, might be present, as also Hyginus on the sphere,[87] and Hermannus on the astrolabe.[88] The *Almagest*, *Centilogium*, and *Quadripartitum* of Ptolemy would be in the better scientific libraries, along with some work of Albumazar[89] on astrology, the commentaries or original writings of Haly,[90] and the *De Electionibus*, the *Liber Interrogationum*, or the *Liber Novem Judicum* of Zael.[91] Perhaps also there might appear Grosseteste on the sphere, or the *Almanac* or the *Composicio Novi Quadrantis* of Profacius.[92]

These are the only scientific works that one could fairly confidently count on finding in even the best equipped library. Some of the most famous of mediaeval scientific writers occur only very rarely and the appearance of works by scientists such as Adelard of Bath, Roger Bacon, Albertus Magnus, Alkindi, Messahalla, and Rasis, is not to be taken for granted in any given library.

A section on medicine is naturally to be found in most of the monastic libraries. It usually contains numerous anonymous and unidentifiable treatises, along with some titles which recur fairly frequently, and are sufficiently individual to be recognised.[93] Of the works of the great doctors, the *Afforismorum* and *Pronosticorum* of Hippocrates are present in most libraries,[94] while rather less common are the same author's *De Regimine Morborum Acutorum* and the *Secreta*. Far and away the most popular of the works of Galen was the *Tegni*[95] but the *Dinamidiarum* and the *Liber Graduum*[96] are fairly frequent, while other works by him are almost certain to be present.[97] In fact, as is to be expected, Galen was the most popular of all the ancient doctors in mediaeval times.

Along with the works of Hippocrates and Galen will appear the *Isagoge in Artem Parvum Galieni* of Hunein ibn Ishaq,[98] as well as Philaretus on the pulse, and the *Liber Urinarum* of Theophilus. The former, of whom nothing seems to be known, is often identified with the latter, Theophilus Protospatarius, a Greek writer of the seventh century. Both works were extremely popular throughout the mediaeval period. Other common mediaeval works dealing with the subject of the second are those by Isaac Judaeus,[99] Maurus,[100] and Gilles de Corbeil.[101] An even more popular work by the first was his *Liber Dietarum*, often divided into *Dietae Particulares* and *Dietae Universales*, while the same physician's *Liber Febrium* is only a little less common.

In the main the Middle Ages depended largely on the great works of the past, particularly on those of Hippocrates, Philaretus, Theophilus, Johannicius, and Isaac Judaeus. These would be found in all libraries which had any appreciable section devoted to medical works. But some of the later medical writers attained to almost comparable popularity. The first, and perhaps the greatest, of the translators from Arabic into Latin was Constantine Africanus.[102] He translated many of the works of Galen, which, consequently, are often attributed to him, but his most popular work was the *Viaticum*, a treatise for less advanced students, translated from the Arabic of ibn al-Jezzar (d. 1009). In addition the *Pantegnum, De Simplici Medicine, De Stomacho, Liber Febrium,* and *De Melancholia,* are all fairly frequent. Equally popular was the *Antidotarium* of Nicholas,[103] and along with it will appear the *De Naturis Herbarum* of Odo of Meung-sur-Loire.[104] The *De Simplicibus Medicinis* of Platearius is more difficult to identify, since there was more than one writer of this name,[105] but the *Summa de Cirurgia* of Roger of Salerno[106] was in many libraries, and so was the *Practica Bartholomaei*.[107]

Other works which might well have been found in any particular library would include the *Canon of Medicine* of Avicenna,[108] perhaps one or other of the works of Bernard de Gordonio,[109] especially his *Lilium Medicine,* Dioscorides,[110] the *Commentum super Tegnum Galieni* of Haly,[111] the work of John of St Amand on the *Antidotarium*,[112] the *Cirurgia* of Lanfranc of Milan,[113] and perhaps the *De Passionibus Mulierum,* an obstetrical and gynaecological treatise produced at Salerno during the first half of the twelfth century and ascribed to a woman physician of the name of Trotula.

Of these three classes of medical works, the first would certainly be in any library that contained any such works at all; the second would be likely to be present, along with some at least of the third, as well as a number of anonymous works, and others by authors less widely known.

The vast majority of the manuscripts in all mediaeval libraries were naturally in Latin, and in many, so far as we can tell, no other languages were represented. What English works there are will in the main be devotional or didactic, but only in the pre-Conquest foundations is there likely to be more than an occasional vernacular work. Some of these have a comparatively large number, but when a later catalogue of the library is available, most of the English books are seen to have disappeared. The sixteenth-century catalogues, and more particularly that of Syon, show again a fair number of English works present, but the average fourteenth- or fifteenth-century library will rarely show anything in English, and what there is will almost certainly be devotional or didactic.

The French element is on the whole rather more marked than the English, though even so it accounts for only a small proportion of the books in the libraries. Here again religious works are the most numerous. Versions of the Bible or the Psalter occur occasionally, and the general religious literature contains a number of treatises of the usual type, some of which were evidently comparatively popular. The commonest is the *Chasteau d'Amour*[114] of Robert Grosseteste, a pious and not unsuccessful predecessor of the *Roman de la Rose*. Other religious works appearing more than once are the *Manuel des Pechez* of William of Waddington, and the *Lumiere as Lais* of Pierre d'Abernon. The former is perhaps better known as the source of Robert Mannyng's *Handlyng Synne*, while the latter is a version of the *Elucidarium* of Honorius, with additional material from the *Sentences*, and provides further evidence for the influence of the two works. In addition a French version of the *Speculum Ecclesie* of St Edmund of Abingdon also appears. Other subjects are sparsely represented. There is a certain amount of history, with French versions of the *Brut*, and of other chronicles of the usual type; occasional treatises on feudal law, and a little grammar. French romances appear sporadically in some of the libraries, more especially at St Augustine's, Canterbury, Dover, St Mary's, Leicester, and Peterborough.

As for works in any other languages, there are very few indeed to be found. An occasional Greek or Hebrew Psalter appears in some of the larger libraries, and a few of the newly printed Greek texts, along with translations from the Greek, are sometimes to be found in some of the sixteenth-century libraries, but these are practically the only signs of the new learning that appear.

To sum up, these are the works which will normally appear in almost all the larger libraries, and many of them will be found even in the smaller ones. But it must be emphasised that in the case of the former they will comprise merely the core of the library. Along with them will appear numerous anonymous, and usually unidentifiable, treatises on the various subjects, and each library will contain also its own selection of the less widely known writers, together with the works of strictly local authors whose writings never spread beyond the district in which they lived. Since monastic and college libraries seem to have grown up in much the same way they will be very similar in content, but the latter are perhaps more strictly utilitarian. They will contain more of the works of the scholastics, and fewer of the more popular religious works. Grammar, medicine, and science, will be represented only by the stock text-books, and there is little of the more entertaining literature sometimes to be found in the monastic libraries.

NOTES TO CHAPTER V

1. This chapter owes much to valuable criticisms and suggestions by Prof. Wormald and Dr C. E. Wright.

2. In fact the survival of actual manuscripts is in some cases in conflict with the evidence of the catalogues, and it cannot be taken for granted that the latter will necessarily give the more correct picture.

3. For bibliography of these catalogues see N. R. Ker, *Medieval Libraries of Great Britain*, London, 1941.

4. Burton, Bury St Edmunds, Christ Church, Canterbury (2), St Augustine's, Canterbury, Dover, Durham (3), Glastonbury, Leominster, Norwich (2), Peterborough (2), Ramsey (2), Reading, Whitby.

5. Bridlington, Lanthony, Leicester, Waltham.

6. Flaxley, Meaux, Rievaulx.

7. Bradsole, Titchfield, Welbeck.

8. Bermondsey, Monkbretton.

9. Aberdeen (2), Exeter (2), Glasgow, Lichfield, Lincoln (3), St Paul's (3), Rochester (2).

10. Bishop Auckland, Eton, Winchester, Windsor.

11. Elsing Spital London, Ewelme, Gateshead.

12. University Library (2), Clare (2), Corpus, King's, Pembroke, Peterhouse, Queen's, St Catherine's, Trinity (various), Trinity Hall.

13. All Souls, Canterbury (2), Durham (3), Lincoln, Merton, New College, Oriel.

14. G. Oliver, *Lives of the Bishops of Exeter*, Exeter, 1861, pp. 301 ff., 366 ff.

15. *Eng. Hist. Rev.*, xlviii (1933), p. 443.

16. Not infrequently in many copies; St Augustine's, Canterbury, for example, had thirty-five, Christ Church twenty-eight, and other libraries in proportion.

17. With *De Genesi ad Litteram*, *De Trinitate*, *Sermones*, and *Soliloquia* not far behind.

18. Usually under the title *De Orthodoxa Fidei*.

19. Probably in the translation by John Scotus Erigena.

20. St Augustine's, Canterbury, for example, had fifteen copies of the work.

21. Perhaps more usually an epitome than the complete work.

22. A canon of Rheims who died c. 1209.

23. Often ascribed to Prosper in the catalogues.

24. Really by Richard of St Victor.

25. A collection of excerpts from Gregory's *Moralia*.

26. But the last two are rather more frequent in the catalogues of the college libraries—as might perhaps be expected.

27. e.g. St Augustine's, Canterbury, had fifteen copies, Peterborough thirteen, etc.

28. Often ascribed to the more famous Hugh of St Victor.

29. Bishop of Mende. His work is not easily distinguishable in the catalogues from the *Summa*, on the same subject, of John Beleth, a much more obscure person who flourished at Paris during the 12th century, and whose work was extremely common.

30. His *De Sacro Altaris Mysterio* was almost as highly regarded.

31. The most important of the writers of the Syrian patristic age, c. 306–73.

32. His *Imago Mundi*, a summary of natural history in three books, was even more popular abroad. It is fairly frequent in English libraries, but a good deal less so than the *Elucidarium*.

33. So-called from its opening words. It is a version, with additions and slight changes, of the *Summa* of William de Monte. Perhaps by Richard Wetherstede, see P. Glorieux, *Répertoire des Maîtres en Théologie de Paris au xiii⁰ siècle*, Paris, 1933, i, 280.

34. Lector of the Dominican Order, d. 1314.

35. Said to have been a monk of Ligugé, near Poitiers, in the 7th century.

36. Abbot of St Mihiel at the beginning of the 9th century.

37. Said to have been begun by John Walleys, and completed in 1306 by a certain Thomas of Ireland, see P. Glorieux, op. cit., no. 322. Works which were only slightly less popular would include the *Moralium Dogma Philosophorum* of William of Conches, the *Expositio Super Missam* of Remigius of Auxerre, the *Verbum Abbreviatum* often ascribed to Petrus Cantor, and the *Templum Domini* of Grosseteste, along with the *Speculum Iuniorum*, and the *Speculum Ecclesiae*.

38. Telling of the conversion of Asenath, wife of Joseph, and of her magnanimity towards her enemies. Present at Christ Church, Canterbury, St Augustine's, Canterbury, Rochester, Dover, Durham, Titchfield.

39. Translated from the Greek by William of St Denis in the 12th century.

40. But, as Prof. Wormald points out, the martyrology in use at any given time was probably kept in the chapter house, not the library.

41. The last at Durham, Rievaulx, Christ Church, Hulne, Flaxley.

42. e.g. St Augustine's, Canterbury, had at least fifteen copies of the *De Interpretatione*, thirty of the *Divisions*, nineteen of Porphyry, seventeen of the *Topics*, etc.

43. Especially the *De Sensu et Sensibili*, *De Memoria et Reminiscentia*, *De Somno et Vigilia*, *De Longitudine et Brevitate Vitae*, and *De Vita et Morte*. The *De Juventute et Senectute* is much less frequent, and the *De Somnis*, *De Divinatione per Somnum*, and *De Respiratione* very rare indeed.

44. Especially the *Liber de Causis*, *De Vegetabilibus et Plantis*, *De Differencia Spiritus et Animae*, and *De Substancia Orbis*. An anonymous work on rhetoric is not uncommon, but it is rarely possible to decide whether or not this is the work of Aristotle. For Latin translations of Aristotle see M. Grabmann, *Forschungen über die Lateinischen Aristoteles Übersetzungen des xiii Jahrhunderts*, Münster, 1916.

45. Abū-l-Walīd Muhammad ibn Ahmad ibn Muhammad ibn Rushd, b. at Cordova 1126, d. 1198 at Marrakūsh. One of the greatest of the mediaeval philosophers. His comments on the *Parva Naturalia* and on the *Physics* are those most commonly met with.

46. Gilles de Rome, archbishop of Bourges, d. 1316. His commentary on the *De Generacione* is the commonest of his works.

47. Abū 'Alī al-Husain ibn 'Abdallāh ibn Sīnā, b. 980 at Afshana near Bukhārā, d. 1037 in Hamadhān. 'The most famous scientist of Islām.' The work most frequently met with is the *Metaphysics*.

48. Especially his comments on the *Ethics* and the *Politics*. Walter Burley (1275–?1345) was a fellow of Merton College, Oxford.

49. William Durandus, bishop of Mende, d. 1296. The *Speculum Judiciale* is the most likely work of his on canon law to appear.

50. Guydo de Baysio, d. 1313, archdeacon of Bologna, hence the usual name under which the works are entered in the catalogues. The *Rosarium* is the most frequent of them.

51. Bishop of Pavia, d. 1213. Especially his *Casus Decretalium*.

52. The *Summa Aurea* of Henry of Susa, bishop of Ostia, d. 1271.

53. Innocent IV, d. 1254.

54. The *Summa Casuum* of Raymond of Penafort, d. 1275.

55. Archdeacon of Bologna during the first half of the 13th century.

56. See P. Glorieux, op. cit., no. 115.

57. William of Mandagout, archbishop of Aix, cardinal-bishop of Praeneste, d. 1321.

58. Pope Gelasius I, 492–6.

59. Giovanni d'Andrea, professor of canon law at Bologna, d. 1348. His *Apparatus super Sextum* is the one most commonly found.

60. Regulations dealing with the spiritual and moral welfare of the people of the diocese or province.

61. e.g. the *Summa que vocatur Cadit Assisa*.

62. The *Heroides* usually appears under the title *Epistolae*, and the *Amores* as *Ovidius sine Titulo*.

63. These include the *De Nuce*—which modern scholars are apparently inclined to accept as genuine—, *De Cuculo*, *De Mirabilibus Mundi*, *De Pulice*, and *De Vetula Fratris*.

64. Though some of the anonymous volumes of *Hymns* are perhaps to be ascribed to him.

65. Fourteen brief letters supposed to have been exchanged between Seneca and the apostle which were already extant as early as the 4th century.

66. Usually appearing in the catalogues under the title *De Mirabilibus Mundi*.

67. Said to be a corruption of Josephus. The seven books of the original have been compressed into five, but additions made from the *Antiquities* and from some of the Roman historians.

68. A translation of the ecclesiastical histories of Theodoret, Sozomen, and Socrates. Usually anonymous in the catalogues.

69. Commonly ascribed to Ivo of Chartres.

70. A 9th-century bishop of Lisieux.

71. This is fairly frequent, usually anonymous, but sometimes attributed to Priscian.

72. A versified grammar. The author flourished at the end of the 12th century.

73. A Paris teacher who wrote c. 1150.

74. Often appearing under its opening words, *Qui Bene Vult Disponere*.

75. Franciscan and lexicographer, d. 1356.

76. A dictionary by John Balbi of Genoa, which appeared in 1286.

77. With his *De Planctu Naturae* a good deal less frequent.

78. Usually under the title *Phaletolum*—its opening words.

79. Ascribed indifferently to St Bernard, Stephen Langton, and others.

80. A Latin epic telling the story of the two biblical Tobits which became popular as a school-book.

81. An extract from Walter Map, *De Nugis Curialium*; often found separately, and attributed to St Jerome.

82. With the *Apocalypsis Golie*, the *Architrenius* of John de Hauteville, and the *Speculum Stultorum* of Nigel Wireker, a good deal less likely.

83. The name comes from Abū 'Abdallāh Muhammad ibn Mūsā al-Khwarizmī, d. c. 850, mathematician, astronomer, geographer. 'One of the greatest scientists of his race.' His trigonometrical and astronomical tables were translated by Adelard of Bath (1126); his *Algebra* by Gerard of Cremona, and his *Arithmetic* by John Hispaniensis.

84. A monk at Auxerre.

85. John of Holywood, or Halifax, fl. 1230.

86. Guido of Arezzo, 11th century. 'The father of modern music.'

87. Gaius Julius Hyginus, fl. 20 B.C.

88. Hermannus Contractus, 1013–54. Monk at Reichenau.

89. Abū Ma'shar Ja'far ibn Muhammad ibn 'Umar al-Balkhī. Lived at Baghdad, 805–85. The *Flores* and the *De Magnis Coniunctionibus* are the most likely works.

90. Abū-l-Hasan 'Alī ibn Ridwān ibn 'Alī ibn Ia'far al-Misrī, d. c. 1061 in Cairo. His *De Electionibus Horarum*, and the commentaries on Ptolemy's *Centilogium* and *Quadripartitum* are the most frequent works.

91. Abū 'Uthmān Sahl ibn Bishr ibn Habīb ibn Hānī, Jewish astrologer, who flourished in Khurāsān during the first half of the 9th century.

92. Jacob ben Mahir ibn Tibbon, Judaeo-Provençal mathematician, astronomer, zoologist, c. 1236–c. 1304.

93. e.g. the *Liber Aureus*, *Liber Graduum*, *De Simplici Medicine*, *De Modo Medendi*.

94. The former probably in the translation made from the Arabic by Constantine Africanus in the 11th century, the latter in that by Gerard of Cremona.

95. Translated into Latin from the Arabic of Hunein ibn Ishaq by Gerard of Cremona.

96. No doubt the anonymous *Liber Graduum* is sometimes this work.

97. Especially the *Liber de Accidente et Morbo*, *De Simplici Medicine*—often anonymous—, *Anathomia*, *Comment. super Librum Afforismorum*, *De Interioribus Membrorum*, *De Creticis Diebus*, *De Febribus*.

98. One of the earliest of the Arabic medical works to be translated into Latin, probably by Marcus of Toledo in the 12th century. It usually appears in the catalogues as *Johannicius*.

99. Isaac ben Solomon, c. 845–c. 940. Court physician at Kairawan. Medical works translated by Constantine and Gerard of Cremona.

100. Died at Salerno in 1214.

101. French humanist and physician to Philip Augustus, d. c. 1220.

102. A monk of Monte Cassino, c. 1015–87.

103. A 12th-century Salernitan physician of whom little is known.

104. An 11th-century writer whose work was known to the Middle Ages as Macer Floridus.

105. John Platearius, an 11th-century Salernitan physician, who wrote a

Practica brevis and a *Regula urinarum*; Matthew Platearius, a physician of the same school of about a century later, wrote a popular commentary on the *Antidotarium*.

106. Fl. c. 1170. 'The greatest Salernitan surgeon.'

107. Of Salerno. Flourished during the first half of the 12th century.

108. On Avicenna, see n. 47.

109. A French physician who flourished c. 1283–1308.

110. A Greek physician, fl. c. 50 A.D. Composed a materia medica which was added to during the Middle Ages.

111. On Haly, see n. 90.

112. A Belgian physician who worked in Paris, and died at the beginning of the 14th century.

113. Practised mainly in France, d. c. 1306. 'The founder of French surgery.'

114. Usually entered in the catalogues as *De Creacione Mundi*, a title taken from the Latin prologue to the poem.

VI

The Private Collector and the Revival of Greek Learning

ROBERTO WEISS

WHEN does the collecting of books by private persons begin to be noticeable in England? During the Middle Ages books were as a rule the property of institutions, such as monasteries or cathedral chapters, and only exceptionally were they to be found in the hands of individuals. Bishops were naturally prominent among such early private owners, but even they seldom possessed books not directly connected with their duties, that is to say volumes outside the spheres of liturgy, theology, or canon law. Thus out of thirty-three items bequeathed in 1095 by William of Saint Carilef, bishop of Durham, to his own cathedral,[1] only two of them contained secular texts. Such a tiny percentage of non-ecclesiastical books is also evident in the collections gathered by other English bishops during this period. And a similar absence of books not strictly essential for the exercise of their professional duties, is noticeable also in most cases in the modest libraries collected by lawyers, physicians, and teachers. The man who acquires books for the sake of acquiring books and not because he needs them for his profession or calling, who does not necessarily study or even read them, in short the type of bibliophile so wittily satirised by Sebastian Brant[2] at the end of the fifteenth century, was definitely not a common figure in the mediaeval scene. It was, however, just towards the very end of the Middle Ages that a new type of book collector closer to his modern counterpart began to make his appearance in England. The rise of the universities and the consequent demand for 'set books' (which Dr Talbot has described in chapter iv), the improvement in the economic climate, the new methods of mass production of manuscript texts, the changes in the standard sizes of books, all these and others were factors which made eventually possible the accumulation of considerable numbers of volumes by private individuals, often on a scale hitherto never reached. Even when the sizes of private libraries were considerably increased, most of the collectors were to be found among the higher clergy. But during the fifteenth century the laity was certainly not lagging behind the ecclesiastics. In fact the two greatest English collectors of books of this century were not members of the clergy, but two cultured laymen with a marked taste for Renaissance learning, Humphrey, duke of Gloucester, and John Tiptoft, earl of Worcester.

Who may be called the first English collector of books?[3] If we think of a book collector as a man who gathers books not so much because he needs them for some particular reason, but just because he loves them, because he appreciates their contents, and also because of their physical appearance and of the delight he draws from the awareness that he possesses them, then such an honour must certainly be assigned to Richard de Bury, that very successful civil servant who held the see of Durham from 1333 until his death in 1345. It is not quite clear whether Richard was the author or merely the inspirer of the famous *Philobiblon*.[4] What is certain is that before his elevation to the episcopate, he had already started to collect books by every means at his disposal,[5] an activity which only ceased with his death. Some of his books were acquired by purchase, others came to him as gifts from religious houses, anxious to secure favours or privileges through his influence at court. Thus between 1329 and 1333 he received a Terence, a Virgil, a Quintilian, and a copy of St Jerome's *Contra Rufinum* from St Albans Abbey, as an inducement to further the monastery's interest with the king.[6] A similar aim was behind the sale of some thirty-two volumes to him arranged by Abbot Richard II of St Albans for the sum of fifty pounds in silver, half of which the abbot characteristically kept for himself.[7] No doubt these were not unsatisfactory transactions for the monastery, since it was, for instance, thanks to Richard's good offices that the abbot of St Albans was granted the right to imprison excommunicated persons.[8] All the same it appears that Richard was not entirely happy as to the way in which some of these books had come to him. It was no doubt because of this, that after his elevation to the see of Durham he eventually returned some of them to the St Albans monks.[9] Besides acquiring books from monasteries, Richard also employed some friars in searching for desirable texts for his library and also in collating and glossing the manuscripts already in his possession.[10] A considerable part of his library was, however, written in his own household, which is known to have included several scribes, illuminators, and binders, that is to say all the personnel essential for the production of books.[11]

What made Richard de Bury collect books on so unprecedented a scale? If we are to accept what we are told in the *Philobiblon*,[12] his aim was not so dissimilar from that of Thomas James, Bodley's first librarian. Just as James saw in the setting up of a library a way to defend the Protestant religion, so Richard de Bury claimed that he acquired books in order to assemble the necessary weapons for fighting successfully against heresy and paganism.[13] This may have been so. What seems, however, much more likely is that he indulged in book collecting because, as was the case with Sir Thomas Phillipps five centuries later, anything written was absolutely irresistible to him. Yet Richard de Bury was certainly more discriminating than Sir Thomas. For instance, law books were rigidly excluded from his library, on the grounds that law was not one of the liberal arts,[14] and there is proof that he paid no little attention to the subject matter of his volumes.

All the books so sedulously collected by Richard de Bury were carefully catalogued under his supervision.[15] Sadly enough this inventory has not reached us, so that we do not know the titles or the actual number of his volumes. The information supplied by a Durham chronicler, according to whom the contents of Richard's library would have easily filled five carts,[16] suggests, however, that he can hardly have possessed less than 1,500 items! This huge collection was quickly dispersed at the owner's death. Like so many mediaeval magnates, Richard died deeply in debt. Hence his executors found themselves forced to sell his books instead of distributing them in accordance with the testator's wishes. Some of those acquired from St Albans and still in Richard's library were purchased back by that abbey early in 1346.[17] Where the others went we do not know. Certainly none of them is at Durham now. Alas, all that remains of his library amounts to but four volumes, each of which finished up at St Albans. One of these is now in the Bodleian;[18] two are among the Royal MSS in the British Museum,[19] and it is but very recently that a Pliny at New College, Oxford,[20] (MS 274) was also found to contain an inscription showing that it had belonged to Richard de Bury.

Compared with Richard de Bury, all the other fourteenth-century book collectors appear rather dim and colourless. Not for nothing was Richard supposed to have owned more volumes than all the other English bishops of his day put together. This must, however, not be taken to imply that none of them had gathered libraries of any significance. For some remarkable collections of books were certainly assembled in this country by members of the episcopate during the fourteenth century. Archbishop Simon Langham, for instance, was able to leave ninety-four volumes to Westminster Abbey in 1376,[21] while William Reed, bishop of Chichester, and William of Wykeham, bishop of Winchester, also possessed a substantial number of theological and canonist texts, which went eventually to New College, Oxford.[22] Among the collections of books formed during the second half of the fourteenth century, the one assembled by the Benedictine cardinal Adam Easton[23] deserves perhaps a special mention, not only on account of the variety of its contents, but also because Easton's books had been acquired both in England and abroad. Naturally enough most of them dealt with theology or canon law. But among them there was also at least one Hebrew manuscript, now at Cambridge,[24] and perhaps also some texts in Greek. Easton died in Italy in 1398 (incidentally his fine tomb can still be seen in St Cecilia's church in Rome); hence at his death his books, which he had destined to his monastery at Norwich, were there and not in England. Fortunately, however, they eventually reached this country in 1407, carefully packed in six barrels.[25] I shall not venture from this an estimate of the actual size of Easton's library. I shall, however, go as far as to say that the volumes formerly in Easton's hands, which still survive at Oxford and Cambridge, certainly point to his having had a large number of books in his possession.

The development of private book collecting, so evident in fourteenth-century England, was but the forerunner of the considerable advance in this field which took place here during the following century. During the fifteenth century prelates were still most enthusiastic where books were concerned. Archbishop Henry Chichele[26] and Cardinal Beaufort, whose ancient copy of Pliny was mentioned in one of Poggio's letters,[27] were certainly not behind their predecessors as book collectors. They lacked, however, the enthusiasm of John Whethamstede, abbot of St Albans from 1420 to 1440 and again from 1452 to 1465, who quite definitely proved the leading ecclesiastical book collector of his day. Whereas all the prelates of his time with bibliophile leanings hardly ever strayed beyond the boundaries of traditional learning, Whethamstede's intellectual appetite found attractions also in the productions of Italian humanism, though whether he really grasped their full significance is quite another matter. During his long career Whethamstede succeeded in securing a very considerable number of books, among which were to be found not only the texts we usually associate with late mediaeval learning, but also many ancient classics and even some of the latest humanist writings from Italy, the latter including several translations of Greek works into Latin.[28] Some of these versions had reached Whethamstede through the good offices of his friend, the papal collector Piero del Monte;[29] others were probably acquired by him directly in Italy, where Whethamstede had attended the councils of Pavia and Siena in 1423.[30] Whethamstede certainly made full use of his books. His voluminous compilations, so dreary and yet so valuable for the study of classical culture in fifteenth-century England, disclose a constant employment of his library. At the same time he was by no means niggardly with its contents. Apart from his benefactions to St Albans[31] and to Gloucester College, Oxford,[32] he also presented books to some of his friends and patrons. Thus he gave a treatise on astronomy to John, duke of Bedford,[33] and a Cato,[34] Plato's *Phaedo* in Latin, and perhaps the chronicles of Matthew Paris, to Humphrey, duke of Gloucester. The Plato is now at Corpus Christi College, Oxford (MS 243); the Matthew Paris is in the British Museum, Royal MS 14 C. vii. We also still possess three of the manuscripts presented to Gloucester College by Whethamstede, namely a copy of Thomas Netter of Walden in two volumes, now respectively in the British Museum, Royal MS 8 G. x and at Worcester College, Oxford, MS LRA 6, and the commentary on Valerius Maximus by Petrarch's friend, Dionigi da Borgo San Sepolcro, now in the Bodleian Library, MS Auct. F. inf. I. 1.

The catholic attitude to books shown by Whethamstede, an attitude different in so many ways from the indiscriminate piling up of Richard de Bury, was also adopted by the greatest collector of the age, Humphrey, duke of Gloucester. The origins of Duke Humphrey's bibiliophily are not difficult to guess. Love of books was traditional in his family, and both his father Henry IV and his brothers, Henry V and John, duke of Bedford, were keen biblio-philes.[35] But Humphrey's passion for books went very much further than theirs, and was also animated by a strong desire to secure the most recent productions by Italian humanists and copies of those ancient Latin classics which were then coming again to light after having been forgotten since the Carolingian age. Many of the books owned by Duke Humphrey were presents from friends or relatives. Thus for instance his copy of the letters of Nicholas of Clemanges now in the Bodleian, MS Hatton 36, was given to him by a canon of Rouen, while others, as for example Harleian MS 1705 in the British Museum, were presentation copies from authors enjoying the duke's patronage. The greater part of Humphrey's library was, however, secured through purchase. British Museum Cotton MS Nero E. v, for instance, was bought by him in London from the heirs of Thomas Polton, bishop of Worcester. His most interesting manuscripts came to him from Italy. While Zenone da Castiglione, the Italian-born bishop of Bayeux, was at the council of Basle in 1434, he was commissioned by Duke Humphrey to ask Italian scholars to send him their works —particularly their versions from the Greek, and also to buy books for him[36] (incidentally Humphrey's copy of Cicero's letters now in the Bibliothèque Nationale, MS lat. 8537, was given to him by Castiglione). Similar instructions were also given to the papal collector in England, Piero del Monte, when he returned to Italy in 1440.[37]

All this was not, however, sufficient to satisfy Humphrey's

I

appetite for new texts from Italy. His desire to secure Latin renderings of Greek writings on politics, which he hoped might also prove of practical value, made him turn to Leonardo Bruni for a translation of Aristotle's *Politics*,[38] and later to Pier Candido Decembrio for one of Plato's *Republic*.[39] Besides translating the *Republic*, Decembrio was instrumental in securing for the duke's library some forty volumes of rare classical texts not available in England,[40] among which was the handsome copy of Pliny's letters now in the Bodleian, MS Duke Humphrey, d.1.

Besides acquiring books in these ways, Duke Humphrey also followed the practice of Richard de Bury of having some texts carefully copied by members of his own household. His Italian secretaries Frulovisi and Beccaria prepared handsome copies of the writings which they had been commissioned to compose by their master, as is shown for instance by Beccaria's Latin versions of works by St Athanasius now in the British Museum, Royal MS 5 F. ii, and at King's College, Cambridge, MS 27. But apart from this, there is also evidence that many of the texts secured from Italy, and probably others too, were copied again here at the duke's command. Accordingly he eventually came to possess not less than four copies of the Latin version of Plato's *Republic*,[41] and at least two of Vitruvius's *De Architectura*,[42] these being works which Decembrio had sent to him from Milan.[43] This explains of course why Humphrey was prepared to give in his lifetime so many of the works which he had acquired to Oxford University: he did so because in many cases they were not the only copies of those writings in his possession.

The actual size of Duke Humphrey's library is unknown. It seems, however, reasonably certain that prior to his benefactions to Oxford he cannot have possessed less than 500 or 600 volumes. As these donations also indicate quite clearly, the subjects covered in his library were fairly varied. Besides classical and humanist texts, it contained a large number of treatises dealing with theology, canon law, medicine, astronomy, philosophy, and history. Books in French were by no means uncommon in it,[44] and it is also interesting to note the presence of Dante's *Divine Comedy* and of a Latin commentary on it,[45] probably the one which Giovanni da Serravalle had prepared at the beginning of the fifteenth century for two English bishops, and which is known to have been available to John Whethamstede.[46] As is shown by the extant remains of his library, it was Humphrey's habit to note in French on his volumes the fact that they belonged to him and also the manner in which they had come into his hands. The formula he employed was 'Cest livre est a moy Homfrey duc de Gloucestre' this being followed by details as to how he had acquired the volume. Thus in MS Hatton 36 of the Bodleian Library this formula is followed by 'du don Maistre Guillem Errard docteur en theologie chanoyne Nostre Dame de Rouen', while in Cotton MS Nero E. v in the British Museum it goes on 'lequel jachetay des executeurs maistre Thomas Polton feu eveque de Wurcestre'. According to Leland, Duke Humphrey also wrote the motto 'Mon bien moundain' as a sign of ownership on his books. This statement by Leland[47] has been questioned,[48] but the discovery of this motto on f. 1 of Duke Humphrey's own copy of the *De Laboribus Herculis* of Coluccio Salutati now in the Vatican Library, MS Urb. lat. 694,[49] confirms it fully.

As it is well known, Duke Humphrey presented 129 volumes to Oxford in 1439,[50] these being followed by others in 1441[51] and by a further gift of 134 in 1444.[52] He also announced his intention of bequeathing all his Latin books to Oxford University.[53] Unfortunately for Oxford this bequest never materialised, for at Gloucester's death his property was granted by Henry VI to King's College, Cambridge,[54] where many of his books were duly entered in the catalogue of the college library drawn up in 1452.[55] Of the books which went to King's only two, a Hebrew psalter now at Leyden (MS Scal. Hebr. 8) and a Latin version of some sermons of St Athanasius by Humphrey's secretary Antonio Beccaria still in the college's possession (MS 27), now survive. In fact only about thirty volumes once owned by Duke Humphrey are now known to exist, though a few more are certainly still awaiting identification.[56] If we consider, however, how very few of the books formerly in the library of John Tiptoft, earl of Worcester, are now known, we may certainly deem ourselves lucky to have still such a number of Humphrey's volumes.

It is possible that the books given to Oxford by Duke Humphrey may have stimulated John Tiptoft, earl of Worcester, to follow his example. As a book collector Tiptoft certainly fired the imagination not only of his English but also of his Italian contemporaries. So much so that in 1460 the Italian humanist Ludovico Carbone stated in his funeral oration for Guarino da Verona that Tiptoft had literally sacked the libraries of Italy in order to enrich England with beautiful books.[57] Needless to say such a remark was not free from exaggeration, although the statement made a few years later by the Florentine bookseller Vespasiano da Bisticci in his own reminiscences of Tiptoft, to the effect that he had collected a very great number of books, and, while in Florence, had purchased all the books he could find and ordered several to be made expressly for him,[58] is certainly true. It was in Italy that a considerable part of Tiptoft's collection was acquired. Furthermore, as several of his extant books show, many of his Italian acquisitions were expressly written for him and sumptuously illuminated with his coat of arms. A group of such manuscripts, including Oxford Bodleian MSS Arch. Selden B. 50, Bodl. 80, Bodl. 646, and Auct. F. 1. 13, British Museum Harl. MS 2639 and St John's College, Cambridge, MS 226 were all decorated by the same artist, an illuminator whose work is remarkably akin to that of the Paduan school,[59] which naturally suggests a link between these volumes and Tiptoft's sojourn in Padua in 1458–61.[60] MS Gl. Kgl. S. 2154 in the Royal Library at Copenhagen, a handsomely decorated Sallust, is on the other hand one of the books purchased in Florence from Vespasiano da Bisticci, and a typical product of Vespasiano's scriptorium.[61] After his return to England in 1461 Tiptoft continued to receive books from Italy.[62] And, what is even more interesting, he imported in 1468 two printed Latin bibles from Cologne,[63] a sign that he did not share the current aristocratic prejudice against the productions of the printing press. What turned Tiptoft into a bibliophile, we may wonder? His interest in the humanities must certainly have influenced him in that direction, but, besides this, there was also the fact that he had the advancement of learning very much at heart and that he wanted to further it by enriching the libraries of the two English universities. Duke Humphrey's role was quite familiar to him and there is no doubt that he aspired to be a second Duke Humphrey. The letter he wrote from Padua to the authorities of Oxford University about 1461[64] certainly points this way, and is confirmed by the provisions of his will, according to which his books were to go after his death to Oxford and Cambridge.[65] Thanks to the intervention of George Neville, archbishop of York, some of his volumes eventually reached the two beneficiaries:[66] but the part of his library that he had taken with him to Ireland never did. Only eleven books once part of Tiptoft's library have been identified,[67] yet even this handful is sufficient to give us a clear idea of the nature of his collection. His copies of Lucretius[68] and Tacitus, *De Oratoribus*,[69] were almost certainly the first ones to reach the British Isles after the discovery of these texts by Poggio and Enoch of Ascoli, and many of the humanist writings he assembled were also undoubted novelties for this country. Works of mediaeval learning were represented in his collection as well, but it was the classical and humanist element which dominated it. This was an element which was well represented, although not overwhelmingly so, in other English private libraries of the time, as for instance in those of William Gray, bishop of Ely, and Robert Flemmyng, dean of Lincoln, and these two collections also included many manuscripts acquired abroad, mainly in Italy. Gray had, however, already started to collect books on a considerable scale in his Oxford days. In fact his collection was so well known in Oxford that Thomas Gascoigne, when mentioning a work by Nicholas of Lyra in his *Liber de Veritatibus*, referred to the copy of it in Gray's rooms in Balliol.[70] Gray's sojourns in Germany and Italy in 1442–54[71] proved most beneficial to his library. He acquired several volumes while studying in Cologne and was also able to secure the services of the scribe Theodorick Werken,[72] whom he employed to transcribe some texts he particularly wanted to possess. Other scribes were employed by him while in Italy. In Florence, two of the leading local copyists of books, Gherardo del Ciriagio and Antonio Mario, produced some very fine classical manuscripts for him.[73] In Rome, Werken and Laurence Dyamant executed for Gray in 1448 the impressive copy of Domenico di Bandino's encyclopedia in five folio volumes now at Balliol College, Oxford, MS 238. Books were also copied for him by members of his household, as for instance the St Augustine, now Balliol MS 78a, written in Cologne in 1442 by his secretary Richard Bole, and the Pseudo-Apuleius *De Diphthongis* and other grammatical treatises now in the Vatican Library, MS Urb. lat. 1180, copied in 1446 by Niccolò Perotti in Ferrara 'apud magnificum et generosissimum virum d. Guilielmum Grai'. A substantial part of Gray's Italian acquisitions came from the scriptorium of Vespasiano da Bisticci, whose *Vite di Uomini Illustri* numbers Gray among its subjects.[74] But Gray purchased books everywhere he went; volumes of theology, particularly Scotist, being acquired by him side by side with the choicest classical and humanist texts. All this collecting did not cease with his return to England in 1454. He probably induced Theodorick Werken, the German scribe who had worked for him in Cologne and Rome, to come over to England, and kept in touch with him,[75] while another German scribe called Rheinbold was also working for Gray in 1461-5.[76] Little wonder then, that by the end of his life Gray had succeeded in assembling a library of about 400 volumes, if not more, among which classics and humanists were certainly well represented although, as in Duke Humphrey's library, the majority of the volumes (which included also one printed book, a Latin Josephus now at Balliol)[77] dealt mostly with mediaeval learning. Gray left his books to Balliol College, where a fairly substantial part of them is still to be found, though not quite all those which originally went there.[78]

Not very dissimilar in character from the library of William Gray was the one collected during the same period by Robert Flemmyng, dean of Lincoln. Like Duke Humphrey Flemmyng was prepared to part with many of his books in his lifetime. This is shown by a generous gift of manuscripts, made by him in 1465 to Lincoln College, Oxford,[79] where the rest of his books also went after his death in 1483.[80] Flemmyng too had pursued his postgraduate studies in Germany and Italy, and while in these countries had purchased a considerable number of books dealing with theology and the Latin classics, and several works by contemporary Italian humanists. Other volumes were obtained by him in Oxford and from monasteries, and at least one of them, a Cicero now at Lincoln College, MS 43, he himself had written while in Italy in a book hand obviously modelled upon Italian contemporary script. Several of Flemmyng's books are fortunately still at Lincoln College, for as a collection it is almost as important as that assembled by Gray; and consequently its significance, particularly to the student of early humanism in this country, is very great.

If we consider the private collections of books assembled by Duke Humphrey, Tiptoft, Gray, and Flemmyng, we find them sharing many common traits. Each of them was undoubtedly still interested in works of mediaeval learning. At the same time the writings of the ancient classics and their humanist imitators exerted a very powerful fascination over them. Moreover, all three clearly felt that their books should eventually contribute to the advancement of learning and that their libraries should include works not available elsewhere in England. Each of them acquired many books on the Continent, and, apart from Flemmyng, they all employed scribes while Duke Humphrey and Tiptoft even went as far as commissioning scholars to turn some works from Greek into Latin. Their example as book collectors was naturally followed by other Englishmen, and especially by those to whom the humanism of Italy appealed strongly. In a way it was in them (with Duke Humphrey, Tiptoft, Gray, and Flemmyng) that the bibliophile traditions established by Richard de Bury found their culmination. One thing that also strikes us about these fifteenth-century collectors is this: that with a single exception, they seemed somewhat indifferent to the physical appearance of their books. Naturally they liked them if possible to be neatly written and on fine vellum, but they were not particularly interested in their decoration. In this Tiptoft stands apart. Like the great Italian bibliophiles of his day, he was not only interested in the contents but also wanted his manuscripts to look beautiful, with the result that all those which were expressly made for him invariably had some handsomely illuminated initials and title pages with his coat of arms beautifully framed.

Plate 8b

This tradition of book collecting so enthusiastically pursued during the fifteenth century ended during this same century. It ended for the simple reason that manuscripts were quickly supplanted by the products of the printing press. The first collections of printed books were in fact already being formed in this country during the last decades of the fifteenth century. John Shirwood, bishop of Durham from 1484 to 1494, really marks the passage from the late mediaeval to the Renaissance type of bibliophile. Shirwood collected several manuscripts, but the main bulk of his collection consisted of the fine printed volumes, mainly of classical and humanist writings, which he purchased during his residence in Rome as king's proctor.[81] An important feature of Shirwood's library was the presence in it of a considerable number of Greek manuscripts, which are unfortunately not with his Latin books at Corpus Christi College, Oxford, and cannot now be traced.[82] But Shirwood was by no means the first English scholar to collect Greek writings.

Greek manuscripts were already to be found in England during the Middle Ages, though admittedly in very small numbers.[83] But then this country did not possess, like France, a centre with an unbroken tradition of Greek studies since Carolingian times, which was the case with the abbey of St Denis.[84] The few Greek books there were, could be found in certain English monastic libraries such as Christ Church and St Augustine's, Canterbury, Ramsey, Glastonbury,[85] and Darley. The earliest extant library list of Christ Church, Canterbury, already shows among its entries a 'Donatus Grece',[86] this being almost certainly a copy of the grammar by Dionysius Thrax. At a later stage other Greek books also found their way to Christ Church, these including a psalter, a copy of the Prophets and an Octateuch. The psalter may perhaps be identified with one now at Trinity College, Cambridge, MS B. 10. 11: the Octateuch is now in the Bodleian, MS Canon. gr. 35, after having migrated from England to Italy, probably during the Reformation period. A Greek psalter now lost was at St Augustine's, Canterbury,[87] and not less than three copies of this text were at Ramsey Abbey during the second half of the thirteenth century.[88] The Ramsey psalters were almost certainly one of the results of the active interest in Greek studies taken by the prior Gregory of Huntingdon,[89] about whose Greek scholarship we wish we knew more. By a lucky chance one of these three psalters has survived and is now at Corpus Christi College, Cambridge, MS 468.[90] This psalter is a very attractive little book with the psalms both in Greek and Latin, written in a characteristically English script of the late thirteenth century, a particularly interesting feature being that the Greek text has also been written in Latin characters. Bilingual texts such as this were of course practically the only means by which one could teach oneself Greek before the Renaissance,[91] and it is my belief that the Corpus psalter may have been used for such a purpose. I also suspect that Gregory of Huntingdon himself may well have been its scribe, or at any rate have been responsible for its execution. Another Greek manuscript containing the liturgy of St Basil, now in the Bodleian, MS Laud gr. 28, was at Darley Abbey in Derbyshire in the fifteenth century,[92] and had probably been there for some time. Unfortunately we are utterly in the dark as to how this book reached the abbey.

This slender number of Greek books may be increased a little if we add to it the volumes available in some of the libraries of the friars and yet other ones, which were certainly in England during the last centuries of the Middle Ages, though we know nothing at all about their owners. To start with, there were two Greek volumes (a copy of the Canticles of the Prophets and a psalter), in the library of the Austin Friars of York in 1372, when they were entered in the library inventory among the books placed at John Erghome's disposal.[93] This is, as far as I know, a unique instance of Greek books in the north of England during the later Middle Ages. On the other hand an important collection of Greek texts could be found in the library of the Oxford Grey Friars. These books came from Robert Grosseteste, the great bishop of Lincoln who died in 1253 and will be mentioned anon.[94] But reference should be made first to those other Greek books which were certainly in this country. A fine Octateuch written in the Eastern Empire in 1152 by the priest Constantine and now at University College, Oxford, MS 52, was already in England during the late twelfth or early thirteenth century—too early a date for supposing that Grosseteste was in some way connected with its importation. During the twelfth century an English scribe, whose name is unknown, wrote the Greek psalter now at Emmanuel College, Cambridge, MS 253.[95] To these can be added the *Nicomachean Ethics* in the Cambridge University Library, MS Ii. v. 44. The possibility cannot of course be excluded that these books were already in private hands before the Reformation. That

Greek manuscripts could be found in private ownership in England during the thirteenth century is indeed actually shown by the fact that Robert Grosseteste possessed not a few of them,[96] though we do not know just how many he succeeded in acquiring. It is, however, certainly not too rash to suggest that besides those few which are still known, he must have owned the Septuagint and at least some of those texts which he turned into Latin. Some of these books probably reached Grosseteste from South Italy, the home of his friend and assistant Nicholas the Greek.[97] Others may have come from Greece, a country which was by no means unknown to another of his intimates, John of Basingstoke, archdeacon of Leicester in the diocese of Lincoln.[98]

Grosseteste's Greek manuscripts, or at any rate a substantial part of them, were left by him to the Grey Friars of Oxford, where they were particularly studied during the second half of the fifteenth century.[99] Three of them still survive. The Cambridge University Library possesses Grosseteste's copy of the Testaments of the Twelve Patriarchs, now MS Ff. i. 24, while a New Testament that belonged to him is also in Cambridge, at Gonville and Caius College (MS 403). On the other hand, the famous manuscript of Suidas at Leyden, MS Voss. gr. F 2, formerly owned by Isaac Vossius and almost certainly acquired by him in England, was wrongly identified by M. R. James as a relic of Grosseteste's library.[100] Two further Grosseteste MSS can be identified in an Aristotle in Corpus Christi College, Oxford, MS 108,[101] and a

Plate 11 pseudo-Dionysius in the Bodleian (Canon. gr. 97).

Whereas something is known about Grosseteste's Greek manuscripts, nothing is known about those at the disposal of Roger Bacon. Yet Bacon's studies, and particularly his Greek grammar, indicate that he must have had some texts in this language in his hands. Incidentally Bacon's grammar appears to have enjoyed some popularity in this country,[102] which argues the presence of an interest in Greek, an interest which is also behind the important Graeco-Latin glossary now at the College of Arms, MS Arundel 9. This glossary is almost certainly the work of an Englishman connected with the circle of Robert Grosseteste.[103]

The decree passed by the Council of Vienne in 1312, ordering the foundation of chairs in Greek and some oriental languages at

Oxford, had apparently no results,[104] and was probably not instrumental in increasing the number of Greek books in this country. The failure of this decree was lamented by Richard de Bury in the *Philobiblon*,[105] which naturally leads one to ask whether Richard de Bury possessed any Greek books. A passage in Walter Burley's commentary on Aristotle's *Politics*[106] clearly indicates that Richard actually had a smattering of Greek, and if we are to take literally (and I do not see why we should not) what we are told in the *Philobiblon*,[107] it would seem that he possessed Roger Bacon's Greek grammar and also some Greek texts. It is also not unlikely that Cardinal Adam Easton may have owned a few Greek books, though here I must add that this is a subject on which I have failed to find any definite evidence,[108] apart from a passage in Bale's *Index*[109] which seems to point to this conclusion.

To find Greek manuscripts again in private ownership we must reach the 1440s. The scarcity of such books in England during the first half of the fifteenth century is vividly brought home to us by the fact that, despite an intensive search, Poggio completely failed to find any in London.[110] The papal collector Piero del Monte, who was here from 1434 to 1440, was more fortunate,[111] but what the books he discovered while in this country were we do not know. However, the fact that they were not exactly of the kind he was looking for suggests that they were not texts of the ancient classics. In spite of this Del Monte had been particularly lucky. Even Duke Humphrey does not appear to have owned anything in Greek beyond a couple of Graeco-Latin glossaries,[112] one of which he gave to Oxford in 1444. At the same time it is, I think, reasonable to assume that some of the writings of Athanasius in the original must also have been available in his household, for a number of them were turned into Latin for the duke by his secretary Antonio Beccaria of Verona.[113] The dearth of Greek books in Duke Humphrey's library was, however, mainly due to his ignorance of the language. It is doubtful if he ever attempted to acquire Greek texts, for the simple reason that translations were obviously quite good enough for him. Had he really wished to acquire some Greek manuscripts, he would certainly have found no difficulty in getting these from Italy.

It was just about the time of Duke Humphrey's death—he died

in 1447—that once more an interest in Greek became noticeable in England. This new wave of interest was the result of the Renaissance. It was in Italy that Robert Flemmyng, dean of Lincoln from 1452 to 1483, succumbed to the attractions of Greek learning, and it is not unlikely that his copy of the Epistles of St Paul and the Acts of the Apostles in Greek, now at Lincoln College, Oxford, MS gr. 82, was acquired by him in that country; his copy of the liturgy of St Basil came on the other hand from Darley Abbey, whence he obtained it on loan on 5 January 1453. It is known that Flemmyng duly returned this manuscript to the abbey,[114] and it eventually ended up in the collection of Archbishop Laud, who gave it to the Bodleian, where it bears the shelfmark Laud gr. 28. If we are to believe Leland,[115] Flemmyng was the author of a Graeco-Latin dictionary, which could still be seen at Lincoln College, Oxford, during the sixteenth century, but that Flemmyng actually compiled this work is a thing which I find hardly credible. What I think was the position is this: Flemmyng had owned a Graeco-Latin glossary, and his name appeared on it, and Leland assumed from this that he was the author. It was a kind of mistake Leland often made. As far as we know, Flemmyng was one of the first Englishmen of the Renaissance period who got together some Greek books. Another was William Gray's protégé, John Free, who not only became a very accomplished Greek scholar, but was also the author of Latin translations of two treatises by Synesius of Cyrene, which he dedicated respectively to John Tiptoft, earl of Worcester, and Pope Paul II.[116] Free's slender means prevented him from collecting a large library, and it is fortunate that one of his few Greek manuscripts, a copy of Theocritus including also some of Pindar's odes, survives now in the Bodleian Library, MS Auct. F. 3. 25, after having belonged during the late fifteenth century to William Worcester the antiquarian.[117] Worcester incidentally appears to have secured other books formerly owned by Free also.[118] Rather than real collectors of Greek books, Free and Flemmyng were actually only owners of a few stray Greek texts. The honour of being the first collector of Greek books in this country belongs perhaps to their contemporary George Neville, archbishop of York from 1465 to 1476. The colophon of a Demosthenes discovered by M. R. James in the

Leyden University Library, MS Voss. gr. 56,[119] shows that this volume was copied expressly for Neville by the scribe Emanuel of Constantinople in 1468, and it is not unlikely that while here Emanuel copied also other volumes for the archbishop, who appears to have been particularly interested in Greek learning. Eleven manuscripts written by Emanuel still survive,[120] ten of which are in English libraries and were almost certainly the outcome of his activity in England. An interesting feature of Emanuel's activity in England is that he did not only transcribe religious texts. A Homer, now at Corpus Christi College, Cambridge, MS 81, a Plato and an Aristotle in Durham Cathedral Library, MSS C. I. 15 and C. IV. 1, a Suidas now in the British Museum, Harl. MS 3100, another at Corpus Christi College, Oxford, MSS 76–77, and the Leyden Demosthenes show a departure from tradition: in fact the beginning of some demand for classical Greek literature in this country.

Emanuel of Constantinople was not the only Greek scribe who enjoyed Neville's patronage. During his visit to England in 1475[121] George Hermonymos of Sparta, who later settled in Paris, where he numbered Erasmus, Budé, and Reuchlin among his pupils, was also in touch with the archbishop, to whom he presented a manuscript now in the British Museum, Harl. MS 3346. At a later date he presented Neville's former secretary, John Shirwood, bishop of Durham, with a text of the pseudo-Aristotelian *De Virtutibus* accompanied by a Latin translation of it made by himself, now MS Auct. G. 9. 3 in the Bodleian. This and a copy of Theodore Gaza's grammar in the Cambridge University Library, MS Ii. iv. 16, are unfortunately all that now survives of Shirwood's collection of Greek books. Unfortunately: for the Greek side of his library appears to have been really quite considerable.[122]

Besides Emanuel of Constantinople and George Hermonymos, two other Greek scribes are known to have worked in England during the period 1475–1500. Hermonymos only stayed a few months, and the same applies to Demetrius Cantacuzenus who was in London in 1475, when he copied, probably for an English patron, a volume of excerpts from Herodotus now in the Bibliothèque Nationale in Paris, MS gr. 1731. On the other hand, John Serbopoulos of Constantinople was in England between 1484 and

1500[123] and perhaps for much longer. The fact that the previously mentioned Suidas at Corpus Christi College, Oxford,[124] was partly copied by Serbopoulos suggests of course that he was active in Oxford and in touch with Emanuel of Constantinople. From 1489 to 1500, however, he was living in St Mary's Abbey, Reading,[125] where he probably worked also for an Oxford clientèle. Several manuscripts written by Serbopoulos are now known,[126] not less than three of them being copies of Theodore Gaza's grammar,[127] an evident sign of a demand for that text. The number of manuscripts written by him which were owned by William Grocin[128] naturally suggests that Grocin himself may have been one of his Oxford patrons. Interest in Greek during the last quarter of the fifteenth century was not, however, circumscribed to Oxford, London, and Neville's circle. Greek studies were also being pursued at Christ Church, Canterbury, from about 1472, when William Worcester took down some observations on Greek grammar put forward in one of his classes by Dr William Sellyng,[129] who was prior of that house from 1472 to 1494. As we saw, a few Greek manuscripts had already been available at Christ Church, Canterbury, in earlier centuries.[130] Their number had, however, increased by Sellyng's time. His turning a sermon by Chrysostom into Latin in 1488[131] naturally implies that the Greek text of it was at his disposal. The Homer and the Euripides now at Corpus Christi College, Cambridge, MSS 81 and 403, were probably also at Canterbury in Sellyng's time,[132] and thanks to John Leland[133] we also know that copies of Cyril on the Prophets, Basil on Isaiah, and of some works by Synesius of Cyrene were also in the library at that time.

It may well have been Sellyng who was instrumental in arousing the interest of Thomas Linacre. With Linacre and William Grocin we find for the first time after John Shirwood a bringing together of a substantial number of Greek manuscripts in this country. They also acquired printed books in this language, though these remained a small minority. Just to give an idea of the Greek sections of their collections, it is perhaps sufficient to say that at least sixteen Greek manuscripts owned by Linacre still survive at Oxford, Brussels, Leyden, and Paris,[134] and that at least thirteen, to which may be added two printed books, were owned by Grocin.[135] Part of Grocin's Greek books went after his death to Corpus Christi College, Oxford.[136] However, the libraries of Grocin and Linacre were not mediaeval but Renaissance collections and are therefore outside the province of this study.

NOTES TO CHAPTER VI

1. *Catalogi Veteres Librorum Ecclesiae Cathedralis Dunelmensis* (ed. J. Raine, Surtees Society, 1838), pp. 117–18.

2. S. Brant, *Narrenschiff*, Basle, 1499, ff. a5b–a6b.

3. Although not actually a book collector, one may recall that Robert Grosseteste, bishop of Lincoln, owned a considerable number of books, on which see S. Harrison Thomson, *The Writings of Robert Grosseteste*, Cambridge, 1940, pp. 25–36; R. W. Hunt, 'Manuscripts containing the Indexing Symbols of Robert Grosseteste', *Bodl. Lib. Rec.*, iv (1953), pp. 241–55; *Robert Grosseteste Scholar and Bishop*, ed. D. A. Callus, Oxford, 1955, pp. 121–45.

4. Even if Robert Holcot was the actual author of the *Philobiblon*, which is by no means established, it is certain that the treatise reproduces Richard's views. Holcot was actually a member of Richard's 'familia', cf. N. Denholm-Young, *Collected Papers on Medieval Subjects*, Oxford, 1946, p. 23. On the authorship of the *Philobiblon* cf. ibid., p. 19; Richard d'Aungerville of Bury, *Fragments of his Register and Other Documents*, Durham, 1910, pp. xxxvii–xli; J. De Ghellinck, 'Un Evêque Bibliophile au xiv Siècle', *Revue d'Histoire Ecclésiastique*, xviii (1922), pp. 301–2.

5. See n. 6.

6. T. Walsingham, *Gesta Abbatum Monasterii Sancti Albani* (ed. H. T. Riley, Rolls Ser. 28. 4, London, 1867), ii, 200.

7. ibid., loc. cit.

8. ibid., ii, pp. 283–4.

9. ibid., ii, p. 200.

10. *Philobiblon*, ch. viii.

11. ibid., loc. cit.

12. ibid., ch. xviii.

13. ibid., ch. xvi.

14. ibid., ch. xi.

15. ibid., ch. xix.

16. *Adae Murimutii Continuatio Chronicarum* (ed. E. Maunde Thompson, Rolls Ser. 93, London, 1889), p. 171.

17. Walsingham, op. cit., ii, p. 200.

18. MS Laud misc. 363.

19. Royal MSS 8 G. i and 13 D. iv.

20. 'Notes and News: Richard de Bury's Books from the Abbey of St. Albans', *Bodl. Lib. Rec.*, iii (1951), pp. 177–9.

21. J. Armitage Robinson and M. R. James, *The Manuscripts of Westminster Abbey*, Cambridge, 1909, pp. 4–7.

22. A. F. Leach, 'Wykeham's Books at New College', Oxford Hist. Soc. *Collectanea*, iii, 1896, pp. 223–30; 234–8; 240–1.

23. N. R. Ker, 'Medieval Manuscripts from Norwich Cathedral Priory', *Trans. Camb. Bibl. Soc.*, i (1949–53), pp. 10, 17–18, 21; R. Weiss, 'The Study of Greek in England during the Fourteenth Century', *Rinascimento*, ii (1951), p. 236, n. 6.

24. Cambridge, St John's College, MS 218.

25. T. Rymer, *Foedera*, viii, London, 1709, p. 151; H. C. Beeching and M. R. James, 'The Library of the Cathedral Church of Norwich', *Norfolk Archaeology*, xix (1917), p. 72, n. 1.

26. E. F. Jacob, 'Two Lives of Archbishop Chichele', *Bull. John Rylands Lib.*, xvi (1932), pp. 469–81.

27. *Poggii Epistolae*, ed. T. de Tonellis, i, Florence, 1832, pp. 158–9.

28. R. Weiss, *Humanism in England during the Fifteenth Century*, 2nd edn., Oxford, 1957, p. 36.

29. R. Weiss, 'Piero del Monte, John Whethamstede, and the Library of St. Albans Abbey', *Eng. Hist. Rev.*, lx (1945), pp. 399–404.

30. Weiss, *Humanism in England*, p. 32.

31. ibid., p. 37, n. 3.

32. ibid., p. 37, n. 5.

33. ibid., p. 37, n. 4.

34. ibid., p. 33, n.9.

35. ibid., p. 39.

36. ibid., pp. 50, 61.

37. ibid., p. 62.

38. ibid., pp. 47–9; R. Weiss, 'Leonardo Bruni Aretino and Early English Humanism', *Mod. Lang. Rev.*, xxxvi (1941), pp. 445–6.

39. Weiss, *Humanism in England*, pp. 54–8.

40. ibid., pp. 58–9.

41. ibid., p. 57, n. 4.

42. ibid., p. 63, n. 11.

43. ibid., pp. 56–7, 59.

44. ibid., pp. 62, 65, 68.

45. R. Weiss, 'Per la conoscenza di Dante in Inghilterra nel Quattrocento', *Giornale Storico della Letteratura Italiana*, cviii (1936), p. 357.

46. ibid., pp. 358–9.

47. J. Leland, *De Rebus Britannicis Collectanea*, ed. T. Hearne, iv, London, 1774, p. 58.

48. K. H. Vickers, *Humphrey, Duke of Gloucester*, London, 1907, p. 410.

49. B. L. Ullman, *Studies in the Italian Renaissance*, Rome, 1955, pp. 345–8.

50. *Epistolae Academicae Oxon.*, ed. H. Anstey, i, Oxford, 1898, pp. 177–84.

51. ibid., i, pp. 203–5.

52. ibid., i, pp. 232–7.

53. ibid., i, p. 295.

54. Weiss, *Humanism in England*, p. 67, n. 4.

55. ibid., loc. cit.; A. L. N. Munby, 'Notes on King's College Library in the Fifteenth Century', *Trans. Camb. Bibl. Soc.*, i (1949–53), pp. 280–4.

56. A list of extant MSS formerly in Duke Humphrey's Library is in Ullman, op. cit., pp. 353–5. For recent additions to the known relics of Duke Humphrey's Library, cf. 'A Manuscript Belonging to Humphrey Duke of Gloucester', *Bodl. Lib. Rec.*, iv (1952), p. 124.; G. I. Lieftinck, 'The *Psalterium Hebraycum* from St Augustine's Canterbury Rediscovered in the Scaliger Bequest at Leyden', *Trans. Camb. Bibl. Soc.*, ii (1955), pp. 97–104; R. Weiss, 'An Unnoticed Manuscript of Humfrey, Duke of Gloucester', *Bodl. Lib. Rec.*, v (1955), pp. 123–4.

57. E. Garin, *Prosatori Latini del Quattrocento*, Milan-Naples, 1952, pp. 398–400.

58. V. da Bisticci, *Vite di Uomini Illustri*, ed. A. Bartoli, Florence, 1859, p. 403.

59. R. Weiss, 'The Library of John Tiptoft, Earl of Worcester', *Bodl. Quart. Rec.*, viii (1935-8), p. 160.

60. ibid., p. 161, n. 5.

61. R. Weiss, 'Another Tiptoft Manuscript', *Bodl. Quart. Rec.*, viii (1935-8), pp. 234-5.

62. Weiss, 'The Library of John Tiptoft', p. 158.

63. R. Weiss, 'The Earliest Catalogues of the Library of Lincoln College', *Bodl. Quart. Rec.*, viii (1935-8), p. 354, n. 19.

64. J. Tait, 'Letters of John Tiptoft, Earl of Worcester and Archbishop Neville to the University of Oxford', *Eng. Hist. Rev.*, xxv (1920), pp. 571-2.

65. Weiss, 'The Library of John Tiptoft', pp. 158-9.

66. ibid., p. 159.

67. ibid., p. 161; Weiss, 'Another Tiptoft Manuscript', pp. 234-5.

68. Oxford, Bodleian Library, MS Auct. F. i. 13.

69. British Museum, Harl. MS 2639.

70. T. Gascoigne, *Loci e Libro Veritatum*, ed. J. E. Thorold Rogers, Oxford, 1881, p. 185.

71. Weiss, *Humanism in England*, pp. 87-90.

72. R. A. B. Mynors, 'A Fifteenth Century Scribe: T. Werken', *Trans. Camb. Bibl. Soc.*, i (1949-53), p. 98.

73. Weiss, *Humanism in England*, p. 92.

74. Da Bisticci, op. cit., pp. 213-15; A. De la Mare, 'Vespasiano da Bisticci and Gray', *Journal of the Warburg and Courtauld Institutes*, xx (1957), pp. 174-6.

75. Mynors, op. cit., pp. 100-4.

76. Weiss, *Humanism in England*, p. 92.

77. Weiss, 'The Earliest Catalogues of the Library of Lincoln College', p. 354, n. 20.

78. Some books noted by Leland in the 16th century are no longer there, see Leland, *De Rebus Britannicis Collectanea*, ed. T. Hearne, iv, pp. 60-7.

79. Weiss, 'The Earliest Catalogues of the Library of Lincoln College', p. 346.

80. Weiss, *Humanism in England*, p. 104.

81. P. S. Allen, 'Bishop Shirwood of Durham and his Library', *Eng. Hist. Rev.*, xxv (1910), pp. 455-6.

82. ibid., pp. 453-4.

83. See on this M. R. James, 'Greek MSS in England before the Renaissance', *The Library*, 4th ser., vii (1927), pp. 337-53.

84. R. Weiss, 'Lo Studio del Greco all' Abbazia di San Dionigi durante il Medioevo', *Rivista di Storia della Chiesa in Italia*, vi (1952), pp. 426-38.

85. Some Graeco-Latin fragments of the Old Testament from Glastonbury are in the Bodleian Library, MS Auct. F. 4. 32. The mediaeval Glastonbury catalogue lists a Graeco-Latin psalter, cf. T. W. Williams, *Somerset Medieval Libraries*, Bristol, 1897, p. 55.

86. M. R. James, *The Ancient Libraries of Canterbury and Dover*, Cambridge, 1903, pp. lxxxv, 7, n. 25.

87. ibid., p. 201.

88. Weiss, 'The Study of Greek in England', p. 220.

89. ibid., pp. 219-20.

90. ibid., p. 220, n. 1.

91. R. Sabbadini, *Il Metodo degli Umanisti*, Florence, 1922, pp. 18-20.

92. See p. 128.

K

93. M. R. James, 'The Catalogue of the Library of the Augustinian Friars of York', *Fasciculus Ioanni Willis Clark Dicatus*, Cambridge, 1909, p. 21.

94. See p. 126.

95. M. R. James, 'On a Greek Psalter in the Library of Emmanuel College', *Proc. Camb. Antiq. Soc.*, viii (1891–4), pp. 168–72.

96. Weiss, 'The Study of Greek in England', p. 212, n. 1; *Robert Grosseteste Scholar and Bishop*, ed. D. A. Callus, pp. 134–5.

97. Weiss, op. cit., p. 211.

98. ibid., p. 213.

99. Weiss, *Humanism in England*, pp. 137–8.

100. G. Mercati, *Ultimi Contributi alla Storia degli Umanisti—Fascicolo I: Traversariana*, Vatican City, 1939, p. 80.

101. On this MS cf. H. J. Drossaart Lulofs, 'Some Notes on the Oxford MS. Corp. Christi 108', *Mnemosyne*, 3rd ser., xiii (1947), pp. 290–301. Mr N. R. Ker tells me that the note at the end of the MS is 'in a hand which I find it difficult to distinguish from genuine Grosseteste'. See also *Robert Grosseteste Scholar and Bishop*, ed. Callus, p. 135. On the pseudo-Dionysius see R. Barbour, 'A Manuscript of Ps.-Dionysius Areopagitica copied for Robert Grosseteste', *Bodl. Lib. Rec.*, vi (1958), pp. 401–16.

102. Weiss, 'The Study of Greek in England', pp. 217–18.

103. ibid., pp. 218–19.

104. R. Weiss, 'England and the Decree of the Council of Vienne on the Teaching of Greek, Arabic, Hebrew, and Syriac', *Bibliothèque d'Humanisme et Renaissance*, xiv (1952), pp. 1–9. Some teaching of Hebrew appears however to have been done at Oxford in accordance with the decree, cf. C. Roth, 'Jews in Oxford after 1290', *Oxoniensia*, xv (1950), pp. 63–4.

105. ch. x, 166, 167.

106. Weiss, 'The Study of Greek in England', p. 228, n. 3.

107. ch. x.

108. Weiss, 'The Study of Greek in England', p. 238.

109. John Bale, *Index Britanniae Scriptorum*, ed. R. Lane Poole and M. Bateson, Oxford, 1902, p. 5.

110. Weiss, *Humanism in England*, p. 14.

111. ibid., p. 26.

112. ibid., p. 63, n. 12.

113. ibid., pp. 45–6.

114. Oxford, Bodleian Library, MS Laud gr. 28, f. 1b.

115. J. Leland, *Commentarii de Scriptoribus Britannicis*, ed. A. Hall, Oxford, 1709, p. 461.

116. R. Weiss, 'A Letter—Preface of John Free to John Tiptoft, Earl of Worcester', *Bodl. Quart. Rec.*, viii (1935–8), pp. 101–3; R. Weiss, 'New Light on Humanism in England during the Fifteenth Century', *Journal of the Warburg and Courtauld Institutes*, xiv (1951), pp. 25–31.

117. Weiss, *Humanism in England*, p. 111.

118. ibid., loc. cit.

119. M. R. James, 'The Scribe of the Leicester Codex', *Journal of Theological Studies*, v (1904), pp. 445–7.

120. Weiss, *Humanism in England*, p. 145, n. 3.

121. ibid., p. 146.

122. See above, n. 82.

123. Weiss, *Humanism in England*, pp. 147–8.

124. See above, p. 129.

125. Weiss, *Humanism in England*, p. 148.

126. ibid., p. 148, n. 2.

127. Dublin, Trinity College, MS 925; Cambridge, Trinity College MS R. 9. 22; Oxford, Bodleian Library, MS Gr. class. e. 96.

128. Oxford, Corpus Christi College, MSS 23, 24, 77, 106, 109.

129. Weiss, *Humanism in England*, p. 157, n. 6.

130. See above, p. 124.

131. Weiss, *Humanism in England*, pp. 157–8, 194.

132. ibid., p. 158, n. 5.

133. Leland, *Commentarii de Scriptoribus Britannicis*, p. 483.

134. R. Weiss, 'Notes on Thomas Linacre', *Miscellanea Giovanni Mercati*, iv (Vatican City, 1946), p. 377. To the list given there should be added Oxford, New College, MSS 240 and 241.

135. M. Burrows, 'Memoir of William Grocin', Oxford Hist. Soc., *Collectanea*, ii (1890), pp. 319–23.

136. J. R. Liddell, 'The Library of Corpus Christi College in the Sixteenth Century', *The Library*, 4th ser., xviii (1938), p. 389.

VII

The Preservation
of the Classics

M. D. KNOWLES

THERE are few if any topics in the whole range of mediaeval studies which are less patient of summary treatment or of what is called vulgarisation than the subject of this chapter. Only a long lifetime ago even serious scholars could make broad or precise statements about the survival of the classics in the Middle Ages without hesitation and with little fear of immediate challenge, but in the past sixty years the rise of scientific bibliography and the careful examination of collections and library catalogues have made what was largely an antiquarian study into an exact historical discipline. Max Manitius in Germany and Montague Rhodes James in England did much to reveal both the riches and the difficulties of the subject; the relevant literature has grown far beyond the powers of intake of the general historian, and both the scattered detail of the acquired knowledge, and the gaps and dark places which the specialists are the first to acknowledge, make general conclusions not only rash but impossible. Above all, for anyone, even a Mynors or a Ker, to give a final summary in a small compass would be out of the question, while to present an exact account of a small section of the field would be useless to all save a few specialists. Nevertheless, an attempt will be made here to say where and by whom what writings of the classical authors were preserved.

Let us begin by defining our subject. The classics, for our purpose, are the works of profane literature composed before c. 200 A.D. We are not expected to consider either the church fathers or the philosophers or the legists or even the poets, half classical, half Christian, of the Empire's Indian summer on the banks of the Moselle and the Garonne. Moreover, the classics for our purpose are the Latin classics. The appearance of Greek studies here and there, and the survival of Greek manuscripts in the West, is an important and fascinating subject, but taken by and large, the libraries of the West had little share in preserving and transmitting the Greek classics. As regards dates, we may fix roughly the limits as A.D. 500 to A.D. 1400. In 500, when Boethius and Cassiodorus were in the prime of life, it was still possible, at least here and there in Italy, to read and even to acquire almost all the Latin classical writers. By 1400, save for a few important exceptions, manuscripts of the classics once more existed in sufficient numbers to ensure the preservation of at least some kind of text of the author so long as no major catastrophe overtook Western civilisation. Doubtless disasters and unexplained losses have occurred since, and down to our own day. Poggio and Scaliger and Casaubon knew of manuscripts that have since vanished without a trace. The only known manuscript of the beautiful Epistle to Diognetus perished in the bombardment of Strassburg in 1870. But we are concerned not with problems and tragedies, but with the main stream of the transmission.

Why, we may first ask, were the Latin classics threatened with destruction on a continent where Latin never ceased to be the vehicle of all higher communication, and why, in fact, did they survive? The answers that have usually been given, now as fifty years ago, are that they were threatened by the barbarians, and saved by the monks. In its main lines this answer is of course correct, but it needs to be given with reservations and additions. It has been shown, in the first place, that the invaders taken as a whole, by the time they reached Gaul and Italy, were no longer destructive barbarians, but children anxious to learn and admiring what they saw. On the other hand it has been shown that monks were by no means always and everywhere preservers of literature, and that churchmen were by no means always interested in its preservation. The survival of important texts as palimpsests is very considerable. We are not here concerned with the variations of Christian sentiment on the subject of profane literature from apostolic times downwards, but we may note that a victorious Church, gradually acquiring a large technical literature of its own, and faced by a militant neo-paganism which regarded itself as the true heir and interpreter of the legacy of the classical past—that a Church in these surroundings was not predisposed in favour of a literature which made intolerable assumptions in both religion and morals. In addition, there is the complex of inferiority, which belittles what it cannot hope to emulate, just as there is the haste of the convert, who uses the very technique he has been bred in to attack the system which had created it. Jerome and Augustine are examples of the latter frame of mind, Gregory the Great and Gregory of Tours, in some degree, of the former. Finally, the newly developed monasticism was by no means anxious to multiply or to enjoy the masterpieces of ancient rhetoric and poetry. St Benedict, though he expected his monks to read the Fathers of the Church and of the Desert, nowhere suggests that the copying or amassing of books is part of the work of a monk.

To all that has just been said of the mental climate of the sixth century there is one notable and possibly weighty exception. Cassiodorus, one of that small band who, themselves having entered upon the heritage of the ancient world as a birthright, now saw it threatened with destruction and knew how to transmit it to a less privileged posterity—Cassiodorus had, at the very same moment as Benedict, founded a monastery in south Italy and endowed it with a splendid library, and had laid upon his monks as one of their primary tasks the digestion and transmission of the classics of the old world. It has often been said that the literary ideal of Cassiodorus was soon mated to the ascetic and laborious ideal of Benedict, and that the issue was the typical literary abbey of the Benedictine centuries. On the high level of historical sequence this is undoubtedly true; the two ideals were in fact fused; but that Cassiodorus's programme had any direct and measurable influence upon the monasteries of Italy in the century after the foundation of Vivarium has not yet been convincingly proved from documentary evidence. One fact, however, should be grasped. In every monastery the liturgy was performed, the Scripture and the Fathers read, the infants and young oblates instructed. In other words, books were needed, some of them accurately and finely written, and others of the class of elementary text-books and readers.

But if the monasteries of the sixth century were not collecting and copying the classics, Italy as a whole was still rich in collections of books. The public libraries had perhaps for the most part been dispersed and the great private collections had diminished in number, but in private hands, and in the collections of books that came to be associated with the cathedrals, the classics were included. How rich some of these collections could be the surviving treasures of Vercelli and Verona and a number of other Italian cathedral libraries show, though it may be noted that the library of Verona in recent centuries has contained no classical texts. But while realising that Italy was still rich in books, it is worth remembering that the whole corpus of classical literature was not in existence in numerous copies. Even now, for one copy of Petronius or Manilius, there are a thousand of Virgil or Horace, and the use of numerous, but standardised, classical texts for education during the course of four or five centuries had tended to a very uneven distribution of numbers, favouring the survival of the principal models such as Virgil and Cicero's rhetorical and philosophical works, and the more rhetorical and sententious writers of the Silver Age such as Lucan, Juvenal and Persius. A few, such as Ennius and Catullus, whom modern taste ranks among the highest, were never popular in the later Empire, and the same is possibly, if surprisingly, true of Tacitus; other poems such as Lucretius' *De Rerum Natura* and the lyrics of Horace were particularly unacceptable to Christians. But in the matter of survival, as in the process of transmission, a great deal depended upon chance or upon circumstances of which we know nothing.

We find then in the sixth and early seventh centuries in Italy and Gaul a mental climate hostile to pagan literature, while at the same time the mass of remaining books was great and the machinery for its transmission was at least potentially in existence in the monasteries. This hostile climate was soon modified by three new cultural currents which ultimately united in what is called the Carolingian Renaissance. The condition for all three was the rise of a young literary discipline in barbarian surroundings, where the only road to progress lay in following ancient models and where the danger to Christian principles was not a practical one.

The first of these cultures was that of Ireland in the late fifth and throughout the sixth century. The exact scope of this, in common with all other phases of Irish history, has been obscured by controversy and propaganda and is still very imperfectly known. Many of the claims made for it have been exaggerated, such as that there existed a wide and deep knowledge of Greek, and some acquaintance with Hebrew, but it is at least certain that the Irish of this period were distinguished by artistic and literary gifts of a high order, that they possessed at least some of the classics and above all Virgil, and that they had no inhibitions in their reading. Their chief part in preserving the classics was, however, not taken in Ireland but when, led by Columban, their monks swarmed into Alpine and sub-Alpine regions and founded such monasteries as Luxeuil (590), Bobbio (613) and St Gall (614). It seems probable that the Irish monks took with them and received later a few, but only a few, Irish classical manuscripts, but they readily accepted and even sought out codices from Italy and elsewhere. Bobbio in particular became a storehouse of ancient manuscripts: a few of these are still in existence; others, erased and written over, have been recovered within the last century. Other houses had almost equally noble collections.

The second focus was in southern England. Here the first impulse came from Italy, with the arrival of the learned Greek Theodore of Tarsus as archbishop of Canterbury in 668, accompanied by the equally learned North African and Neapolitan abbot Hadrian. These brought books, including classical authors, with them: what is more, they brought a definite educational programme which was entirely literary and included the teaching of Greek. That the books that they brought with them contributed to the further transmission of the classics is very probable; what is even more important is the impetus they gave to education, which certainly included Virgil and other poets and which affected the whole of south-west England. Verse writing was part of the curriculum, and Persius and Juvenal were added to Virgil.

Meanwhile yet another focus was developing between the Wear and the Tyne. Here three streams converged—from Canterbury and the south, filtering northwards; from Iona and ultimately from Ireland, running south from the western isles; and, finally, a fresh inflow of books from Rome and Gaul brought by that indefatigable traveller, Benedict Biscop. We know from the citations of Bede that his working library, particularly in patristic and what may be called technical literature was very large; we know also that he had a working knowledge of patristic and gospel Greek. He also knew Virgil and parts of Cicero and Horace, but he appears to have been considerably more narrow in his range than his older contemporary Aldhelm of Malmesbury and Sherborne.

Important in themselves as were the two English intellectual movements in Kent-Wessex and in Northumbria, each was still more powerful in its consequences. From Wessex went forth Bede's exact contemporary Winfrith or Boniface of Crediton, who was responsible for founding in south Germany Fulda and Reichenau, among other monasteries, and for giving them the literary education then widespread in England and some at least of its books. Other books he took with him to Germany from Rome. From Jarrow and Wearmouth, a little later, the learning of Bede passed through his pupils to York, where a library was collected during the eighth century which contained not only a large number of patristic writings but also a representative collection of the classics. Indeed the author of a work which is still standard does not hesitate to write that it 'far surpassed any, even in the XII cent. in England or France', and he explicitly includes in this comparison the Canterbury library of 1170. Certainly no other library of that age of comparable size was also, as we know York to have been, the working library of a cathedral school and the scene of active copying. When therefore Charles the Great, with his genius for choosing the best, asked the most illustrious master of the school of York, Alcuin, to become head of his own palace-school and to take charge of the intellectual rebirth of the Empire, he was in fact diverting back to the Continent a great stream that had gone across the Channel in a previous century.

Besides the training and the literary resources of York, Alcuin brought to the heart of the Empire a wholly new attitude to the ancient literature widely differing from that of Jerome and Augustine. To him, inheriting the traditions of Ireland and Northumbria and Wessex, the ancients are a marvel; all knowledge comes from them; they are the only models; to imitate and reproduce them is the only hope. Alcuin would even go a stage further: the liberal arts are not the work of man, but of God, who has created them as a part of nature for men to find and develop; the ancients did this—how much more eagerly and successfully should a Christian do so! And Alcuin in a well known passage enunciates the functions of Christian humanism. In the morning of life he had sown in Britain; in the evening of that life he ceased not to sow in France. His one desire was to build a new Athens in France, or, rather, an Athens better than the old, for the old had only the science of the seven arts, but the new has in addition the seven Gifts of the Holy Spirit. Alcuin, indeed, precisely reverses Jerome. Jerome had turned to the monastic life as a flight from profane letters; Alcuin exhorts his monks to abandon the spade for the pen: 'Fodere quam vites melius fit scribere libros.'

With such a programme from the man who has been called 'the first minister of public instruction', 'the premier in things of the mind', 'the school master of France', and with an emperor resolved to further the cause of letters and commanding resources which, however limited, were nevertheless wider than those of any previous European ruler since Constantine, it is easy to see why the Carolingian renaissance was a new thing. Though it was not, like the movement two centuries later, the intellectual adolescence of half a continent, it was certainly a new epoch in the world of books. It was now that there began that quest and interchange of manuscripts, that multiplication of texts and that imitation of the Latin authors that continued for almost four centuries, dying down and breaking out here and there like a forest fire. It was to the activity of the monks and bishops of this age that the transmission of the Latin classics was largely due. They collected the exemplars from Italy and elsewhere and multiplied the texts. For many of the Latin writers our printed text rests upon a basis, often very incomplete, of ancient manuscript authority extended and supported by copies of the Carolingian age. In not a few cases the oldest existing manuscript is Carolingian.

The movement began from two centres, at Aachen and at Tours, and it was at this time that the *scriptoria* of such monasteries as Stavelot and Corbie in the north, and Fleury in the south, became celebrated and their libraries rich. In the next generation

Paschasius Radbert and Lupus of Ferrières passed the torch to south Germany and north Switzerland, to Fulda and Reichenau and Wurzburg. St Gall revived, Tegernsee and Blaubeuren rose, and a little later Gorze and St Evroult les Toul. In Germany and Lorraine there was always life at one monastery or another, and recent research has shown that in Italy a surprisingly lively literary culture existed in the urban schools at least from c. 950.

But it was in Italy, still the treasure house of manuscripts, that a deliberate and magnificent attempt was made to preserve the classics a century later. This was at Monte Cassino in the golden age that culminated in the abbacy of Desiderius (1058–87). Already rich in books, the abbots obtained codices for copying from Italy, Dalmatia and even farther afield; patristic, historical, encyclopedic and medical works were copied as well as the classics. It is to the Monte Cassino of this age that we owe the unique surviving manuscript of Tacitus *Annals* xi–xvi and *Histories* i–v, as also that of Apuleius' *Metamorphoses*. Nor should we forget the treasures that still existed at Bobbio, Farfa, Nonantola and other Italian monasteries, which received new life at this time either from Cluny or from the Gregorian reformers.

Almost contemporaneously with the Reform two important provinces were added to the monastic world in Normandy and the new plantation of England. Here also, the following century was one in which books were imported and multiplied. The peak of the purely literary movement was reached by 1200. The new orders of the twelfth century explicitly renounced profane learning, and the new schools of law and dialectics had other tastes. The great age of the classical revival had ceased by 1200, and during the next century the craft of writing, along with that of illumination, passed to professional clerks and laymen. If the centuries before 1100 had been Virgilian the twelfth century was that of Horace and the satirists and the thirteenth that of Ovid. It was only with the fourteenth century that Virgil came back with Dante and Petrarch, to begin a new age and a new renaissance.

We have now glanced at the process of transmission. What did in fact survive that process? Here we may perhaps make three observations. The first is, that the bulk of classical Latin literature of the first rank is not overwhelmingly large. The second is, that a certain amount was lost before 500 A.D., especially of the primitives such as Lucilius, Naevius and Ennius, and of the pre-Ciceronian orators. The third is, that a very appreciable section of what survived hibernated, so to say, for some or all of the Middle Ages—Tacitus in bulk, the *Silvae* of Statius, some of the speeches and letters of Cicero—and were therefore warehoused or kept in cold storage by the monks rather than transmitted.

After having said so much, let us glance at some of the statistics that can be ascertained of classical authors in mediaeval libraries. It will, of course, only be a glance of the most superficial kind. The most accurate list of all Latin authors in all European libraries is in the posthumous work of Max Manitius (1935) which gathered up a lifetime's study and collection.[1] Yet excellent as it is, the entries for England have been increased by about one-third by Professor R. A. B. Mynors—an indication that the field of research is still open; indeed, it stretches wide and out of our sight. Professor Mynors has kindly allowed his notes to be used in what follows, and has added to his kindness by lending an unpublished paper on the (itself not wholly published) catalogue by John Boston, the monk of Bury at the beginning of the fifteenth century, who set out upon the ambitious task of listing all pagan and secular books in the English libraries of his day[2].

In what follows the figures given will, for brevity's sake, be almost exclusively English. The numbers given from Manitius indicate the *houses* where a particular author is found; those of Mynors indicate the *copies* of a particular author; the additions made by Mynors do not therefore represent such a great proportional increase as might appear, since at many of the houses noted by Manitius two or more copies occur under his entry. The year 1400 will be taken as the latest limiting date, as after that the manuscripts of the humanists begin to filter in.

Of PLAUTUS Manitius lists only two occurrences in the whole of Europe during the Middle Ages, viz. at Bamberg in 1120 and at Halberstadt in 1147. Mynors, however, has been able to add a Bury St Edmunds' book from John Boston.

TERENCE is much more common. Manitius finds him in England

at six houses, with five copies at Canterbury and two at Dover. Mynors adds five more copies.

LUCRETIUS is found only at Murbach (ninth century), Bobbio (eleventh century) and Corbie (twelfth century), though a few later writers, such as Alain de Lille and Honoré d'Autun quote him. Mynors adds nothing from England.

Of CATULLUS no instance occurs, though Rathier of Verona quotes him in the ninth century. Likewise there is no instance of TIBULLUS or PROPERTIUS, though Richard of Furnival quotes both c. 1250.

VIRGIL is of course ubiquitous, but it is worth noting that while manuscripts and quotations abound before 1200, both are rare in the thirteenth century, but return to frequency in the fourteenth.

HORACE is very frequent, though the Odes less so than the Satires and Epistles. Manitius finds him in nine houses (Canterbury had ten copies in 1170 and Dover five, with commentaries in addition, in 1389). Mynors adds six more copies.

OVID is very frequent, especially in the thirteenth century. Canterbury had ten copies in 1170 and Durham ten in the twelfth century; Peterborough had four in the fourteenth.

PERSIUS, whom we find difficult, was of common occurrence. Manitius lists ten instances, with nine copies at Canterbury. Mynors adds six.

LUCAN is frequent. Manitius lists nine houses, with five copies at Canterbury and four at Durham. Mynors adds four.

JUVENAL is frequent. Manitius lists eight houses, with three and a half copies at Canterbury. Mynors adds five.

MARTIAL is fairly common. Manitius lists three houses; Mynors adds three copies.

CICERO is common but unevenly distributed. The Rhetorics, *De Senectute*, *De Amicitia*, *De Officiis* are very common in earlier centuries; the philosophical works, the Philippics and the Catilines less common. Other speeches and the Letters range from rare to non-existent.

CAESAR is very rare save in northern France. Manitius lists none in England, but Mynors gives two from Bury St Edmunds.

SALLUST is common. Manitius lists nine houses, with eight copies at Canterbury. Mynors adds two.

LIVY is rare. Manitius found two occurrences in England.

TACITUS is not found in any mediaeval catalogue.

PLATO (*Timaeus*) is common. Manitius lists six houses with six copies at Canterbury. Mynors adds five.

All these of course are the literary classics, used as school-books.

The survival of the technical classics—grammar, medicine, astronomy—is more impressive still.

We may now consider the same subject from another point of view. What manuscripts are in fact behind our best modern critical texts? Are they of mediaeval and monastic date? It will be realised that here we are dealing with manuscripts that either still exist or at least were in existence later than 1400. Hitherto we have been dealing, not with numbers of manuscripts, but with mediaeval catalogue references to manuscripts. Hence there may well be in existence for editors a mediaeval manuscript which is not in fact listed in any mediaeval catalogue. Here, then, is a selection of Latin classics, with brief notes on the principal manuscript authorities for the printed text:

LUCRETIUS rests on two manuscripts, one of Mainz (ninth century) the other of St Bertin (tenth century), both deriving from a fourth- or fifth-century manuscript existing in France in Carolingian times.

CATULLUS rests on an ancient manuscript of Verona.

VIRGIL rests chiefly on six manuscripts dating from before 500 A.D., one of which was preserved at Bobbio, one at St Denis, Paris, and one probably at Luxeuil.

PERSIUS rests partly on monastic manuscripts, including two English pre-Conquest ones of the ninth century.

STATIUS rests entirely on monastic manuscripts, including the unique one of the *Silvae* found by Poggio at St Gall.

CICERO and CAESAR both depend chiefly on monastic manuscripts.

TACITUS depends entirely upon manuscripts from Corvey, Fulda and Monte Cassino.

If we consider the same question from a slightly different angle again, and ask what classical authors owe their *preservation* (as distinct from their best text) to monastic care, we find similar results. In general, we may say that we do not know of any classical work which disappeared between the eighth and the twelfth centuries. Considering works more in detail, we may say that all TACITUS depends on unique texts preserved in abbeys. *Annals* i–x are in a Corvey manuscript of the ninth century, the rest of *Annals* and *Histories* in a Florence manuscript copied at Monte Cassino in the eleventh century. *Germania*, *Agricola* and *Dialogus* are in a ninth- or tenth-century Fulda manuscript of Hersfeld provenance. The five last books of LIVY come from a Lorsch manuscript now at Vienna; Lorsch also preserved the *De Clementia* and *De Beneficiis* of SENECA; Hersfeld the *De Grammaticis* of SUETONIUS. Eleventh-century manuscripts of Monte Cassino are unique for the *Golden Ass* of APULEIUS, part of VARRO *De Lingua Latina*, and CICERO *Pro Cluentio*. Unique texts at the same abbey give us FRONTINUS *De Aquaeductis Urbis Romae* and thirty-six verses that are lacking in all other manuscripts of JUVENAL, Satire vi. The unique source of CICERO *De Republica* is a Vatican manuscript of Bobbio provenance. The oldest manuscript of CAESAR's *Commentaries* is from Fleury and the most complete collection of CICERO from Corvey.

Our final conclusion must therefore be: first, that for the preservation of the ancient texts libraries of all sorts in Italy and the Irish and Anglo-Saxon monasteries are equally responsible; second, that in the work of transmitting the text the monastic scriptorium played a very great, but not always an effective part; and thirdly, that taste and accident had a very large share in determining the selection of texts to be copied. No attempt was ever made or even imagined to make a complete collection of the classics. On a balance, immeasurable as is the benefit they conferred on posterity in this respect, the monasteries have probably received somewhat more than their share of praise from recent historians. Without the great old Italian depositories of books they could have done nothing. Yet if they had never existed the survival of the classics would indeed have been precarious.

NOTES TO CHAPTER VII

1. M. Manitius, *Handschriften antiker Autoren in mittelalterlichen Bibliothekskatalogen* (Zentralblatt für Bibliothekswesen, Beiheft 67), Leipzig, 1935.

2. cf. R. A. B. Mynors, 'The Latin Classics known to Boston of Bury', in *Fritz Saxl, 1890–1948: A Volume of Memorial Essays from his Friends in England*, ed. D. J. Gordon, Edinburgh, 1957, pp. 199–217.

VIII

The Dispersal of the Libraries in the Sixteenth Century

C. E. WRIGHT

AFTER the Danish wars in the Anglo-Saxon era, and the unrest that was the immediate result of the Norman Conquest, political conditions in England during the Middle Ages were fortunately such, that it is possible for us to consider the dispersal of the mediaeval libraries in terms of one period—the sixteenth century. Apart from the 'nineteen winters' of Stephen's reign when, as the Peterborough chronicler reports, conditions were so terrible that men openly said that Christ and his angels slept,[1] and the disturbances natural to the prolonged Wars of the Roses (1455–85), this country was singularly free from internal political strife. There was, of course, the incident of the Peasants' Revolt in 1381, which, as we have proof, was destructive of manuscript material—records were burnt on Market Hill in Cambridge and of the colleges there only Corpus Christi appears to have escaped damage, a piece of good fortune which it owed to the powerful protection of John of Gaunt.[2] And earlier in the same century, in 1327, there was the famous attack on the monastery of Bury St Edmunds, when the townspeople forced their way into the abbey and are reputed to have carried off, among other things, all the writings they could lay their hands on.[3] This country, however, was spared the devastation that befell France in the Hundred Years War.[4] That there was continuous wastage in the libraries throughout the Middle Ages is not of course denied; books lent sometimes failed to come back, and all the time (particularly in the later centuries) there was deliberate mutilation of books no longer in current use, a process which is evidenced today by the leaves or portions of leaves to be found as paste-downs or flyleaves in mediaeval bindings. From the beginning of the Middle Ages we may cite, for example, the fragments of a ninth-century sacramentary which were used for strengthening the beautiful 'Romanesque' binding of the Winton Domesday of about 1160, now preserved in the library of the Society of Antiquaries (MS 154), and examples from the fifteenth century are legion. Sometimes, too, the monastic libraries were deprived of books *en bloc* by transfer elsewhere; for instance, a collection of manuscripts was sent in two batches from the library of the Cathedral Priory of Durham to Durham College at Oxford in 1409;[5] the total of books so transferred amounted to thirty-six volumes. Nevertheless, we can say that the monastic libraries remained for the most part intact until the dissolution of the houses effected by the various Acts passed between 1536 and 1539. This is the great dividing line; it meant the immediate dispersal of the library contents of all the monasteries with the exception of the cathedral priories.

First, something must be said, by way of preface, of the steps by which the monastic life was brought to an end by Henry VIII and his advisers.[6]

The royal commissioners appointed to visit the monasteries began their work in July 1535. The legal instruments necessary to enable action to be taken followed quickly in 1536, first by the Act for the Court of Augmentations (27 Henry VIII, c. 27) whereby the machinery necessary for handling the monastic properties was established and, secondly, by the Act for the Dissolution of the Lesser Monasteries (27 Henry VIII, c. 28). A large number of the greater monasteries almost immediately took the hint and surrendered in the following year; such action was further stimulated by a second visitation in January of 1538. Even after this date however twelve of the more powerful houses declined to come to terms, although other events of a disquieting kind had intervened; some abbots had found themselves faced with charges of treason, their houses becoming forfeit to the Crown as if they had been the private property of the abbots. Thus, as a result of the Pilgrimage of Grace (October 1536 to February 1537) Jervaulx, Whalley, Kirkstead and Bridlington were dissolved, the abbot of Furness was forced to surrender, Barlings was involved

L

in the Lincolnshire rebellion (October 1536), and finally three abbots—those of Glastonbury, Reading and Colchester—were hanged in November and December of 1539. The last house to surrender was Waltham, on 23 March 1540, and by this date the Act for the Dissolution of the Greater Monasteries (31 Henry VIII, c. 13) had already been passed. The whole process was to be rounded off in the next reign, in 1547, by the Act for the Dissolution of the Chantries (1 Edward VI, c. 14) which the church historian Fuller happily characterised as 'the last dish of the last course, and after chantries, as after cheese, nothing to be expected'.[7]

What the dissolution meant to the inmates themselves is difficult to assess; it must have varied with individuals. So far as the necessities of life were concerned they had nothing to fear; as long as half-empty houses survived (and there were many such at this time) the members of the dissolved houses were transferred to vacant 'cells' in the others, and when the final steps were taken by which all the houses were dissolved then the ex-religious received the benefits of the pension system instituted by the Crown in the first place for the heads of the houses.[8] Many of the senior members of the houses were men well-versed in worldly affairs so that, despite the penalties threatened to those who broke the provisions of the Acts, a large amount of monastic property of every kind passed into the possession of the ex-religious and their relatives; for example, it has been pointed out that the abbot of Alnwick in Northumberland was able to found a county family on the lands of his former house,[9] and if land could be so transferred or retained we may be sure that the same process happened often enough with movables. It would be no difficult thing for abbots and priors to convey such to their country houses, which indeed often formed part of their pensions, and among such movables, books were undoubtedly sometimes included. This is one channel through which the library contents might be dispersed, and we shall have something to say about it in detail later on. Large numbers of the ex-religious secured what were called 'capacities', that is to say, licences which enabled them to hold benefices as secular priests, and they were thus absorbed into the parochial clergy. All at any rate had to face one tremendous fact; the monastic way of life no longer existed in this country and those who found themselves unable to adapt their lives to the change had no option but migration overseas. The number that availed themselves of this was however very small.

This then in broad outline is the background of events to our subject.

Finally, before we go on to discuss it, it is important to be quite clear as to the kind of material with which we are going to be principally concerned. The manuscripts in the possession of the monasteries fell into three well-defined groups according to their contents.

(a) First, there were the muniments; their subsequent history is normally that of the house and the major properties to which they relate—thus, several of the monastic chartularies, for example, are preserved, or were until very recently preserved, in the possession of those families to whose ancestors the properties had passed;

(b) secondly, there were the service books necessary for liturgical purposes; one of several fates might befall these at the Dissolution itself, but they were to be expressly dealt with subsequently by Edward VI in 1550 by the Act against Superstitious Books and Images (3 and 4 Edward VI, c. 10), an Act which was the complement of the 1549 Act of Uniformity (2 and 3 Edward VI, c. 1);

(c) thirdly and lastly, there were the contents of the libraries proper, and it is with the fortunes of these that we are to be primarily concerned, though I shall necessarily have something to say about the service books.

Now let us see if contemporaries themselves have anything to tell us of what happened to the libraries when the monastic life was brought to an end. John Aubrey, the seventeenth-century antiquary (1626–97), has preserved for us a picturesque, and lamentable, story of a day in the sixteenth century when the leaves of illuminated manuscripts from the despoiled abbey of Malmesbury fluttered like butterflies through the streets of the town. Aubrey's authority for this, as for much else that went into his notebooks, was probably his grandfather Isaac Lyte (1577–1660) and the story may contain a kernel of truth. Lyte could have obtained such information from the rector of Malmesbury, who was related to William Stump the rich clothier who purchased the site of the abbey[10] and was one of those selected by the nineteenth-century editors of Spelman's *History of Sacrilege* as a signal example of the misfortunes that befell those who laid hands on monastic spoils.[11]

Whatever truth there may be in Aubrey's tradition it is one that was recorded long after the event and must, therefore, be used with reserve. *Contemporary* evidence, however, does exist which enables us to deduce pretty clearly what must have happened during the period that elapsed between July 1535 when the commissioners began their work and 23 March 1540 when the last house (Waltham) surrendered. This evidence is supplied chiefly by two people: first, John Bale (1495–1563), a Suffolk man of varied gifts but stormy character, a Carmelite converted to Protestantism, bishop of Ossory until Mary's accession, then one of the Marian exiles at Basle, and at the time of his death (in 1563) a prebendary of Canterbury, and, secondly, John Leland (?1506–52), whose journeys throughout England in 1534 and the immediately following years were of immense importance to posterity. Roughly speaking the critical years for the history of the dispersal of the volumes from the monastic libraries may be said to have been 1530 to 1565 or thereabouts and the evidence we possess does in fact coincide for the most part with those thirty-five years. Briefly the most significant documents are: (1) a letter from Leland to Cromwell, 16 July 1536; (2) Leland's New Year's Gift presented to Henry VIII in 1546 and printed by Bale in 1549 at the beginning of his edition of Leland's works entitled *The laboryouse Journey 7 serche of Johan Leylande for Englandes Antiquitees . . . with declaracyons enlarged: by J. Bale* (*S.T.C.* 15445); (3) Bale's own preface to Leland's New Year's Gift inserted in the 1549 edition referred to above; (4) a long and most interesting letter from Bale to Matthew Parker, written on 30 July 1560 in answer to a questionnaire from the latter; (5) a letter from Parker himself to Sir William Cecil, 24 January 1565/6; and (6), finally, a Privy Council letter of 7 July 1568, which was almost certainly drafted by Parker himself.

The first of these, Leland's letter of 1536 to Cromwell, opens on a practical note; it was without doubt inspired by the experience gained on his journeys throughout England undertaken as a result of that royal commission which Leland alleged that he had received in the twenty-fifth year of Henry VIII's reign (1533/4). In this letter Leland begs Cromwell's assistance in pursuing his researches and in getting the books that were being dispersed brought into the Royal Library; this last point receives some illumination from a document which we shall have occasion to discuss later (the Lincolnshire monasteries list preserved in B.M. Royal MS Appendix 69).

The most vigorous statement on the subject is that made over ten years later—1549—by Bale in the preface which he published with Leland's New Year's Gift of 1546 in *The Laboryouse Journey*; Bale had a gift for happy and striking expression:

Neuer [he writes] had we bene offended for the losse of our lybraryes, beynge so many in nombre and in so desolate places for the more parte, yf the chiefe monumentes and most notable workes of our excellent wryters, had bene reserued. If there had bene in euery shyre of Englande, but one solempne lybrary, to the preseruacyon of these noble workes and preferrement of good lernynges in oure posteryte, it had been yet sumwhat. But to destroye all without consyderacyon, is and wyll be vnto Englande for euer, a moste horryble infamy amonge the graue senyours of other nacyons. A great nombre of them whych purchased those superstycyous mansyons, reserued of those lybrarye bokes, some to serue theyr iakes, some to scoure theyr candelstyckes, and some to rubbe their bootes. Some they solde to the grossers and sopesellers, and some they sent ouersee to the bokebynders, not in small nombre, but at tymes whole shyppes full, to the wonderynge of the foren nacyons. Yea, the vnyuersytees of thys realme, are not all clere in this detestable fact. . . . Yea, what maye bryng our realme to more shame and rebuke, than to haue it noysed abroade, that we are despysers of lernynge?

His raciest language however he put in the reply which he made (30 July 1560) to Matthew Parker, then newly appointed archbishop of Canterbury:

And as concernynge bookes of antiquite, not printed; when I was in Irelande [i.e. February–September 1553] I had great plenty of them, whom I obtayned in tyme of the lamentable spoyle of the lybraryes of Englande, throgh much fryndeshypp, labour and expenses. Some I founde in stacyoners and bokebyndeers store howses, some in grosers, sope sellers, taylers, and other occupyers shoppes, some in shyppes ready to be carryed over the sea into Flaunders to be solde—for in those uncircumspecte and carelesse dayes, there was no quiyckar merchaundyce than lybrary bookes, and all to destructyon of learnynge and knowledge of thynges necessary in thys fall of antichriste to be knowne —but the devill is a knave, they saye—well onle conscyence, with a fervent love to my Contrey moved me to save that myghte be saved.

For this eloquent picture of what happened there is plenty of evidence in our libraries today: the mediaeval service books were of course early and obvious victims and their destruction went on continuously throughout the sixteenth and well into the seventeenth century, their pages being cut up to provide flyleaves or strengthening binding strips for all sorts of books (of examples from as late as the seventeenth century I will just mention two volumes of heraldic material in the Harleian collection in the British Museum (Harl. MSS 5852, 5862), which have as flyleaves pages from service books with the name Richard Kimbe written across them). In order to set the sixteenth-century picture more vividly before you let me quote a passage from Dr Rowse's description of the active industrialisation that contributed so powerfully to the prosperity and strength of sixteenth-century England; in dealing with the iron works in the Weald of Sussex, Surrey and Kent, Dr Rowse writes:[12]

From the moment Sir William Sidney got possession of Robertsbridge Priory he set to work mining for iron and building a forge, with the vicar of Salthurst in charge. It is fortunate that many accounts and forge-books remain, *some of them covered with leaves from the Priory psalters* [my italics]. Miners were brought in from abroad. The forge was set up in the abbey gate-house; the abbot's lodgings served to house the workers; when steel-making was tried out [in 1565 by Sir Henry Sidney] the steel forges were set up in the brewhouse. . . . The forge there was still in use up to the mid-eighteenth century. Now there is little left: not much in the way of remains: abbey and forge, monks and iron-workers are alike gone.

And we may add—library books, too. Is it any wonder that of the Robertsbridge library only three specimens—two certain and one doubtful—remain?[13] And what was true of the south was true of the midlands. William Sheldon of Beoley, receiver of monastic estates for the Crown in Warwickshire, who developed the tapestry works which produced the famous tapestry maps of the English counties, set up his looms in the buildings of Bordesley Abbey (in Worcestershire); [14] from this house only three manuscripts remain. Farther north, in Nottinghamshire, Sir Francis Willoughby was developing his coal mines near Wollaton, and from the muniments of his descendants comes eloquent evidence of the truth of Bale's outburst; eleven leaves from a bible executed in Northumbria about 700 and one of two manuscripts related to the Codex Amiatinus were found in Lord Middleton's muniments at Wollaton used as bindings to estate papers, and were in 1938 acquired by the British Museum (Add. MS 45025),[15] and in 1946 one leaf and a fragment of a second from an eleventh-century chartulary of Worcester Cathedral Priory which had served a similar purpose in the same muniments were also secured by the British Museum (Add. MS 46204).[16] The latter were found in the nineteenth century in a bundle of estate documents (no. 168) at Wollaton Hall and the strips had been used in the binding of an account book bearing the title 'Colpyt Book from the Nativitie of Our Lorde in anno regni Regis Edwardi Sexti secundo' (1548/9). Here is an exact parallel to the Sidneys' utilisation of manuscripts at their Robertsbridge enterprise; and note the date, that of Bale's preface. The complete leaf *may* have been rescued by Francis Willoughby, the seventeenth-century naturalist (1635–72), in whose autograph the notes on the leaf are alleged to be. The journey of these from Worcester to the Willoughby estates at Wollaton it is impossible to trace: it has been suggested with some plausibility that these and the group of leaves now preserved in the second part of Cotton MS Nero E. i (ff. 181–4) formed part of a chartulary which was inserted at the time of its writing in the eleventh century in the manuscript of the great bible said to have been presented to Worcester by King Offa,[17] fragments of which have been identified with the bible leaves to which I have referred above (B.M. Add. MS 45025).

Of course, the removal of individual leaves *may*, exceptionally, have been due to the collecting instinct; satisfactory evidence of this is obviously difficult to obtain, but a story recounted by the nineteenth-century bibliographer, Beriah Botfield, in 1849[18] may point to an example of this kind. He writes as follows:

In arranging the fasciculi of the Exon Domesday [preserved in the library of the Dean and Chapter at Exeter] in their proper order, Mr [Ralph] Barnes [the Chapter Clerk, who catalogued the Exeter manuscripts in 1810–11] had the mortification of observing that at page 233, a single leaf had been extracted, [a fact] which he recorded in 1810. Subsequently to this period Mr Trevelyan called to see the Domesday, and upon the book being opened, produced from his pocket a leaf, which exactly supplied the previous hiatus in the record. This leaf it appeared came into the possession of Mr Trevelyan, by descent from his ancestor, Dean Willoughby, who in the time of Henry the eighth was the Dean of Exeter,[19] and doubtless he it was who abstracted this identical leaf, either from curiosity or a less venial motive.

At any rate, the presence of detached leaves or portions of leaves, in the bindings of manuscripts and early printed books, is painfully frequent and the greater part of the destruction to which such leaves are a witness may certainly be attributed to the period of Henry VIII and his successor, Edward VI. Unfortunately for the history of our early vernacular literature Anglo-Saxon manuscripts suffered very heavily; the important heroic poem of Waldere, for example, is preserved for us today in only fragmentary state in a few leaves that were in all probability (though not certainly) used in a binding and are now in the Royal Library at Copenhagen.[20]

What has been said above confirms Bale's remarks in ample measure. The position was not unknown to or disregarded by those in authority: Matthew Parker in a letter to Cecil, 24 January 1565/6, when returning a manuscript borrowed from Cecil's library says 'in the riches whereof . . . I reioice as moche as thei wer in myn owne. So that thei maye be preserved within the realme, & not sent over seas by couetouse statyoners, or spoyled in the poticarye shoppis.' This form of destruction was therefore clearly apprehended, as likewise was the fact that many manuscripts dispersed were in the hands of 'private persons'. The Privy Council (almost certainly under the guidance of Cecil and Parker) went so far as to issue on 7 July 1568 a letter, in all probability drafted by Parker himself, dealing specifically with a portion at any rate of such manuscripts.[21] In this letter the Council, after emphasising the queen's interest in the preservation of the ancient records which had been preserved in the monasteries and which were now in the 'possession of sundry private persons', notifies the queen's subjects that the archbishop of Canterbury has been appointed to have 'a speciall care' for such records; the Council directs therefore that they should be handed over to his deputies for inspection. And in the letter accompanying the draft of this, dated three days before (4 July 1568), Parker significantly observes: '. . . if this opportunity be not taken in our time, it will not so well be done hereafter.'[22]

This was most certainly true. The sixties were undoubtedly critical years. The names of several of the 'private persons' were well known to Parker; Bale himself in his 1560 letter to the archbishop disclosed those known to him. Let us see who they were: Sir John Cheke (Edward VI's tutor); John Pekins, a canon of Westminster; a 'Wyllyam Carye'[22a]; 'Maistre Peter Osburne' (presumably the keeper of the privy purse to Edward VI, the friend of Cheke, and later executor of Parker himself); 'the wydowe of Johan Ducket' at King's Lynn; the executors of Robert Talbot— a notable man this, an antiquary, and fellow of New College, Oxford, who had died in 1558; Nicholas Brigham, another antiquary, memorable to us today as the author of an epitaph on Chaucer, for whose bones he gave the tomb at Westminster; then there is John Twyne, master of the Grammar School at Canterbury and mayor in 1554 (he did not die until 1581); the executors of Robert Recorde, the mathematician; William Paget, first Baron Paget of Beaudesert (1505–63), a staunch Roman Catholic who had relinquished his offices on Elizabeth's accession; Sir John Mason (1503–66); and, lastly, 'my Lorde of Arundell'—this refers to Henry Fitzalan, earl of Arundel, who died in 1580, and was a notable collector—who owns, adds Bale, Matthew Paris which 'belongyth to the quenes majestyes lybrary, lent by Bartylmew Trihearn such time as he had the kepynge of that lybrarye in kyng Edwardes tyme'.[23]

This is not the only such list; another important one, undated, but probably, I think, belonging to 1565 or thereabouts in its original nucleus, is in the handwriting of John Joscelyn, Archbishop Parker's Latin secretary,[24] and adds a few other names— Iohn Stow, the antiquary; John Nettleton (of Hutton Cranswick in the East Riding of Yorkshire);[25] Nicholas Wotton, dean of Canterbury and of York (?1497–1566); and William Darrell, prebendary of Canterbury.

These are names to be borne in mind when we are studying this problem of the dispersal and subsequent regathering of the contents of the mediaeval libraries. What alas are so often lacking are inscriptions or any notes at all in the manuscripts themselves which would furnish us with the simple and yet essential clue to their wanderings. Such notes of course do occasionally occur; for example, the name of John Nettleton of Yorkshire (referred to in Joscelyn's list cited above) occurs with that of Henry Savile, another Yorkshireman (whose estate was at Banke also in the East Riding), in a shorthand inscription (at ff. 4, 5b) in a fine manuscript of the Orations of St Gregory Nazianzen from the Yorkshire abbey of Byland (now B.M. Royal MS 5 E. xxii). Again, in a manuscript (Mm. 1. 25) in the University Library at Cambridge occurs the following note by Sir Thomas Knyvett: 'This book I found among the books of Fakenham, late Abbot of Westminster. Thomas Kny[vett]. Feb. 1560.'[26] Similarly we find on a roll of the Statutes of Edward I, of thirteenth/fourteenth-century date (now preserved in the library of the dean and chapter of St Paul's), the following note in a late sixteenth-century hand: 'Found in the Abbey of Coxall in Essex at the Time of the dissolution'—that is, the Cistercian house of Coggeshall in Essex.[27] To my mind, however, the most interesting inscription of this type is that which occurs in an eleventh-century copy of Ælfric's Homilies now in the University Library at Cambridge (MS Ii. 4. 6; inscription at folios 1 and 311b); it was written by Francis Russell, second earl of Bedford, a strong Protestant, and is to the effect that the manuscript was found 'cum altero consimile . . . in Domo quondam Cenobio de Tavistocke in devinshire' in 1566 by R. Ferror, a servant of the earl's. The earl in his turn, as a second note (on f. 308b) in the manuscript discloses, handed it over in the Star Chamber to Matthew Parker, archbishop of Canterbury—'Dedit Matthaeo Cantuar. 29° Decembr. An° 1567°: in camera stellata'.[28] Sometimes indeed the probable original home of a manuscript and the channel of its abstraction may be disclosed by sixteenth-century notes written in it. This is a point to be commended to students for particular attention. Here are two instances, which are specially worthy of notice: first, two manuscripts now preserved in the libraries of Hereford Cathedral and Jesus College, Oxford, contain contents lists in the autograph of Sir John Prise (who was one of the visitors of the monastic houses and who died in 1555), both are Cirencester manuscripts, and, as Mr Neil Ker has pointed out, 'So far as is known Price [sic] wrote notes of this kind only in the manuscripts which he obtained from Cirencester.'[29] Such a clue is worth noting. Secondly, autograph marginalia of Robert Talbot, the antiquary, occur in a large number of manuscripts which certainly came from Norwich Cathedral Priory. The connection in this instance would seem to be explained by Talbot's presence at Norwich as a prebendary between 1547 and 1558 the year of his death; it will be remembered that Bale in his letter to Parker, mentioned, among those known to him as possessing manuscripts, the executors of Robert Talbot 'which dyed at Norwyche'.[30]

It is relevant to remind ourselves at this point also of what was said earlier about the abstraction of movables from their monastic homes by the ex-religious. Books were certainly appropriated individually or even in blocks. One or two instances will suffice. A fine small early twelfth-century manuscript of St Augustine's Meditations, now in the possession of the Society of Antiquaries (MS 65), belonged in the Middle Ages to Durham Cathedral Priory—an inscription in it indicates as much and it is also recorded in the Priory's catalogue; on folio 4, however, occurs the name John Tutyng accompanied by the date 1541. There is no doubt about Tutyng's identity; he was one of the last monks and the first canons of Durham and in 1556 was presented by the dean and chapter to the rectory of Brantingham in the East Riding, a place some ten miles west of Hull.[31] Presumably the book went with him, and in the north it remained, for it was in the possession of the Darlington antiquary, George Allan, in the eighteenth century and was presented by him to the Society of Antiquaries in 1798.[32] Again, there is a strong probability that when St Mary's Abbey at Kells, in Kilkenny, was surrendered by its abbot, Richard Plunket, on 18 November 1539, the famous Book of Kells (now preserved in the Library of Trinity College, Dublin) remained in his hands, it being noteworthy that an inscription in the manuscript (f. 334b) bearing the date 1568 was written by 'Geralde Plunket' of Dublin.[33] Furthermore, Prior Hart of Lanthony Secunda, a house on the outskirts of Gloucester, appears to have had certainly a great part of the library of that priory in his manor house at Brockworth, four miles south-east of Gloucester, which had been granted to him by the king with firewood out of 'Bukwolde' and a pension of one hundred pounds per annum.[34] Hart left most of his property to his brother-in-law, Thomas Thayer, of the same place. His books and thus this portion of the Lanthony library had however quite a different descent; by his will Hart left to Thomas Morgan, 'the heire of Hurst, *all my books of Latyn* [my italics] and my bowe and arrowes', and Dr M. R. James has demonstrated that most of the Lanthony manuscripts now extant are in the library at Lambeth, whither they were brought in Archbishop Bancroft's time (1604–10).[35]

But the most remarkable instance of such removal is supplied by the history of the library of the Cluniac Priory of Monk Bretton in the West Riding. The catalogue of the library of this house was compiled on 21 July 1558, that is, nearly twenty years after the dissolution of the house (which had surrendered on 21 November 1539); it was written up on blank leaves at the beginning of its chartulary.[36] This extraordinary document shows that the books at that date were preserved at Worsborough, a village a few miles from the priory, in the house of William Brown, the last prior.[37] The catalogue falls into six sections. The heading of the first tells us that the books listed were in the house of William Brown, formerly prior of Monk Bretton and had been purchased at his expense, presumably while still prior; the books in the second section are shown by the heading to have been in the room of Thomas Wilkinson and Richard Hinchclyff at Worsborough at the same date and, it is added, were the gift of and at the expense of Thomas Frobyscer, a former sub-prior ('in camera Thomae Wilkinson et Ricardi Hinchclyff apud Worsburgh . . . et fuerunt ex dono et sumptibus Thomae Frobyscer, quondam subprioris monasterii supradicti'). The third section records those books in the room referred to that belonged apparently only to Thomas Wilkinson, now also called 'alias Bolton' ('libri sequentes sunt

Thomae Wilkinson, alias Bolton, et in eadem camera apud Worsburgh remanentes die et anno et supra'). Then follow three sections (iv, v, vi of the series) of books all of which belonged to Richard Hinchclyff, now also called 'alias Woollay'; the first (that is, section iv) is headed 'the books which are described on the following page were those of Richard Hinchclyff, alias Woollay, acquired at his own expense and by his own hand'; the heading merely adds that they are at Worsborough in his own room and repeats the date we have already given.[38] The second (section v) lists his 'libri . . . de Physicis' and the third (vi) his 'Libri grammaticales'. The number of volumes under each of the six headings is as follows: thirty-one (under i), one item being in eleven volumes; twenty-eight (under ii); fifteen (under iii); fifty-two (under iv); ten (under v), and six (under vi). This catalogue yields a total of 142 books. This is a most interesting picture of the way in which the library of their old home had been withdrawn and distributed amongst a small group of the ex-religious who had settled down at one of the priory's manor houses in its neighbourhood; they were the prior (William Brown), and two of the monks (Thomas Wilkinson alias Bolton and Richard Hinchclyff alias Woollay); both the latter appear under their aliases as monks in receipt of pensions and were two of the thirteen in the house at the time of its surrender—the aliases are interesting of course as indicating in all probability their native place.[39] What happened here we may with confidence suppose to have happened elsewhere, but the telltale evidence has not survived; even so only two manuscripts may with certainty today be ascribed to Monk Bretton.[40]

To judge from the evidence which we have accumulated, it is doubtful if any such concerted and organised effort as that for which Leland had appealed to Cromwell in the summer of 1536 had been carried very far; that a modified programme was envisaged by the king's advisers and perhaps even by the king himself and did in fact bear some fruit is proved by, first, a very important document preserved among the manuscripts in the Royal Library (now B.M. Royal MS Appendix 69) and, secondly, by the large numbers of monastic books already in the Royal Library by the time of the 1542 inventory.

The first document is a list, in a contemporary hand, of manuscripts of history and theology seen by Leland in Lincolnshire houses, presumably on one of the journeys made by him about *Plate* 12 1534; thirty-five houses are noted but not all were visited. There is at least one annotation in the king's own hand and the rough crosses inserted against a number of the items may also have been made by Henry with the object of indicating those manuscripts that were to be appropriated for the Royal Library. The list is of a kind similar to others preserved in Leland's manuscript collections (which were published by Thomas Hearne at Oxford in six volumes in 1715); the way in which this list was used suggests strongly that Leland's other lists of books were compiled not merely as personal records of his own antiquarian curiosity but with the very definite purpose of enabling his master to secure suitable manuscripts for the Royal Library.[41] An analysis of it is extraordinarily revealing. Let us take a few examples. At Lincoln Cathedral eleven manuscripts were noted and six of them are starred; of these six, no less than four are in the Royal Library now (Royal 8 G. iii, 11 B. i, 11 D. vii, and 13 E. i) and, of these four, two are certainly identifiable in the Westminster Palace inventory of 1542. At the Premonstratensian house of Barlings three manuscripts were noted; one bears a star and this is now Royal 3 B. xv and also appears in the 1542 list—it has the added interest that at the top of its first leaf is scribbled in an unidentified early sixteenth-century hand, 'Barlinges'. Of the books noted at another Premonstratensian house, Tupholm, only one is starred and this is now Royal 4 A. iv and is likewise recorded in the 1542 inventory. Other places that yield similar results are Hagneby, Markby, the Dominican friary at Boston, Kirkstead and Revesby. Tattershall College is particularly interesting; there the titles of nine books were recorded and of these, six were starred, of which five are now in the Royal Collection and the sixth in the Bodleian, but this sixth volume did not get to the Bodleian until 1604 (by the gift of Charles Howard, earl of Nottingham) and it too had in fact belonged to Henry VIII—in other words it had got out of the Royal Library at some time in the sixteenth century; that is, all the six starred manuscripts went to the king. Two houses could not be visited because of the plague, the library of another (the

Minorites at Boston) could not be examined because of the absence of the prior, and against others it is merely noted that there are many books. But I think that the evidence quoted makes it quite impossible to avoid the conclusion that this Lincolnshire list was scrutinised for the specific purpose of earmarking items for the Royal Library, and further that in fact instructions must subsequently have been issued for such books to be sent to the king.

The Royal Library was indeed one of the few repositories in existence at the time of the Dissolution into which the scattered spoils of the monastic libraries could have been gathered. Its foundation is probably to be attributed to Edward IV, who may in this have been inspired by the example of his brother-in-law, Charles the Bold, duke of Burgundy. At any rate the king's stay at Bruges in 1470 and 1471 must have been of signal importance, for it is with the Bruges and Ghent illuminators that the Edward IV books now in the Royal Collection at the British Museum are associated. It is worth observing, too, that the Flemish association so established was preserved later, since both of the first recorded royal librarians were Flemings, namely, Quintin Poulet, who was appointed in 1492, and Giles Duwes (Du Wes or Du Gues: in Latin Egidius de Vadis), who is described in the first year of Henry VIII (1509/10) as keeper of the King's Library 'at Richemounte', that is, the palace built by Henry VII after the destruction of the old royal residence at Sheen in 1497. The earliest inventories that survive, however, both date from the later years of Henry VIII's reign. The earlier is the Richmond list of February 1534/5;[42] it contains 143 items. The second, the first Westminster inventory, bears the date 27 May 1542; and significantly enough it is preserved in an Augmentation Office Book, where it forms part of a long account of household stuff drawn up by Sir Anthony Denny, keeper of the King's Palace at Westminster since 1536. In this 1542 inventory 250 items at least out of its 910 are manuscripts; shortly afterwards the overall total had risen to 1,450. This sudden increase can only be explained by the incorporation of spoils from the monastic libraries; the additions included no less than one hundred books from Rochester and about thirty from St Albans, and yet the numbers from several houses are curiously small—

eight came from Merton Priory, six from Worcester, five from Gloucester, and five from Sempringham—and so on. Even the contribution from Rochester is not large when we reflect that it probably possessed some six hundred books at the Dissolution. Indeed the example of Rochester serves to remind us of the enormous losses that have been sustained, for of the Rochester books that survive today this block of one hundred in the Royal Collection represents by far the greater number; outside this, as a matter of fact, only thirty can now be traced.

This emphasises very forcibly what Dr M. R. James said in his study of the library of the Austin Friars at York:

The fact that an establishment so obscure as this of the Austin Friars at York should have owned a library of 646 volumes a century or more before its dissolution on 28 November 1538 gives scope for serious and indeed depressing reflection. Depressing, because after a lengthy search among catalogues and libraries I cannot find that more than four of the whole number have survived. . . . It is hardly open to doubt that nine-tenths of the books have ceased to exist.[43]

There can be no possibility of dispute that the losses were very great. With the surrender of Waltham, the last house, in 1540 the number of monasteries dissolved amounted to over eight hundred; almost all of these must have had libraries of some kind, the larger houses indeed very considerable ones. The cathedral priories (Canterbury, Durham, Ely and Norwich, Rochester, Winchester, Worcester, and Carlisle) and the secular minsters, such as York and Lincoln, had a continuing life though on an altered constitutional basis, and yet this did not save their libraries. As we have seen, Rochester's has suffered heavily; the Norwich books have been largely scattered; and those in the great library of Christ Church at Canterbury almost entirely so. Only Durham, Worcester, Salisbury, Hereford, and Exeter have retained any considerable portion of their mediaeval libraries *in situ*.

But the dissolution of the monasteries is not the end of the story of the dispersal of the books in the mediaeval libraries. Henry VIII's settlement of the church involved their scattering and destruction only, in a certain sense, incidentally. A more serious enemy to their survival was the alignment of the king with the New Learning and his reform of the universities, which was effected by the issue of royal injunctions in the same year (1535) that the commissioners began their visitation of the monasteries. What happened at Oxford is revealing. The visitors there were Dr London and Dr Richard Layton: here is what the latter had to say in the report which he sent back to the vicar-general, Cromwell:

We have set Duns [Scotus] in Bocardo [that is, the old gatehouse which was used as a prison], and have utterly banished him Oxford for ever with all his blind glosses. . . . The second time we came to New College, after we had declared your injunctions we found all the great Quadrant Court full of the leaves of Duns, the wind blowing them into every corner. And there we found one Mr Greenfield, a gentleman of Buckinghamshire, gathering up part of the same book leaves, as he said, to make him sewells [i.e. shewels = scarecrows] or blawnshers [i.e. blanchers = obstructions] to keep the deer within his wood, thereby to have the better cry with his hounds.[44]

This was the end of the Middle Ages and of the old scholastic teaching in the universities. The reform had, of course, its credit side; it included, for example, the establishment of the Regius professorships in Divinity, Hebrew, Greek, Medicine, and Civil Law, but the scene recorded by Layton adds point to Bale's hit at the end of that 1549 Preface which recorded the destruction of the library books by the 'sopesellers' and others: 'Yea, the unyuersytees of thys realme, are not all clere in this detestable fact.'

In the reign of Henry's successor, however, the destruction of the heritage of the Middle Ages became with the quickening of the reforming tempo a more sharply defined act of policy, especially after Somerset's fall in October 1549 and in the days of the unscrupulous Northumberland. The First Act of Uniformity (2 and 3 Edward VI, c. 1) was passed in 1549; it was followed in 1550 by the Act against Superstitious Books and Images (3 and 4 Edward VI, c. 10). This was admittedly expedient if the terms of the Act of Uniformity were to be fulfilled; by ordering the destruction of the old service books the 1550 Act removed all rivals to the new Book of Common Prayer. Its operative clause as regards the books was in these terms:

Be it therefore enacted . . . that all books called antiphoners, missals, grails, processionals, manuals, legends, pies, portuises, primers in Latin

M

or English, couchers, journals, ordinals, or other books or writings whatsoever heretofore used for the service of the Church, written or printed in the English or Latin tongue, other than such as are or shall be set forth by the King's Majesty, shall be by authority of this present Act clearly and utterly abolished, extinguished, and forbidden for ever to be used or kept in this realm or elsewhere within any of the King's dominions.[45]

Furthermore, the books were to be delivered up to certain officials of the town where they were and had to be surrendered *openly* by these officials within three months to the archbishop, bishop, chancellor, or commissary of the diocese, to be immediately 'openly burnt or otherways defaced and destroyed'.

This Act gave to the zealots the legal sanction they required. What a destruction of mediaeval art, a sort of second Savonarola holocaust, was here envisaged! For of the kinds of books specified several were just those that carried in the Middle Ages the richest illumination: the antiphoners, missals, graduals, the 'portuises' (that is, the portable breviaries) and the 'couchers' (that is, the large breviaries which were kept on desk or table). Let us reflect for a moment on what the provisions of this Act meant by thinking in terms of some of the more notable manuscripts that survive today: the Lytlington Missal (1383/84) at Westminster Abbey, the Sherborne Missal at Alnwick, and the Chichele Breviary at Lambeth; and the great gospel books and the psalters, which, though not specified by title, fall well within the category of 'other books or writings whatsoever heretofore used for the service of the Church'—the Lindisfarne Gospels from Durham; the 'Golden Gospels' from Christ Church, Canterbury, now in the Royal Library at Stockholm; the Peterborough Psalter executed for Robert de Lindeseye and now a treasured possession of the Society of Antiquaries; and the Lovel Lectionary, prepared by Siferwas for John, Lord Lovel, for presentation to Salisbury Cathedral and now in fragmentary form preserved among the Harley manuscripts (7026) in the British Museum. There is no need to specify more examples.

And yet extreme measures of this kind are not easily enforced with complete success; the bigotry of the reformers hardened the opposition of those devoted to the old faith. The very fact that the masterpieces referred to do survive shows that there were many people who were ready to save and conceal such works, notwithstanding the penalties. The shortness of Edward VI's reign of course may have helped. Some manuscripts also were undoubtedly smuggled abroad; the 'Golden Gospels' from Canterbury, now at Stockholm, to which I have referred may possibly have been one of these; it is at any rate worth observing that the manuscript was bought *in Madrid* by the great Swedish collector, Count Sparwenfeldt, in 1690. Did it go to Spain in the sixteenth century in the hands of Catholic refugees? The first part of the late eleventh century Gundulf Bible (now MS 62 in the Huntington Library at San Marino, California) was a Rochester manuscript which disappeared from sight at the Dissolution; it went apparently to Holland, ending up finally in the collection of Van de Wal, burgomaster of Amsterdam, and was sold with his library in 1734; the authors of the *Histoire littéraire de la France*[46] describe it in 1750 as 'entièrement perdu de vue' but it turned up in England early last century in the collection of Sir Thomas Phillipps at Middlehill.[47] Attempts to send fine manuscripts overseas are interestingly confirmed, of course, by the well-known failure of one such attempt (which, however, occurred not in Edward VI's reign but in that of Queen Mary); one of the finest fourteenth-century psalters of English provenance now preserved (B.M. Royal MS 2 B. vii) owes its very title of 'Queen Mary's Psalter' to the fact that when on the point of being conveyed abroad it was stopped by a London customs officer, Baldwin Smith, and presented to the queen in October 1553.

The descent of the Luttrell Psalter on the other hand illustrates the channel through which many such manuscripts were to be saved for this country. This psalter was executed shortly before 1340 for Sir Geoffrey Luttrell of Irnham in Lincolnshire. An inscription of 1703 in the manuscript itself records that in that year it was given to Sir Nicholas Shireburn of Stonyhurst by Mary Charlton, the wife of Sir Edward Charlton of Hesley Side in Northumberland and by birth a Widdrington, while on folio 1 occurs the signature of Lord William Howard of Naworth (1563–1640).[48] Now, all of these were members of staunch Catholic families and it is undoubtedly to the zeal of such families in the sixteenth century that we owe the preservation of several master-pieces of mediaeval illumination.

Nevertheless, the provisions of Edward VI's Act were en-forced, and how they were put into operation with regard to one library at any rate we do know. An order in council, passed 25 February 1550/1 and recorded in the Acts of the Privy Council runs as follows:

The Kinges Majesties lettre—for the purging of his Highnes Librarie at Westminster of all superstitiouse bookes, as masse bookes, legendes, and suche like, and to deliver the garnyture of the same bookes, being either of golde or silver, to Sir Anthony Aucher in the presence of Sir Thomas Darcie, etc.[49]

It is not surprising then that hardly any of the books in the Royal Collection now retain their original bindings or that the elaborate ornamental metal work and jewelled binding of the Lindisfarne Gospels has long since disappeared. We may feel quite confident that not only the 'garniture' of many manuscripts disappeared.

To Henry VIII's 1535 visitors and Edward VI's commissioners may be chiefly attributed the large gaps in the contents of the non-monastic libraries that survived from the mediaeval period. These libraries were, it is true, few in number but not necessarily unim-portant—Duke Humphrey's Library at Oxford, the University Library at Cambridge, the libraries of the Oxford and Cambridge colleges of mediaeval foundation, and that at Eton College.

For an illustration, let us look at what happened to Duke Humphrey's Library. The number of volumes given to the uni-versity of Oxford by Humphrey, duke of Gloucester, in several batches between about 1411 and 1444 seems to have amounted in all to approximately 300; this was a quite unusually large number —Henry VI's gift of books to All Souls College amounted to no more than twenty-three volumes.[50] The university made special arrangements to preserve the duke's gifts. There appears to have been from 1412 a librarian who looked after the books in the room over the porch of St Mary's, and with the completion of the new divinity school about 1487 the library was housed there.[51] Yet within eighty years, as Anthony Wood records, the library had been so rifled as to be almost non-existent. In 1550 Edward VI's commissioners went to Oxford and as a result of their activities there the University Library seems to have been almost completely pillaged. The picture drawn by Wood is claimed by him to be based on facts 'credibly reported from ancient men and they while young from scholars of great standing',[52] and there is at any rate some confirmatory evidence for his story; first, of Duke Humphrey's books only two that may be certainly identified as having been his now remain in the Bodleian,[53] and secondly, and most significantly, we find in Queen Mary's reign that a decree passed Convocation on 25 January 1555/6 appointing certain members ('venerabiles viri') of the Senate to sell in the name of the university the book-desks in the public library—'ad vendenda subsellia librorum in publica Academiae bibliotheca, ipsius Universitatis nomine'. As Macray, the historian of the Bodleian, comments with reference to this decree: 'The books of the "public" library had all disappeared; what need then to retain the shelves and stalls, when no one thought of replacing their contents, and when the University could turn an honest penny by their sale? and so the *venerabiles viri* made a timber yard of Duke Humphrey's treasure-house.'[54] So the library-room remained destitute until Sir Thomas Bodley wrote his famous letter to the vice-chancellor on 23 February 1597/8, offering to take the charge and cost upon himself of reducing it again to its former use. What happened to the public library happened also in all probability to the college libraries; Wood claimed that a cartload of manuscripts was taken from Merton and destroyed and that large numbers also were removed from Balliol and from New College.

The same story appears to be true of Cambridge. Trinity Hall, for instance, has suffered the loss of nearly the whole of its ancient library and Dr James notes that of the books bequeathed to it by its founder, Bishop Bateman (d. 1355), two at most survive.[55] Also of the 175 manuscripts recorded in the 1452 inventory of the library of King's College only one (MS 27) now survives, and this again certainly suggests some deliberate removal and not mere wastage, since already by 1600 only seven were recorded by Thomas James, in his *Ecloga Oxonio-Cantabrigiensis*.[56] Of the University Library at Cambridge, Henry Bradshaw, its famous nineteenth-century head, who made a very thorough investigation into its history, says: 'In 1547, the commencement of Edward VI's reign, a clean sweep was made of the old common library, and for the next forty years it was used as a second Divinity school, now wanted for the Regius Professor. The hatred of the old learning seems to have been for a time so intense, that few things having the semblance of antiquity about them were spared.'[57]

In the years immediately following the accession of Elizabeth in 1558, however, we detect a change; the process of dispersal and destruction is arrested. Men begin to be not only aware of the need to preserve but become very soon even intensely interested in bringing together again the material that had been scattered, and not by any means for sentimental reasons.[58] The lead was taken by those in authority, who now realised the great importance of much of this material for the purpose of propaganda for the government's policy in church and state alike. Parker early discerned the purposes to which the writings of Ælfric and the early church historians could be put for the more secure establishing of the Ecclesia Anglicana over which he had been appointed by Elizabeth to rule, and Cecil was equally anxious to secure historical material which should feed the rising tide of nationalism and supply the groundwork of the closely-reasoned state papers which were expedient to strengthen Elizabeth's position against hostile controversialists here and abroad. Both men used the opportunities which their office gave them to further the discovery and acquisition of the scattered manuscripts, as we have indeed seen from the Privy Council letter of 7 July 1568 which was inspired by them. Parker's great collection of manuscripts went at his death to Corpus Christi College, Cambridge, except for a group of twenty manuscripts and seventy-five printed books which were given by him to the university in 1574 (24 May), a year made memorable in the history of that library by this and two other gifts—one of twenty volumes by James Pilkington, bishop of Durham, on 16 May, and another of seventy-three volumes by Sir Nicholas Bacon on 22 September. Cecil's large collection remained more or less intact until its sale in 1687, when it was unfortunately dispersed.[59] But many others were active, the more notable being Henry Fitzalan, earl of Arundel, who seems to have secured the greater part of the collection of manuscripts which

Archbishop Cranmer had rescued; in the north, Lord William Howard of Naworth and Henry Savile of Banke; elsewhere, Sir Robert Cotton and Sir Thomas Bodley; and such less highly placed individuals as John Dee, the astrologer, and Cecil's friend, Laurence Nowell, who owned the famous manuscript of *Beowulf.* As a result of the activities of these and others we may say that some considerable portion of the libraries scattered at the Dissolution had by 1600 been reassembled in the collections in which they have remained 'frozen' to this day: Parker's at Corpus Christi College, Cambridge, Fitzalan's in the Royal Collection now in the British Museum, Cotton's in the same institution, and Bodley's at Oxford. To these great collectors and to the hundreds of lesser men all over the country who were rescuing the *membra disjecta* of the mediaeval libraries we today owe an immense debt of gratitude.

NOTES TO CHAPTER VIII

1. 'Hi sæden openlice ðæt Xrist slep. 7 his halechen', E. text (Bodl. MS Laud Misc. 636, f. 89b) of the Anglo-Saxon Chronicle, s.a. 1137 (*Two Saxon Chronicles Parallel*, ed. C. Plummer, i, Oxford, 1892, p. 265).

2. E. Powell, *The Rising in East Anglia in* 1381, Cambridge, 1896, p. 53; C. H. Cooper, *Annals of Cambridge*, i, Cambridge, 1842, pp. 124–5; and also *The Anonimalle Chronicle*, 1333–1381, ed. V. H. Galbraith, Manchester, 1927, p. 150.

3. John Stow, *Annals*, 1600 edn. (*S.T.C.* 23335), p. 353; for a reference to the passage see also F. S. Merryweather, *Bibliomania in the Middle Ages*, London, revised edn. 1933, p. 228, footnote.

4. See H. Denifle, *La désolation des églises, monastères et hôpitaux en France pendant la Guerre de cent ans*, Paris, 1897–9.

5. For the list of manuscripts so transferred see *Catalogi Veteres Librorum Ecclesiae Cathedralis Dunelmensis* (ed. J. Raine, Surtees Society, i, 1838), pp. 39–41; and H. D. Hughes, *A History of Durham Cathedral Library*, Durham, 1925, p. 58. The Durham College lists have also been printed by H. E. D. Blakiston, in Oxford Hist. Soc.'s *Collectanea*, iii, 1896, pp. 1–76.

6. On this subject and the evidence from contemporary sources dealt with below see also the present writer's paper, 'The Dispersal of the Monastic Libraries and the Beginnings of Anglo-Saxon Studies. Matthew Parker and his Circle: A Preliminary Study', *Trans. Camb. Bibl. Soc.*, i (1949–53), pp. 208–37.

7. For the documents referred to above see J. R. Tanner, *Tudor Constitutional Documents A.D. 1485–1603 with an Historical Commentary*, Cambridge, 1940.

8. For a concise statement of the position see G. Baskerville, 'The Dispossessed Religious after the Suppression of the Monasteries', *Essays in History presented to R. Lane Poole*, Oxford, 1927, pp. 436–65, and for a fuller study the same author's *English Monks and the Suppression of the Monasteries*, London, 1937.

9. For details see *History of Northumberland*, ii, Newcastle-upon-Tyne, 1895, p. 436.

10. On Isaac Lyte and the story of the manuscripts destroyed see Anthony Powell, *John Aubrey and his Friends*, London, 1948, pp. 34–7, especially 37. The story has also been referred to recently by Prof. Stuart Piggott, 'Archaeology in Wessex, Part I', *The Archaeological News Letter*, vol. 4, no. 3 (October 1951), p. 34, and by June Wilson, 'John Aubrey's Country', *Country Life*, 23 May 1957, pp. 1044, 1045.

11. 'The descendants of this wealthy merchant now exist *as labourers* in or near Malmesbury' (1895 edn. of Spelman's *History of Sacrilege*, Appendix I).

12. A. L. Rowse, *The England of Elizabeth*, London, 1950, pp. 135, 136.

13. The two certain volumes are a formularium (of 14th–15th-century date) in the possession of the marquess of Bath at Longleat and a St Augustine (of 13th-century date) in the Bodleian Library, Oxford (Bodl. MS 132). The doubtful manuscript is St John's College, Cambridge, MS 113. See N. R. Ker, *Medieval Libraries of Great Britain*, London, 1941, p. 89.

14. On the Sheldon family see E. A. B. Barnard, *The Sheldons*, Cambridge, 1936.

15. See *Brit. Mus. Quart.*, xii (1937–8), pp. 39, 40.

16. The complete leaf came from a portion of the same chartulary now preserved in B.M. Cotton MS Nero E. i, part 2, ff. 181–4, its original position being between ff. 182 and 183 (the strips come from an earlier portion of the chartulary).

17. See *Hemingi Chartularium Ecclesie Wigorniensis*, ed. T. Hearne, i, Oxford, 1723, pp. 95, 319, and also *Catalogus Librorum Manuscriptorum Bibliothecae Wigorniensis*, ed. I. Atkins and N. R. Ker, Cambridge, 1944, pp. 77–9.

18. *Notes on the Cathedral Libraries of England*, London, 1849, p. 139.

19. This is Edward Willoughby, who was dean about 1500 and died in 1508.

20. For an account of these leaves see F. Norman's edn. of *Waldere*, London, 1933, pp. 1–5. Other examples worth recording here are: the Sigmaringen leaves of Ælfric's Anglo-Saxon/Latin Grammar (fragments which were collated by Zupitza for his edition, *Ælfrices Grammatik und Glossar*, 1880, pp. 201–3); fragments of Ælfric's homilies show that MSS of these were frequent victims—two fragments from these (and the grammar) removed at some time in the 17th century from either a MS or printed book are preserved in a volume of John Bagford's collections in B.M. Harley MS 5915; a leaf of a fine 11th-century MS of these homilies is bound in at the beginning of the Register of Castle Acre Priory (now B.M. Harley MS 2110) (see C. E. Wright, in *Medium Ævum*, vii (1938), pp. 50–5), and small pieces with scraps of the homilies on them used as binding strips in MS 133 D. 22 in the Royal Library at The Hague were identified in 1938 by Mr Neil Ker; a leaf from an 11th-century MS of the Anglo-Saxon version of the Rule of Chrodegang that belonged in the 18th century to Thomas Astle, the antiquary, is preserved now in B.M. Add. MS 34652, f. 3 (on this leaf see A. S. Napier, 'The Rule of Chrodegang in Old English', *Modern Language Notes*, xviii (1903), p. 241, and *Enlarged Rule of Chrodegang*, etc. (E.E.T.S., O.S. 150, 1916, p. x), and in the same composite B.M. MS is also preserved (f. 2) an 11th-century leaf containing a portion of the Anglo-Saxon Chronicle which came from the library of Thomas Tanner (bishop of St Asaph, 1732–5), an active promoter of Anglo-Saxon studies especially during his sojourn at Oxford late in the 17th century—this leaf actually belongs to two MSS in the Cotton collection, Otho B. xi and Otho B. x (see N. R. Ker, 'Membra Disjecta, 2nd Series', *Brit. Mus. Quart.*, xiv (1939–40), pp. 81, 82).

21. Contemporary printed copy in Corpus Christi College, Cambridge, MS 114, p. 49; printed in normalised form in *Correspondence of Matthew Parker*, ed. J. Bruce and T. T. Perowne (Parker Soc., 1853), pp. 327–8.

22. ibid., p. 328.

22a. John Dee bought a MS from the widow of a Mr Carye in 1573 (B.M. Harley MS 3: inscr. f. 3, 'Joannes Dee emit aº 1573. Augusti 3. a vidua Mri Carye').

23. This is Bartholomew Traheron, an ex-Franciscan, appointed librarian to Edward VI in 1549 (see *Catalogue of Western MSS. in the Old Royal and King's Collections*, ed. G. F. Warner and J. P. Gilson, i, London, 1921, p. xvi). This manuscript is now once again with the Royal MSS (B.M. Royal MSS 14 C. vi and vii).

24. Now preserved in B.M. Cotton MS Nero C. iii, ff. 208–212b. On the lists of Bale and Joscelyn see for further details present writer in *Trans. Camb. Bibl. Soc.*, i (1949–53), pp. 213–16, 218.

25. His name occurs among the list of owners in a Book of Hours of East Anglian execution, c. 1490, in the possession of Messrs Maggs Bros. in 1949 (Cat. 786, item 1750).

26. This was John (Howman) de Feckenham, abbot of Westminster Abbey as refounded by Queen Mary, from 1556–9. I owe this reference to my colleague, Dr Schofield. On Sir Thomas Knyvett as collector see *The Knyvett Letters*, ed. B. Schofield, London, 1949, p. 17. In a Westminster Abbey inventory of c. 1541 the library is not mentioned (see *The Manuscripts of Westminster Abbey*, by J. Armitage Robinson and M. R. James, Cambridge, 1909, p. 12). A 13th-century bible with the signature of Edward Howman, a kinsman of John de Feckenham, was lot 91a in Sotheby's sale, 3 April 1957.

27. I owe this reference to Mr Neil Ker.

28. The other manuscript may be B.M. Cotton MS Vitellius C. v (on which see Wanley's Catalogue of Anglo-Saxon Manuscripts in Hickes' *Thesaurus*, ii, 1705, p. 208).

29. In a private communication. The MSS in question are: Hereford Cathedral MS O. ii. 4, a late 12th-century MS of Porretanus, and Jesus College, Oxford, MS 26, a 12th-century MS of the Panormia of Ivo of Chartres. Sir John Prise is now the subject of a detailed study by N. R. Ker in *The Library*, 5th Ser., x (1955), pp. 1–24.

30. The history of the Norwich Cathedral manuscripts has been most recently discussed by N. R. Ker, 'Mediaeval Manuscripts from Norwich Cathedral Priory', *Trans. Camb. Bibl. Soc.*, i (1949–53), pp. 1–27.

31. See S. L. Greenslade, 'The Last Monks of Durham Cathedral Priory', *Durham Univ. Journ.*, N.S., x (1949), pp. 107–13. (Tutyng is no. 44 in Greenslade's list.)

32. On this MS see R. A. B. Mynors, *Durham Cathedral Manuscripts*, Oxford, 1939, no. 65.

33. See *The Book of Kells*, iii, Berne, 1951, p. 16.

34. *Letters and Papers Hen. VIII*, xiv, pt. 1, p. 596.

35. *The Manuscripts in the Library at Lambeth Palace* (Camb. Antiq. Soc., Octavo Publications, no xxxiii, 1900), pp. 1–6, and index of owners under Morgan of Carmarthen, and *A Descriptive Catalogue of the MSS. in the Library of Lambeth Palace: The Mediaeval MSS.*, ed. M. R. James, Cambridge, 1930–2, index under 'Morgan, Canonicus de Kermerd'.

36. Known from its place of custody in modern times (Woolley Hall, near

Wakefield) as the Woolley chartulary; it is now on permanent loan to the York-shire Archaeological Society at Leeds.

37. Printed by Joseph Hunter, *English Monastic Libraries*, 1831, pp. 1–7; most recently with translation in *Abstracts of the Chartularies of the Priory of Monkbretton* (ed. J. W. Walker, Yorks. Arch. Soc., Record Ser., lxvi, 1924), pp. 5–9. See also J. Hunter, *South Yorkshire*, ii, London, 1831, pp. 274–6.

38. 'Libri qui in pagina sequenti sunt depicti fuere Richardi Hinchclyff, alias Woollay, sumptibus ejus et manu adquisiti: sunt modo apud Worsburg in camera predicta sua, anno a Christo nato M.D.LVIII° die vero xxi° Julii.'

39. On this house see Dugdale, *Monasticon Anglicanum* (ed. J. Cayley, H. Ellis, B. Bandinel), v, London, 1825, 131–41.

40. See N. R. Ker, *Medieval Libraries of Great Britain*, p. 73.

41. The document was printed with identifications of many items by J. R. Liddell, 'Leland's Lists of MSS. in Lincolnshire Monasteries', *Eng. Hist. Rev.*, liv (1939), pp. 88–95.

42. Now preserved among the papers of Philibert de La Marc and Febret de Fontelle in the Moreau Collection (MS 849) in the Bibliothèque Nationale in Paris; printed H. Omont, *Etudes romanes dediées à Gaston Paris*, Paris, 1891, pp. 1–14.

43. M. R. James, 'The Catalogue of the Library of the Augustinian Friars at York', *Fasciculus I. W. Clark Dicatus*, Cambridge, 1909, p. 16.

44. Quoted by Cecil Headlam, *The Story of Oxford*, London, 1907, pp. 310, 311.

45. See Tanner, op. cit., p. 114.

46. ix, p. 374.

47. The Bible was no. 48 in the 1202 Rochester Catalogue and was noted by W. B. Rye, in *Memorial of the Priory of St. Andrew*, 1861, pp. 2 and 48; it is also recorded in the mid-12th-century catalogue printed in *Arch. Cant.*, vi (1866), p. 124.

48. See *The Luttrell Psalter*, ed. E. G. Millar, London, 1932, pp. 6, 7, 57.

49. Printed in *Acts of the Privy Council*, N.S., vol. iii, 1550–1552 (1891), p. 224.

50. See B.M. Add. MS 4608, ff. 100, 100b.

51. For Duke Humphrey's books see chapter vi above, and also K. H. Vickers, *Humphrey, Duke of Gloucester*, 1907, pp. 426–38. For an analysis of his library and its reflection of his tastes see especially op. cit., chapter x. The best concise account of Duke Humphrey is G. E. C[okayne], *Complete Peerage*, v, 1926, pp. 730–7.

52. Anthony Wood, *History and Antiquities of the University of Oxford*, ed. J. Gutch, ii, 1796, p. 106.

53. Namely, Hatton 36 and Auct. F. 2. 23. A doubtful one is Auct. F.5. 27 (Bodl. MS 2143).

54. W. D. Macray, *Annals of the Bodleian Library*, *1598–1867*, Oxford, 1868 edn., p. 12.

55. M. R. James, *A Descriptive Catalogue of the MSS. in the Library of Trinity Hall*, Cambridge, 1907, p. v; a list of the bishop's gifts is preserved and has been printed in the *Proc. Camb. Antiq. Soc.*, ii (1864), p. 73. When Thomas James catalogued the MSS in his *Ecloga Oxonio-Cantabrigiensis*, London, 1600, p. 138, there were even then only seven.

56. M. R. James, *Descriptive Catalogue of the MSS. in the Library of King's College, Cambridge*, 1895, pp. 69–71 (for the inventory) and introduction *passim*. On the library in the 15th century see A. N. L. Munby, 'Notes on King's College Library in the fifteenth century', *Trans. Camb. Bibl. Soc.*, i (1949–53), pp. 280–6,

and in the 16th century see W. D. J. Cargill Thompson, 'Notes on King's College Library, 1500–1570, in particular for the Period of the Reformation', ibid., ii (1954), pp. 38–54.

57. H. Bradshaw, *Collected Papers*, Cambridge, 1889, p. 190.

58. Even in Queen Mary's reign Dr John Dee had prepared a petition to the Queen, 15 Jan. 1556-7, proposing the appointment of a commission to collect and copy manuscripts dispersed from the monastic libraries and the establishment of a royal library to counteract 'the spoil and destruction of so many and so notable libraries' at the Dissolution (B.M. Cotton MS Vitellius C. vii, f. 310).

59. Some of the MSS from Matthew Parker's library subsequently found their way into other collections; for instance, several are to be found at Trinity College, Cambridge (see M. R. James, *A Descriptive Catalogue of the Western MSS. in the Library of Trinity College, Cambridge*, iv, Cambridge, 1904, Index s.n. Matthew Parker).

IX

The Elizabethan Society of Antiquaries and the Formation of the Cottonian Library

C. E. WRIGHT

IN 1628, when John Earle published his *Microcosmographie*, the 'antiquary' was a person sufficiently familiar to his contemporaries for Earle to include him in his gallery of 'characters'.

Hee is [writes Earle] a man strangely thrifty of Time past. . . . Hee is one that hath that unnaturall disease to bee enamour'd of old age, and wrinckles, and loves all things (as Dutchmen doe Cheese) the better for being mouldy and worme-eaten. Hee is of our Religion, because wee say it is most ancient; and yet a broken Statue would almost make him an Idolater. A great admirer he is of the rust of old Monuments, and reades onely those Characters, where time hath eaten out the letters. Hee will goe you forty miles to see a Saints well, or ruin'd Abbey. . . . Printed bookes he contemnes, as a novelty of this latter age; but a Manuscript he pores on everlastingly, especially if the cover be all Moth-eaten, and the dust make a Parenthesis between every Syllable. He would give all the Bookes in his Study (which are rarities all) for one of the Romane binding, or sixe lines of Tully in his owne hand. His chamber is hung commonly with strange Beasts skins, and is a kind of Charnel-house of bones extraordinary. . . .[1]

This is, of course, a composite sketch, carefully worked up for effect by a young wit—Earle was twenty-eight when he wrote it; but substantially it is a fair enough description of the various types who went at that time under the name of 'antiquary'. When John Manningham the diariest met Stow in December 1602, the latter told him that in Recorder Fleetwood's study there had been found a portrait of himself with the circumscription 'Johannes Stowe,

Antiquarius Angliae';[2] when Sir Robert Cotton died Sir Symonds D'Ewes prefaced his account of Cotton in his *Autobiography* with the words: 'On Friday, the 6th day of May [1631] . . . died that Great Antiquary, Sir Robert Cotton, my kind acquaintance';[3] and when Richard James, Cotton's librarian, died in 1638 he was described in the burial register of St Margaret's, Westminster, as 'Mr Richard James, That most famous antiquary'.[4] To their contemporaries Stow, the chronicler of London and compiler of annals, Cotton, the collector of manuscripts and coins, and politician, Richard James, anti-papist controversialist and librarian, Selden, the legal controversialist, and Camden, the author of *Britannia*, could all be designated as antiquaries, as could, equally well, the Tradescants, whose museum at Lambeth Earle had perhaps in mind when he says of the antiquary's chamber that it 'is hung commonly with strange Beasts skins, and is a kind of Charnelhouse of bones extraordinary', which describes a sort of late survivor of the 'Wunderkammer' of the German princes of the Renaissance.[5]

Up to a point therefore Earle's sketch is not unfair, in spite of that element of mockery, which anticipates some eighteenth-century accounts of Sir Hans Sloane's collections. Certainly Earle is no less than just when he says, 'Hee will goe you forty miles to see a Saints well, or ruin'd Abbey.' Cotton and Camden went very much more than 'forty miles' when they made together their antiquarian tour—their 'itinerarium curiosum' as Stukeley would have called it—in 1599 to see the Roman remains in the North of England, some of the results of which are preserved in B.M. Cotton MS Julius F. vi and in print in the later editions of Camden's *Britannia*.[6] And as for the ruins of abbeys and the antiquaries' feelings about them, this point receives striking illustration in a book published in the very same year as Earle's *Microcosmographie*, written by William Lithgow, the indefatigable Scot who had journeyed in the East, measured the ruins of Troy and found the 'tombs of Priam and Hecuba his Queen', and adorned his *Totall Discourse, of the Rare Adventures and Painfull Peregrinations of Long Nineteene Years Travayles* (1632) with a portrait of himself clad in 'Turkish suite'; the sight of the ruined abbeys in Scotland provoked this outburst from Lithgow:

Mr. Knoxe did with our glorious Churches of Abbacies and Monasteries (which were the greatest beauty of the Kingdome) knocking all downe to desolation; leaving naught to be seene of admirable Edifices, but like to the Ruines of Troy, Tyrus and Thebes, lumpes of Walls and heapes of stones.[7]

This is a fine anticipation of Dr Johnson's utterance when he visited St Andrews with Boswell on 19 August 1773.

The choice of the 'antiquary' for Earle's portrait gallery is eloquent witness then that such a man was not an isolated phenomenon, and wherever men find that they share a common interest they tend to group themselves together to discuss their problems and exchange information. Unfortunately, in periods earlier than the eighteenth century it is not easy to find records of such gatherings, although ten years *after* this date (1638) four notable antiquaries (Dugdale, Dering, Hatton, and Shirley) actually entered into a formal contract for the exchange of antiquarian material.[8] In the sixteenth century however I suppose the earliest gathering —this time a convivial one—at which antiquarian subjects were discussed and of which we have record is the supper party which took place in the summer lodgings of John Foche, the last abbot of St Augustine's, at Sturry, near Canterbury, and was described by John Twyne, the Canterbury schoolmaster. The date was about 1530. The principal speaker was John Foche; the second speaker was Dygon, a monk of St Augustine's; yet another of the party was Nicholas Wotton, at this time a young man, afterwards a diplomat and the first dean of Canterbury.[9] Wotton and Dygon had just returned from conducting the scholar Vives from Louvain to Oxford. Foche happily opened the conversation by referring to the Channel crossing and telling his guests that there was a time when this island was joined to France and thus they would once have been able to make the journey to Louvain on foot. This led of course to talk about the early history of England, about Albion as it was then called, about the meaning of the word 'Britannia', about the early inhabitants of this island and so to Geoffrey of Monmouth, Twyne wittily observing that it was a great pity that Geoffrey had not looked after his authority, the precious 'vetustissimus liber' more carefully.

We can well imagine that discussions such as this were a not

unusual occurrence in the household of Matthew Parker, archbishop of Canterbury, at Lambeth and elsewhere, in which John
Joscelyn, among others, would have spoken weightily, and there
must have been similar meetings in Cecil's household, where
Laurence Nowell was domiciled for several years.[10]

The strongest continuous force in the fostering of antiquarian
studies in the sixteenth century, however, was, I think, the College
of Arms and its officers. The contribution of the heralds to the
furtherance of antiquarian studies was considerable and arose
naturally out of their duties, more especially out of the researches
necessary to the compilation of the genealogies associated with the
visitations that were carried out regularly from the time of
Henry VIII's grant of a commission under the great seal to Benolt
(Clarenceux from 1511 until his death in 1534) for the visitation
of his province. The heralds examined private muniments as well
as the public records, and in the books of the visitations made by
Robert Glover, Somerset, who died in the year of the Armada,
there appear for the first time copies of charters and drawings of
seals. The heralds' journeys up and down the country gave them
the opportunity of recording the monuments and inscriptions in
the churches of the towns and villages through which they passed
and out of these came that invaluable class of manuscripts usually
designated as 'Church Notes', the earliest of which are those of
Robert Cooke in 1569.[11] The heralds were antiquaries perforce
and the controversies in which they found themselves frequently
engaged either with one another or with outsiders were a further
incentive to antiquarian researches.

The circumstances and the atmosphere of the later decades of
Elizabeth's reign were peculiarly propitious to the formation of a
society in which antiquaries might gather with that degree of
formality characteristic of the age to discuss subjects of common
interest, and we are fortunate in that one of the original members
of the society has left an account of when and how it came into
being.[11a]

The author of this was Sir Henry Spelman, and his story is preserved in the preface which he subsequently added to his treatise
on *The Original of the Four Terms of the Year* under the title 'The
Occasion of this Discourse'. The treatise itself was written, as

Spelman tells us, in 1614; 'The Occasion', that is to say the preface, bears no date, however, but certain internal evidence allows us to date it almost precisely; it is certainly the earliest account of the society, the only other seventeenth-century one independent of it being that of Dr Thomas Smith in the life of Sir Robert Cotton which he prefixed to his Catalogue of the Cottonian Manuscripts published in 1696.[12]

In 'The Occasion' Spelman writes as follows:

About forty two Years since, divers Gentlemen in London, studious of Antiquities, fram'd themselves into a College or Society of Antiquaries, appointing to meet every Friday weekly in the Term, at a Place agreed of, and for Learning sake to confer upon some Questions in that Faculty, and to sup together. The Place, after a Meeting or two, became certain at Darby-house, where the Herald's Office is kept: and two Questions were propounded at every Meeting: to be handled at the next that followed; so that every Man had a Sennight's respite to advise upon them, and then to deliver his Opinion. That which seem'd most material, was by one of the Company (chosen for the purpose) to be entr'd in a Book; that so it might remain unto Posterity. The Society increased daily; many Persons of great Worth, as well Noble as other Learned, joining themselves unto it.

Thus it continu'd divers Years; but as all good Uses commonly decline; so many of the chief Supporters hereof either dying or withdrawing themselves from London into the Country; this among the rest grew for twenty years to be discontinu'd. But it then came again into the mind of divers principal Gentlemen to revive it; and for that purpose upon the – – Day of – – in the Year 1614. there met at the same Place Sir James Ley Knight then Attorney of the Court of Wards, since Earl of Marleborough and Lord Treasurer of England; Sir Robert Cotton Knight and Baronet; Sir John Davies his Majesty's Attorney for Ireland; Sir Richard St. George Knt. then Norrey, Mr. Hackwell the Queen's Solicitor, Mr. Camden then Clarencieux, my self, and some others. Of these the Lord Tresaurer, Sir Robert Cotton, Mr. Camden, and my self, had been of the original Foundation; and to my knowledge were all then living of that sort, saving Sir John Doderidge, Knight., Justice of the King's Bench.

We held it sufficient for that time to revive the Meeting and only conceiv'd some Rules of Government and Limitation to be observ'd amongst us; whereof this was one, That for avoiding Offence, we should neither meddle with Matters of State, nor of Religion. And

agreeing of two Questions for the next Meeting, we chose Mr. Hackwell to be our Register, and the Convocator of our Assemblies for the
present; and supping together, so departed. . . .

But before our next Meeting, we had notice that his Majesty took a
little Mislike of our Society; not being inform'd that we had resolv'd to
decline all Matters of State. Yet hereupon we forbare to meet again, and
so all our Labours lost. . . .

There is in fact very little that we do not know about the
Society thanks to Spelman. We are told that it was formed 'about
forty two years since', that it met every Friday in Term time, that
its place of meeting was Derby House—this was Derby House in
the City, just south of St Paul's, in Paul's Wharf Hill next to
Woodmongers Hall[13]—that the method of proceeding was to
propose at each meeting two questions for discussion at the next
and that each member was expected to give his opinion on the
subjects, the most important points of the discussion being recorded by one of the Society; we are told the names of some of the
original members; we are also told that for certain reasons the
Society 'grew for twenty years to be discontinu'd', and that in 1614
an attempt was made to revive it—unsuccessfully, because in
Spelman's words, the king 'took a little Mislike of our Society'.

The Original of the Four Terms of the Year is dated by Spelman
to the year 1614, it having been prepared for the meeting of that
year. Unfortunately it has been assumed by nearly everyone who
has written about the Elizabethan Society of Antiquaries that
Spelman's preface (that is, 'The Occasion') is of the same date.
But let us see what Spelman's information would yield if this were
in fact the case. If 'The Occasion' and *The Original* belong to the
same date, Spelman's assertion that the Society was formed 'about
forty two years since' would give a foundation date about
1572 and the twenty years' discontinuance would begin about
1592. These deductions however, as the most recent investigator
of the subject, Miss Van Norden, has shown,[14] are quite at variance
with the other evidence available. The five foundation members
were Ley, Cotton, Camden, Doderidge and Spelman himself. In
1572 Spelman would have been nine years of age and Cotton
would have been one year old! Obviously there is something very
wrong with this interpretation. And it will not help us to shelter

N

behind the word 'about' unless it is to be so loosely interpreted as to become meaningless. Other evidence also is against such an interpretation. The documents that survive from the archives of the Society show, where they are dated, that in fact the most active years of the Society's life were those from 1590 to 1605 or thereabouts, that is within the twenty years of discontinuance on the old interpretation. As a matter of fact internal evidence suggests for 'The Occasion' a date some twelve or more years *after* the writing of *The Original of the Four Terms*; the titles and offices cited by Spelman for the foundation members are useful pointers, the most important for this purpose being Sir James Ley, who is referred to as earl of Marlborough and lord treasurer. Ley was created earl of Marlborough in February 1626 and ceased to be lord treasurer in July 1628. If we take then 1627/28 as the year of the composition of 'The Occasion' we shall obtain as an approximate foundation date for the Society 1585/6. 1586 was the year in which Cotton took his degree at Cambridge and Smith in his life of Cotton (pp. iv, v) tells us that Cotton came to Westminster almost at once. Moreover, 1586 saw the publication of Camden's *Britannia*, and by that year all the original members would be in or around London—Camden was teaching at Westminster School, Spelman had just been admitted to Lincoln's Inn, and Doderidge was a bencher of the Middle Temple. And the twenty years prior to the writing of 'The Occasion' which constitutes in Spelman's phrase twenty years' discontinuance would give 1608 as the year of the abandonment of the meetings and this accords with the evidence of the surviving Discourses, few of which seem to date from much after 1605.

Briefly then the probable chronological sequence consistent with Spelman's statements and the other evidence is that the Society or College of Antiquaries came into being in or about 1586 and that it continued until about 1608 and for the twenty years that elapsed between that date and the writing of 'The Occasion' was discontinued, with the exception of an abortive effort in 1614 to revive it.

A portion of the Elizabethan Society's archives fortunately still survives. From these it is possible to learn the dates of the meetings over quite a considerable part of its existence, the titles of the subjects discussed at each meeting, and what sort of discourses were submitted by the various members.

One of the most interesting supplementary items is a small journal that was kept by Francis Tate from 1590 to 1601.[15] This opens with one extraneous item—an epitaph on Sir Christopher Hatton, lord chancellor, who died in 1591, written in a neat italic hand on a blank leaf (f. 4). On the verso of this is a list (not indisputably in Tate's hand but certainly contemporary) of the members of the Society presumably about 1590. This is the list as written:

William ffletewode, seriant and Recorder of London: Garter kinge of armes: Mr Broughton of ye Inner Temple: Mr Heneage: Mr Leye of Lincolns Inne: Mr Bouchier of the inner Temple: Mr Savel of the Middle Temple: ffrancis Tate of the middle Temple: Mr Paten: Mr Holland of the inner temple: Mr Robert Cotton of the middle temple: Mr Agard: Mr Thynne: Mr Stowe: Mr Talbot: Mr Cliffe: Mr Strangman: Mr Wiseman: Mr Lambart: Mr Beale.[16]

Most, but not all, of these can be identified with some certainty. William Fleetwood was recorder of the city of London, the owner of a number of important manuscripts, and well known as an antiquary; he died in 1594. The list is therefore earlier than 1594 and the 'Garter kinge of armes' must be Sir William Dethick, who died in 1612. 'Mr Broughton of the Inner Temple' was Richard Broughton, subsequently justice of North Wales in James I's reign; 'Mr Heneage' was Michael Heneage, keeper of the records in the Tower, who died in 1600 and some of whose collections were acquired by Cotton (B.M. Cotton MS Claudius C. i); 'Mr Leye' was the James Ley to whom reference has already been made; Francis Tate was admitted to the Inner Temple in 1587 and died in 1616; Cotton and Stow require no comment; 'Mr Agard' was Arthur Agarde, deputy chamberlain of the exchequer from 1570 until his death in 1615; 'Mr Thynne' was Francis Thynne, subsequently (1602) Lancaster herald, a notable antiquary who died in 1608; 'Mr Talbot' was Thomas Talbot, clerk of the records in the Tower; 'Mr Strangman' was James Strangeman who compiled antiquarian collections about Essex and elsewhere (some of which are preserved in B.M. Lansdowne MSS 860. A. and B.); 'Mr Wiseman' was Thomas Wiseman of Great Waltham in Essex, a considerable landowner; 'Mr Lambart' was, of course, William Lambarde the historian of Kent who died in 1601; and the last name on the list is that of Robert Beale, clerk to the council and a notable figure in Elizabethan political life: it was he who had the unhappy task of informing Mary Queen of Scots of the sentence of death passed on her; born in 1541, he died in 1601.[17] The absence of some names is surprising, for example those of Camden and Spelman, but the list may be merely a roll of those present at one particular meeting. It is worth noting that the list receives confirmation from two rough lists scribbled by Francis Tate on the back of a manuscript of one of the discourses delivered at a meeting of the Society in 1591 and now preserved in Cotton MS Faustina E. v (f. 108): the first list is dated 21 February 33 Elizabeth [1591], and the second 13 May of the same year. The first meeting was attended by Ley, Tate, Garter (i.e. Dethick), Patten, Bourchier, Thynne, Agarde, Stow, Talbot and Cliffe, and at the second, rather more fully attended, presumably because of the time of year—May, were present Broughton, Camden, Ley, Garter, Holland, Patten, Thynne, Talbot, Stow, Agarde, Wiseman, Bourchier and Tate.[18]

Tate appears to have acted as secretary and as such was presumably responsible for sending out to each member one of the formal summonses to attend, of which several examples have fortunately survived. Hearne in the preface to his *Curious Discourses* published the two addressed to Stow and Bowyer.[19] That addressed to Bowyer reads as follows:

The place apointed for a conference upon the question followinge, is Mr Garter's house, upon All Soules day, beinge Thursday the Secound of November 1598, at one of the Clocke in the afternoone, where your opinioun either in writinge or otherwise is expected upon this question

Of the antiquitie of armes in England.

Yt is desired, that you bringe none other with you, nor give anie notice unto anie, but to such as have the like somouns.

To Mr Bowyer.

A number of the summonses addressed to Sir James Ley is also preserved; these are, generally speaking, uniform in wording with that quoted, but one has the additional phrase 'we desire that . . . you determine that we maie suppe togeather if yow convenyentlie maie'.[20] The proposal that they should sup together confirms what Spelman tells us in 'The Occasion'.

As to the dates of meetings and the subjects discussed, Francis Tate's notebook is again a most important authority. Tate's first date is 27 November 1590 and the two subjects set down for the meeting on that day were, first, 'Of what Antiquity the name of dux or duke is in England & what is the estate thereof', and secondly, 'What is the Antiquitye and exposition of the word Sterlingorum or Sterling'. Then follow three meetings for 1591 (11 February, 23 June, and 25 November), only one in 1592 (6 May), none in 1593, but four in 1594 (12 February, 11 May, 19 June, 27 November); in 1595 there appears to have been only one meeting (29 May), and after that no meetings took place until the end of 1598, when one was held on 25 November; this gap may be due to occurrences of the plague in London.[21] In 1599 however five meetings were held (9 February, 16 May, 23 June, 2 and 23 November) and in 1600 the same number (9 February, 30 April, 7 June, 3 and 28 November). The last entry in Tate's journal has a dramatic historical interest: it is headed '13 Febr. 1600.43 Eliz[abeth]' (that is, 13 February 1601) and beside it Tate has added this note: 'M^d by reson of the trobles stirred by the erle of Essex This day of meeting held not but a new day appointed ye next time 22.Maii.1601.43 Eliz.' The date of the postponed meeting, 13 February 1601, was five days after Essex made his dramatic ride into the city up Ludgate Hill and along Cheapside, closely followed by a herald proclaiming him traitor, the dread word that broke the courage of many of his supporters. On Thursday the 12th, the day before the antiquaries were due to meet, one of Essex's followers, Captain Lea, who had planned to seize the queen, was arrested in the Palace, and a week later Essex was tried in Westminster Hall. The unrest and uncertainty in the city were naturally considerable, and as the antiquaries' place of meeting was Derby House just south of St Paul's, the reason for the postponement of their discussion is easily understood. 22 May 1601 is then the last date cited by Tate in his journal, but manuscripts of the discourses that are dated supply evidence for other and later dates. Most of the manuscripts are now preserved in Cotton MS Faustina E. v, and the one bearing the latest date is in fact Tate's own contribution to a discussion as to 'What knights the abbots made in the time of Henry I and before', the arguments being grounded on the wording of Henry I's charter to Reading: at the top of Tate's paper is written the date '3. James 21. June./' (that is, 1605).[22] No less than two hundred discourses survive and the meetings of which we have record number thirty-eight.[23] The names of the members are of course sufficient to indicate something of the Society's status. Evidence of this is supplied also by the fact that Lancelot Andrewes had apparently hopes of becoming a member; in a letter[24] dated 30 November 1604 Andrewes (at this time master of Pembroke College, Cambridge, prebendary of St Paul's, and dean of Westminster) wrote to Abraham Hartwell, 'I talked with Mr Clarencieux [that is, Camden], and he could not certifie me that I was made of your number and yet he was at y[e] last meeting, wher (as he saith) such things use to be agreed on before eny come in'; he adds that in view of this he will 'committ no error in comming' to the next meeting. That the meetings were a regular and much anticipated event in the lives of those who participated in them is, I think, fairly deducible from a letter that Richard Carew, the Cornish historian, wrote from East Antony on 7 April 1605 to Cotton;[25] in his letter Carew expresses regret at his absence from the meetings. 'I praie you,' he writes, 'geeve me leave to impart unto you my greef, that my so remote dwelling depriveth mee of your sweete and respected Antiquarum society, into which your kyndenesse towardes mee and grace with them made mee an Entrance, and unto which (notwithstanding so long discontynuance) my longing desire layeth a Contynuall clayme.'

Matters of law, the history of the Inns of Court and the privileges of members of the legal profession, the development of various offices of state, heraldic problems, or the early history of this country and the meaning of the antiquities that remain, whether these be in the form of coins or monuments or manuscript records, are the subjects that occupy the antiquaries, and bearing in mind the professional interests of the members of the Society this is what we might reasonably expect. Thus, we find them discoursing of the antiquity of the law terms for the administration of justice in England, the history and privileges of the Inns of

Court and the privileges of the serjeants-at-law. Or they argue with much wealth of evidence as to which is the most ancient court for the ministering of justice universally within the realm, and they have much to say about the antiquity and privileges of Sanctuary. On 27 November 1594 one of the subjects put down for discussion was the origin and jurisdiction of the County Palatines in England. In 1598 and 1599 they devoted themselves to the history and the rights of cities, then of castles, next of towns, and lastly of parishes. In the early nineties they had occupied themselves with a group of subjects falling rather within the province of the heralds: the antiquity of marquesses in England and the manner of their creation, and they proceeded then to consider from the same standpoint viscounts, barons, knights and esquires. Other topics were the origin of mottoes and of sealing. They also interested themselves in the various ways in which land is divided: as for example, what terms are used for the dimensions of land in England, how the shires are divided, and the various methods by which land is measured in Cornwall. Of a more general character are their discourses on epitaphs, and on tombs and monuments. Very much a heralds' subject was the discussion of the ceremonies used at funerals, and a long paper on this survives from the pen of Sir William Dethick, Garter; this occupied them on 30 April 1600. The last subject recorded in Tate's notebook was 'The antiquity, use & ceremonies of lawful combattes in Englande' (13 February 1600/1).

The subject for discussion is usually treated on a strictly historical basis, the facts being arranged chronologically with supporting quotations. A remark made by Francis Thynne towards the end of his paper on the Inns of Court may be quoted as typical of the spirit in which most of the antiquaries handled their material. 'For the rest of the inns of chancery', writes Thynne, 'I can say little both because I pleasure not to favour every fiction and supposal of their original, as for that I have determined to deliver nothing but notes of record and history.'[26] Ample documentation is indeed one of the most interesting features of these papers. A good example is supplied in the discourse which Arthur Agarde contributed on dimensions of land (24 November 1599); he tells us that he bases his remarks on the records in his custody and on 'those notes I have quoted out of ancient registers and books which have fallen into my hands within these xxx. years'; thus we find him citing for a 'solin of ground' a note taken out of a leiger book, 'which the Bishop of Norwich Doctor Redman hath',[27] for a 'carucate', 'an ancient writer called Henry Knighton, a chronicler of Leicester who wrote in H.V[th's] time, and in the custody of a gentleman in Leicester, named Mr. John Hunt'. And in support of his contention that a carucate was twenty-six acres he writes, 'I find mentioned in a book intituled *Restauratio Ecclesiae de Ely* (which Mr. Cotton lent me and now Mr. Cop[?e] hath) these two places worth noting' and he refers his readers or listeners to a passage on 'leaf ix';[28] for 'virgate' he refers to 'a register book of Ely, which now the Dean hath'. In his discourse ('Of the Antiquity of the Christian Religion in this Island') delivered on 29 November 1604, Agarde writes,[29] 'Mr. Robert Hare, that worthy antiquary, lent me a large booke of St. Augustine's of Canterbury, wherein was a full story of our island wrote about H. the 5 his time, *Anno domini* 1406, where he saith that that which he writeth, he collected out of Bede, Cestrensis, Sprot, and *ex aliis scriptoribus illius monasterii.*' Agarde then quotes a passage from 'his 13th leaf'. This manuscript is almost certainly Thomas of Elmham's chronicle of St Augustine's, now at Trinity Hall, Cambridge; we know that it belonged at one time to St Augustine's, Canterbury and subsequently to Robert Hare.[30] For us today these references to the manuscripts used and quoted and the names of their owners are of great interest and importance.[31] Joseph Holland frequently refers to charters in his own possession,[32] some of which (along with coins) he occasionally exhibits to the Society, thus inaugurating a custom which persists to this day in the present successor of the Elizabethan Society. The paper on epitaphs, a subject congenial rather to the genius of Sir Thomas Browne, may preserve inscriptions now lost; John Weever, whose *Ancient Funerall Monuments* was not published until 1631, was a contemporary of this group and acknowledges in his 'Epistle to the Reader' the help he received from manuscripts in Cotton's library. Some also refer to antiquities which they had seen. Agarde in his paper on 'The Antiquitie of Ceremonies used at Funerals in England' (30 April 1600) tells us of the pyramids of stone at

'Borowghe-brigge' which are supposed by the local inhabitants to mark the burial place of 'some notable persons slaine theere at a battell' (a reference presumably to the standing stones near Boroughbridge called 'The Devil's Arrows') and which he himself saw 'these xxxiiij yeares agoe [i.e. 1566], when I was attendinge on Sir Nicholas Throkemton, who wayted on the duke of Richemount, who reported what he had heard xxx. yeares before that tyme to the like effect'. And in his essay on epitaphs he gives as his third reason why so few epitaphs remain, the destruction that followed 'the dissolution of our most ancient religious houses', and yet, he continues:

I sawe at Burton uppon Trent this somer, the monument of Ulricus Spot, father of the Earles Algar and Morcar, who was founder of that abbeye before the Conqueste, whereon lyeth his figure cross-legged, armed with his shielde, swerde, and spurres, but without any epitaph or inscription. The preservation of this monument I think came by this meanes. The first Lord Paget [William Paget, first Baron Paget of Beaudesert], who had the same abbaye geven him upon the dissolution, removed this monument out of the chauncel, first into an isle, and afterwards into the churche.

All these antiquaries, like their predecessors, were keenly aware of the losses that had followed the 'dissolution of our most ancient religious houses' (as Agarde puts it) and did their best individually to rescue what they could. Three of their number—Cotton, Doderidge, and Ley—also moved collectively in the matter in an attempt by way of a petition to the queen to secure a charter for the formation of an 'academy for the study of antiquity and history'. The primary object of this was to be the safeguarding and management of a library which it was proposed should be formed 'to preserve old books concerning the matter of history of this realm, original charters, and monuments'.[33] It was to be founded 'for the better information of all noblemen and gentlemen studious of antiquity; whereby they may be enabled to do unto her Majesty and the realm such service as shall be requisite for their place'. And the library was 'to be well furnished with divers ancient bookes and rare monuments of antiquity, which otherwise may perish; and that at the costs and charges of divers gentlemen which will be willing thereunto'. There can be no doubt at all that this project was intimately connected with the Society of Antiquaries which we have been considering. Not only are the three names which appear on the petition witness to that but in speaking of the officers of the proposed academy or corporation the petitioners say: 'There are divers gentlemen studious of this knowledge [that is, of the antiquity and history of this country], and which have of a long time assembled and exercised themselves therein, out of which company and others that are desirous, the body of the said corporation shall be drawn.' The phrase 'of a long time' may be observed; the Society, as we have seen, probably came into existence in 1586 or thereabouts, and as for the date of the petition there can be little doubt that it belongs to the closing years of Elizabeth's reign, perhaps 1602. This petition shows that there was among the members of the Society a strong consciousness of what their predecessors had been striving for; indeed, there are in the wording of the petition echoes not only of the sentiments but of the actual phrases of earlier antiquaries. We may refer, for example, to John Dee's address to Queen Mary made in 1557 in which he appealed for the recovery and preservation of ancient writings and monuments, lamenting the destruction and dispersal of the monastic libraries, and begging that a library be established to ensure the preservation of works of ancient writers.[34] Had not Leland written, twenty years before Dee's letter, to Cromwell begging for his assistance in seeing that some of the books that were being dispersed should be brought into the Royal Library, with, as a matter of fact, some success? But the closest parallel in phrase and sentiment is to be found in the letter which the Privy Council issued on 7 July 1568 and which opens by way of preamble with a statement as to the interest of the queen and her 'progenitors' in the 'conservation of . . . auncient recordes and monuments' and goes on to indicate what should be done with such material as was then in the 'possession of sundry private persons'. In the letter accompanying the draft of this and dated three days earlier Parker observed to Cecil—'if this opportunity be not taken in our time, it will not so well be done hereafter'.[35]

In actual fact, as one would expect, the work of rescue was left to private individuals—to John Bale, to Dee, to Matthew Parker and Cecil, to Henry Savile of Banke, and others. And this tradition of private enterprise persisted to the end: at the very moment when this petition was being drafted for presentation to Elizabeth one of the three signatories had already been actively engaged for some time in acquiring for his own library such manuscript material as he could come on. Dr Thomas Smith in his life of Cotton tells us that his first purchases for his library were made in 1588 and from then until his death in 1631 Cotton was persistently active in enlarging his collection.

It seems to me that the essential historical background to the formation of the Cotton Library is to be sought in, first, the anti-quarian pursuits in which Sir Robert participated with his fellow members in the Society of Antiquaries, secondly, in the widespread desire to rescue and preserve in one place the records of the past, and thirdly, in the perplexed politics of the early seventeenth cen-tury in which Cotton, it must not be forgotten, took an active part, as may be most easily seen by turning over the pages of the *Calendars of State Papers* for the reigns of James and Charles I; Sir Symonds D'Ewes indeed in his *Autobiography*, in describing the Overbury murder and the events that followed it, observes that Cotton by reason of his standing with the earl of Somerset might have been made one of the secretaries of state[36]—instead, adds D'Ewes, 'this fatal business had almost swallowed up Sir Robert Cotton'.

Of the details of Cotton's life it is not necessary to say more than will explain certain strands in his character and thus account for the direction of some of his actions.

Cotton was born on 22 January 1571 at Denton, about three miles from the Cotton seat of Conington Castle, which lies in the pleasant undulating country that forms the northern fringe of Huntingdonshire along the Northamptonshire border. It is not many miles from the manor of Little Gidding where Nicholas Ferrar was many years later to establish his Protestant community; not far south lies Hinchingbrooke, the seat of the Cromwells and in Cotton's early years the home of the 'Golden Knight'; to the east is Ramsey Abbey, and northwards across the flat outliers of the Fen country is Peterborough. The Cottons be it noted had done well out of the dissolution of the monasteries, having secured at various dates in the forties and fifties of the sixteenth century

lands in Conington that had belonged to Chicksand, to St Mary's
Priory in Huntingdon, to Sawtry Abbey, and to the Leper Hos-
pital of St Margaret near Huntingdon.[37] The core of the Conington estate however came to the Cotton family through Sir
Robert's ancestress Mary de Wesenham; this fact is not unimportant because Mary de Wesenham was the granddaughter and
ultimate heiress of Sir John de Brus who claimed descent from the
Scottish kings, a claim of which Cotton made the most. Indeed
when Cotton was knighted on 11 May 1603 he was compli-
mented by James I on his descent from the Bruces; henceforth
Cotton normally signed himself 'Robert Cotton Bruceus' and
was formally entitled Sir Robert Bruce Cotton. Not unimportant
either was the fact that his mother was one of the Shirleys of
Staunton Harold in Leicestershire, a family famous for its pride of
ancestry and its interest in antiquarian researches. As to Cotton's
education it is significant that he was sent to Westminster School
where the second master at the time was William Camden. And
lastly it is worth noting carefully the position of the town residence
in which Cotton settled when he came to London about 1586.
It was situated in the very heart of the palace of Westminster,
lying between Westminster Hall and St Stephen's Chapel on the
east and the old House of Lords on the west, with, in front of it,
a pleasant garden running down to the Thames, to which it had
direct access by Cotton Stairs.

It may be that today most people think of the Cotton Collection
in terms of some of its more spectacular treasures, such as the
Lindisfarne Gospels, the Coronation Book of Charles V, the Cotton Genesis, Henry VI's Psalter, or the Golden Charter of King
Edgar to New Minister at Winchester. But when John Evelyn
(who made his famous journey to Normandy in 1644 in the company of Sir Robert's grandson Sir John Cotton) paid a visit to the
library on 12 March 1668 he made the following entry in his diary:

Went to visit Sir John Cotton, who had me into his library full of
good MSS. Greek and Latin, but most famous for those of the Saxon
and English antiquities, collected by his grandfather.[38]

Evelyn was right, for it is indeed on this side that the library is
richest, in its great wealth of historical material in Latin and in the

vernacular from the pre-Conquest period, through the Middle
Ages, right down to the Tudor period and Cotton's own day.

The range of the collection may be brought home more vividly
if we instance a few examples from its major categories.

For the pre-Conquest period we are indebted to Cotton for
most of the important surviving manuscripts. He possessed manuscripts of almost all the versions of the Anglo-Saxon Chronicle:
two manuscripts of the Abingdon version (Tiberius A. vi, ff. 1–34,
and Tiberius B. i, ff. 115–64), both substantially of eleventh-
century date; one of the Worcester version (Tiberius B. iv),
dating from about 1050 with some later additions; the only manuscript of the Canterbury bilingual epitome (Domitian A. viii),
which was written at St Augustine's, Canterbury about 1100; and
a manuscript (Otho B. xi) of a version closely related to that preserved in the Parker MS at Corpus Christi College, Cambridge.
In his possession also were some fragments, such as a leaf (Domitian A. ix, f. 9) of a Winchester version recording events of 1113
and 1114, of great importance as showing the preservation of the
Anglo-Saxon literary tradition into the twelfth century in greater
purity than at Peterborough, and some annals from 988 to 1268
(in Anglo-Saxon up to 1110) written at Christ Church, Canterbury (Caligula A. xv, ff. 132b–9). Indeed, the only manuscripts of
the Chronicle outside the Cotton collection are the Parker MS at
Corpus Christi College, Cambridge, and the Laud MS in the
Bodleian Library at Oxford. To Cotton also was due the preservation of the unique manuscripts of Æthelward's chronicle (Otho
A. x) and of Asser's life of Alfred (Otho A. xii) (both alas destroyed in the fire of 1731). Of the five oldest surviving manuscripts of Bede's *Historia Ecclesiastica*, Cotton possessed two
(Tiberius A. xiv and Tiberius C. ii), both of the eighth century.
Of the most important document of the English monastic revival
of the tenth century, the *Regularis Concordia*, he owned the only
surviving manuscripts of both the earlier and later versions. We
owe to his activities also the best manuscripts of the Anglo-Saxon
Laws, of King Alfred's translations of Orosius' *Historia Universalis*
(Tiberius B. i) and Gregory's *Cura Pastoralis* (Tiberius B. xi);
of Ælfric's Homilies (Julius E. vii); and of the Anglo-Saxon
Martyrology (Julius A. x). Of the gospel books I need mention

only the Lindisfarne Gospels (Nero D. iv) and those of King Athelstan (Tiberius A. ii). And but for Cotton's activities the history of Anglo-Saxon poetry would certainly have presented a very different picture, for he was responsible for preserving the unique manuscript of *Beowulf* (Vitellius A. xv), the only extant Anglo-Saxon epic, and our knowledge of numerous other works is due to his preservation of their texts.

Of the manuscripts relating to the mediaeval period it is impossible to speak in detail: the library contains manuscripts of all the most important chroniclers—Matthew Paris, John of Wallingford, William of Malmesbury, Langtoft and Knighton—the last-named in what is almost certainly the author's autograph (Tiberius C. vii).[39] It also preserves a rich selection of monastic registers and chartularies from all parts of the country—including no less than six from Ely, the 'Red Book of Canterbury' (that is, St Augustine's, Canterbury), and others from Waltham, Dunstable, Rievaulx, Abingdon and Worcester (the famous Hemming's Chartulary).[40] Hagiographical material is well represented and includes the most important extant manuscript of the lives of the Welsh saints (Vespasian A. xiv). The history of Middle English literature might be largely written from the material supplied by the Cotton manuscripts. Of the *Ancrene Riwle* Cotton possessed manuscripts of each of the three versions—English (no less than three—Cleopatra C. vi, Titus D. xviii, and Nero A. xiv), French (Vitellius F. vii), and Latin (Vitellius E. vii), and he also owned the best manuscripts of the Southern English Legendary, and of Layamon's *Brut* (Caligula A. ix and Otho C. xiii). Most important of all, he had the unique manuscript (Nero A. x) of the group of alliterative poems of which *Sir Gawain and the Green Knight* and *Pearl* are the best known examples; the loss of this manuscript would have affected the story of Middle English literature as vitally as the loss of the *Beowulf* MS would that of Anglo-Saxon. The library was also rich in legal manuscripts and it was not lacking in important heraldic material, such as the Camden Roll of c. 1280 (Cotton Roll XV. 8) and the Caerlaverock Poem of 1300 (Caligula A. xviii, ff. 23b–30b).

But it was exceptionally rich in original material relating to the political and religious history of this country in the reigns of

Henry VIII, Edward VI, Mary, Elizabeth, and James I; the quantity of the state papers that found their way into Cotton's hands is nothing less than astonishing. In the Caligula press (B. i to E. xii)[41] were no less than forty-three volumes of these papers for the reigns of Henry VIII and Elizabeth, relating not only to domestic affairs but to relations with France, and many, especially those relating to Scotland, bearing notes by Cecil. In the presses under the busts of Nero and Galba were fifty volumes of similar papers (Nero B. i–xii; Galba B. i–E. i) concerning relations with Portugal and Spain, Russia and Poland, the Scandinavian countries, the Hanseatic towns, Holland, and Turkey and the Near East, the last volume (Nero B. xii) being in fact the official letter-book of Edward Barton, our ambassador at Constantinople from 1593 to 1596.

This accumulation of State Papers is very remarkable: how did Cotton obtain them and why? In answer to the first question consider the position of Cotton House. It lay in the centre of the Palace of Westminster, with, on the east, Westminster Hall and St Stephen's Chapel (formerly the House of Commons) and, on the west, the old House of Lords; within the Palace precincts lay a number of the State Paper offices.[42] It would not be difficult for a man in Sir Robert Cotton's position to obtain the loan of papers from various offices and to remove them to his own study for perusal, nor with his circle of influential friends would it be easy to compel him to return them, especially during James's reign, when he was in favour with the king. I think that it was known to a number of people what was going on and that it was either connived at or officials found themselves powerless to oppose it. I will refer to three significant statements in letters from Thomas Wilson, who was Keeper of the State Papers. On 24 August 1615 we find Wilson writing to Ambrose Randolph reporting the death of Arthur Agarde, deputy chamberlain of the exchequer records and an antiquary of whom we have already said a good deal: this office was in the gift of the chamberlain and Wilson urged Randolph to apply for the place, adding significantly that it would be dangerous to the State should Sir Robert Cotton (who will strive for it) succeed in putting in a person devoted to him, because, says Wilson, he already injures the Keepers of State Papers, by 'having such things as he hath coningly scraped together'.[43] On the same day Wilson wrote also to Sir Ralph Winwood, the secretary of state, about Agarde's papers, noting that they included a book on the exemption of the kings of England from the power of the pope, abstracts of treaties, and other state matters, and that they were claimed by Sir Robert Cotton on the pretext that they were left him by Agarde's will but, observes Wilson, Cotton was at the making of the will. Wilson emphasises to Winwood the importance of having such things in the possession of the king's officers, as otherwise they may be suppressed when most wanted.[44] Lastly, in 1618 Wilson received from Cotton an application for the subscriptions and signatures of princes and great men attached to letters otherwise unimportant, the alleged reason being that he was collecting such for curiosity's sake; Wilson very wisely took the precaution of referring this to the king (on 1 March) and noted on the letter (on 3 March) that the king's answer was to approve Sir Robert's request.[45] Here is a clear instance of the royal favour at work.[46]

And why did Cotton acquire these papers? It was on the knowledge derived from them that such political power or influence as Cotton possessed was based—it was the sort of knowledge that made him of course at one time useful and at another a nuisance. Thus, in 1600 he was consulted by the queen's advisers as to the precedency between England and Spain, a question which had been occasioned by Sir Henry Neville, the English ambassador to France, and the ambassador for Spain being together at Calais,[47] and in 1615 the question concerning the right of Lord Roos to carry the sword before the king was, reports John Chamberlain to Carleton in a letter of 13 July of that year, settled by Sir Robert Cotton—'who has ever some old precedent in store', adds Chamberlain with scorn.[48] On the other hand, the same writer reporting on 29 April 1612 that the king had refused to grant baronets precedence over the younger sons of barons mentions that Cotton was sent out of the way when the case was heard because he was furnished with records in their favour.[49]

It is true also that Cotton had projected, at the king's request, a history of the church of England down to the Reformation, a task subsequently undertaken by Archbishop Ussher,[50] and much of the material may have been ostensibly brought together for this purpose. It is arguable moreover that in collecting such papers he was influenced by the example of contemporary French scholars and bibliophiles. The collection of manuscripts made by Jacques Auguste de Thou was for the most part of a political character, and de Thou's influence was certainly not unknown in England. Sir Symonds D'Ewes, Cotton's younger contemporary and friend— in Cotton's last years busy with forming a collection of his own[51] —bears witness to de Thou's influence in his *Autobiography*, which he admits to have written in the form he adopted 'in imitation of that unmatched historian Thuanus or De Thou'.[52] It is not without significance that the acquisition of materials of historical interest was one of the main objects of the brothers Pierre (1582–1651) and Jacques du Puy (1586–1656) (the Puteani), of Jacques Bongars (1554–1612), and Paul Petau (1568–1614).[53] With one famous French scholar and antiquary Cotton was certainly in contact; this was Nicholas Fabri de Peiresc, to whom Cotton in 1606 presented a beautifully executed fifteenth-century manuscript of French laws now in the Sloane collection at the British Museum (Sloane 2423).[54]

At any rate, whatever the reasons that prompted Cotton to collect this sort of material it is today one of the richest parts of the library. Certainly he did not restrict himself to English material; he possessed, for example, manuscripts of the chronicles of Flanders (to 1404, Nero E. iii), of the chronicle of the Dutch monastery of Hoorn on the Zuyder Zee (Nero A. xiii), of the chronicles of Holland (to 1470, Vitellius E. vi), and of one Russian chronicle (Vitellius F. x). And among his manuscripts relating to geography and travel may be mentioned that of John de Castro's voyages of the Portuguese round Africa written in 1542, which may have belonged to Sir Walter Raleigh (Tiberius D. ix).

Lastly, as one would expect, his antiquarian collections were considerable. Agarde left Cotton his collections at his death in 1615, and a further accession by bequest came from Camden who died in 1623.[55] He possessed also portions of the collections of John Leland[56] (Julius C. vi), Francis Thynne (Julius C. viii), Robert Bowyer (Tiberius D. i), Michael Heneage (Claudius C. i), John Joscelyn (Vitellius E. xiv, etc.), William Lambarde (Vespasian

O

A. v), Laurence Nowell (Domitian A. xviii, etc.), and Thomas Talbot (Vespasian D. xvii).

It is certain that Cotton pursued the acquisition of manuscripts for his library with immense zest and pertinacity. An amusing story illustrative of his reputation in this way (even if the details are apocryphal) is told by John Aubrey in his *Brief Lives* with reference to certain of John Dee's manuscripts. Aubrey reports[57] that Meredith Lloyd, a chemist who lived about 1660, told him that 'John Dee's printed booke of Spirits'[58] was 'not above the third part of what was writt, which were in Sir Robert Cotton's library; many whereof were much perished by being buryed, and Sir Robert Cotton bought the field to digge after it'. A glimpse of him at work in his own county is supplied by John Selden in the postscript of a letter to Archbishop Ussher, written on 14 September 1625. Selden writes: 'There is a hope (as Sir Robert Cotton tells me) that a very ancient Greek MS. copy of the Council of Nice[a], the first of that name, is to be had somewhere in Huntingdonshire; I thought it was a piece of news that would be acceptable to your lordship: he is in chace for it.'[59]

We should indeed be very glad to know more about the dates at which and the names of those from whom Cotton obtained his manuscripts.

The earliest catalogue of the library falls well within Cotton's own lifetime and is, in part, in his autograph; it is preserved in B.M. Harley MS 6018 and bears the date 1621. The manuscripts in it are numbered from 1 to 413, but either by inadvertence or by the misplacing of some manuscripts fifteen of the descriptions are repeated and the actual total is therefore just under 400.[60] Almost all of the manuscripts listed have been identified, and we can see that by 1621 most of the better known and more important items of the collection were already in Cotton's hands: such as Æthelward's Chronicle (290 = Otho A. x), the Anglo-Saxon Heptateuch (81 = Claudius B. iv), the Lindisfarne Gospels (323 = Nero D. iv), the Æthelstan Gospels (6 = Tiberius A. ii), and the Cotton Genesis (267 = Otho B. vi). Some items are unfortunately not identifiable since the information against the number is confined to one word, 'Saxon' (against 98, 153, 177, and 401) or 'Irishe' (against 221), or—slightly more helpful—'Irishe physique' (against

Plate 13

229 and 230). There are some other difficulties which however we may ignore here. Neither the *Beowulf* MS (Vitellius A. xv) nor the *Pearl* and *Sir Gawain and the Green Knight* MS (Nero A. x) are identifiable, but both may be concealed under the word 'Saxon'.

A second source of information is supplied by inscriptions in the manuscripts themselves, although these are fewer than we could wish. A good example is the MS Nero D. vii which has a statement in Cotton's hand to the effect that it was given to him in 1623 by the Viscount St Albans, better known to us of course as Sir Francis Bacon; this is of rather special interest because the subject-matter of the volume (which dates from the end of the fourteenth century) is the lives of the abbots of St Albans. It was therefore presumably a family possession dating from the time of Sir Nicholas Bacon (1509–79), Sir Francis's father, who had been high steward of St Albans. Another book that has a useful inscription is Julius A. xi, a manuscript from Byland Abbey, which has (at f. 114) the memorandum 'Ex dono magistri Henrici Savell mense Novembri anno 1609'; this refers to Henry Savile of Banke, who died in 1617 and in whose manuscripts Cotton took a particular interest. He owned, or at any rate had in his possession for some time, a catalogue of Savile's library (B.M. MS Add. 35213), two entries in which, as my colleague Mr Skeat has noted, are in Cotton's own hand. The second (no. 280) is in fact now a Cotton book—Nero D. iii. It is possible that it is from this source that Cotton obtained the famous *Pearl* MS (Nero A. x), since an entry in the Savile catalogue under no. 274 runs: 'An owld booke in English verse beginning Perle pleasant to princes. Paper in 4°. limned', the four words quoted being the opening words of the poem. The only difficulty to identification is the word 'paper', since the manuscript is a vellum one. In all, Cotton secured no less than forty-six of Savile's books. Others among his contemporaries from whose libraries, as we know from inscriptions, he obtained books were Thomas Allen, the Oxford mathematician, William Cecil, Lord Burghley, Robert Hare, the Cambridge antiquary (most of whose surviving manuscripts are at Trinity Hall, Cambridge), Joseph Holland, the antiquary, Lord William Howard of Naworth, John Selden (from whom he obtained Titus D. xi), John Stow, Thomas Talbot, and Patrick Young.

Sometimes Cotton writes the date of acquisition after his signature: thus, in the Æthelstan Psalter (Galba A. xviii), which had belonged in 1542 to Thomas Dakcombe, a minor canon of Winchester, Cotton has written 'Robertus Cotton: Bruceus. 1612' and in an important heraldic manuscript (Nero D. vi) which had belonged to Sir Gilbert Dethick, Garter, who had died in 1586, and then to his son Sir William Dethick, likewise Garter, Cotton has added below William Dethick's memorandum, 'Et nunc liber Roberti Cotton anno 1608', and at the foot of the first page of the text has had painted a shield of arms with mantling, crest, and motto ribbon, the arms showing an unusual disposition of the quarterings of those borne by Cotton. Again, the Coronation Book of Charles V of France (Tiberius B. viii) has (on f. 3) the inscription 'Robertus Cotton Bruceus 1604'.

Plate 14a

It might seem at first sight that the form of the signature would help, since it will be remembered that after he was knighted by James I in 1603 Cotton added 'Bruceus' to his signature, but deductions based on this are hazardous. It is true that a few manuscripts do in fact have only 'Robertus Cotton' as signature (for example, Vitellius A. xvii) and it might be argued that these must therefore have been acquired before 1603; also, one manuscript (Cleopatra C. xi) in the library, has the inscription 'Ro[bertus]: Cotton: Conningtonensis' (that is, Robert Cotton of Conington) without a date, and another (Titus A. xxii, f. 2b) a similar inscription with the date 1596, which suggests that the use of Conington in the inscriptions indicates early acquisition, a supposition that derives some support from the fact that in the manuscripts given by Cotton to Bodley in 1601 the same form occurs. On the other hand it will have been noticed that the 1608 inscription quoted from the Dethick MS was in the short form of Robert Cotton, while the St Augustine's Psalter (Vespasian A. i) has the signature Robert Cotton Bruceus in association with the date 1599! I think it would be wiser therefore not to place too much weight on the signature forms for determining dates of acquisition.

A third important source of information is provided by the loans lists in Cotton's autograph that survive in a number of manuscripts, the most important being those in B.M. Harley MS 6018. The lists range in date from about 1606 to 1621. They are of threefold significance: first, of course, they tell us the names of those who were privileged to borrow manuscripts from the library; secondly, they disclose what manuscripts were in the library at the date of the loan; and thirdly, by reason of the fact that Cotton sometimes by way of identifying a book adds a note as to where he obtained it we glean some information about the sources of the collection. Thus, about 1609 Cotton lent Mr Williams the king's goldsmith (Harl. 6018, f. 158b) 'Howell Daw his lawes in Welsh given me by Mr. Griffith person of Hinckley' (that is, Hinckley in Leicestershire); this is presumably Titus D. ii, which was written perhaps at or near St Asaph in the second half of the thirteenth century and preserves the North Wales (or Gwynedd) recension of Howel Dda's laws. About the same date Cotton lent Sir John Harington '5 or 6 plotts of the Forts of Ireland sent me from Sir Oliver St John'. This refers to Sir Oliver St John, master of the ordnance in Ireland from 1605 to 1614 and subsequently (1616–22) lord deputy of Ireland. To Patrick Young (1584–1652), the royal librarian, he lent a Greek manuscript of Philostratus 'finely written' which he 'had of Mr. Thompson' (Harl. 6018, f. 159b). The list of loans made to Agarde on 27 November 1612 is particularly useful; from this we learn that the Osney Register (Vitellius E. xv) once belonged to Sir Walter Cope, chamberlain of the exchequer (1609) and master of the court of wards (1613), who died in 1614, and is better known as the builder of Holland House, Kensington; that the *Registrum Roffense* (Domitian A. x) once belonged to William Lambarde; that Sulchard's account of the Westminster Abbey privileges (now Titus A. viii) came from Agarde himself; and that a volume containing the 'History of Henry of Huntingdon and Register of Ramsey' (which *may* be Vespasian A. xviii) came from a 'Mr. Many of Ramsey'.

A fourth source of information is supplied by the letters written to Cotton, especially those that accompanied or promised gifts. In 1629 Sir James Ware sent Cotton 'a Map of one of the baronyes of the county of Longford to be added to the rest', and goes on in his letter, 'Your many favours to me do always put me in mynd of thankfulnes and I could wish I had the happines by having some imployment (fitting the small talent God hath given mee) in

England, to injoy your company and the use of your excellent
Library oftener than I doe'.[61] The manuscripts in question are in
the portfolio Augustus II, artt. 24–26, 28, 47, 48. It was Ware who
presented Cotton in 1627 with the register of St Mary's Abbey,
Dublin (Tiberius A. xi)—'as a small token of my love'.[62] Another
frequent correspondent was James Ussher, archbishop of Armagh,
who wrote in 1628 promising Cotton his 'ancient Copy of the
Samaritan Pentateuch' which he had, he says, 'long since destinated
unto that Librarye of yours to which I have ben beholden for so
many good things no where else to be found',[63] and he sent the
manuscript in the following year—it is now Claudius B. viii.
Many of the most important pre-Conquest charters were presented to Cotton by Sir Edward Dering, who also gave him the
copy of Magna Carta now numbered Cotton Charter XIII. 31a;
Dering's covering letter with this was written from Dover Castle
(of which Dering was lieutenant) on 10 May 1630.[64]

If however Cotton benefited by the generosity of friends, he was
himself most generous in the help he gave either by way of loans
or gifts. For instance, in 1601 he presented to Sir Thomas Bodley
for his new library at Oxford eleven manuscripts in each of which
he had written an elaborate inscription in the form of a votive
altar bearing in capitals the words: 'Genio Loci Bodleo Restitu:
Plate 15   Bono Publico Robert: Cotton Connington: Hic LL.M.D.D.'[65]
In 1606 he gave, as we noticed above, a manuscript (now B.M.
Sloane 2423) to the French antiquary Nicolas Fabri de Peiresc.
And we find Augustine Baker writing from Cambrai on 3 June
1629 appealing to Cotton for English books, printed or manuscript, for the English Benedictine nunnery there, specifying
such works as those of Hampole, Hilton's *Scale of Perfection*, Saints'
Lives, and so on.[66] Sometimes he made exchanges of manuscripts,
as for example in 1616 with Patrick Young who thus obtained
three manuscripts that are now among the Royal MSS in the
British Museum (Royal MSS 15 B. vii, 15 C. vi, and 16 C.
xxiii);[67] another exchange was made in 1606 with Robert Bowyer, clerk of the parliaments, to whom he gave four volumes of
records in return for the Anglo-Saxon Orosius (presumably
Tiberius B. i), Bede's *De Ratione Temporum* (4to), 'A Book in
laten Poetry' (8vo), and 'Flores Historiarum in Parchment' (4to);[68]

Bowyer also borrowed largely—he had at one time or another Tiberius C. viii, Faustina A. iii, and Otho C. i. Sir Robert Cecil borrowed on 24 February 1617 a volume of state papers relating to foreign affairs in Elizabeth's reign (Galba D. vi)[69] and seems not to have returned it. Ben Jonson, a near neighbour of Cotton's in Westminster, is noted in 1621 as having had Ælfric's Saxon Grammar and the 'Vita Henrici quinti per Titum Livium and a great boundell of Originall things of Hen. 5 unbound'.[70] Roger Dodsworth borrowed the chronicle of Kirkstead and the register of St Mary's, York. The Anglo-Saxon Heptateuch (Claudius B. iv) was lent to William Lisle, the Cambridge Saxonist, a fact also attested by the manuscript notes in his hand still to be seen at various places in the manuscript.[71] To Lord Keeper Coventry Cotton lent 'My Book of Chancery bound with my Armes.' Several books were lent to scholars for the purpose of publication: thus Julius B. viii was used by John Selden as the basis of his edition of *Fleta* published eventually in 1647[72] and Titus A. ix for his edition of Eadmer's *Historia Novorum* in 1623. His manuscript of the account of the reception in Paris of Mary of England, the daughter of Henry VII and wife of Louis XII in 1514 (Vespasian B. ii) was apparently lent (with Titus A. xvii) to Inigo Jones some time before 1631 (according to Harl. 6018, f. 179b). Cotton also lent books to Sir Walter Raleigh during his captivity in the Tower (to which he was committed in 1605) and furnished Bacon with material for his important *Historie of the Raigne of King Henry the Seventh* (*S.T.C.* 1159), published in 1622, a fact acknowledged by Bacon in a marginal reference (p. 154) to Cotton—'a worthy Preserver and Treasurer of rare Antiquities: from whose Manuscripts I have had much light for the furnishing of this Work'; he gave Camden great help with the fifth edition of his *Britannia* (which Camden acknowledged) and in 1609 revised the proof-sheets of Speed's *The History of Great Britaine* (*S.T.C.* 23045), which was published in 1611, contributing to it a list of the revenues of the abbeys and full notes on Henry VIII's reign, besides lending Speed material. His help was also given to John Weever for his *Ancient Funerall Monuments* published in 1631 (*S.T.C.* 25223). And we find William Burton, the Leicestershire antiquary, writing from Lindley on 9 June 1627 begging for notes

Plate 13

for the second edition of his *Description of Leicestershire* and asking
for the loan particularly of Knighton's chronicle (Tiberius C. vii),
a copy of which, he says, Cotton had shown him at his last visit.[73]

It is not surprising that many manuscripts known to have belonged to Cotton are no longer in the library. Thus, Galba D. vi,
the volume lent to Sir Robert Cecil in 1617, appears not to have
been returned. One manuscript (Otho B. xiv), which contains the
registers of Sheen and Pipewell and a chronicle down to Henry
VIII, was missing for a considerable time and thereby fortunately
escaped the fire of 1731 in which so many Cotton manuscripts
were destroyed; it appeared at a bookseller's in 1787 and was
bought for the British Museum. Another manuscript, missing
when Dr Thomas Smith drew up his catalogue of the Cotton
manuscripts in 1696, was restored in 1854 from the collection of
Sir Thomas Phillipps at Middlehill in Worcestershire. But of the
manuscripts recorded in the 1621 catalogue and known to have
been missing from the library in the later seventeenth century the
most famous is undoubtedly that bearing the press-mark Claudius
C. vii, better known from its presence in the university library at
Utrecht as the 'Utrecht Psalter'. In the 1621 catalogue it was no.
207 (Harl. 6018, f. 98), in 1625 it was lent to Archbishop Ussher
and in 1631 to the earl of Arundel, and in 1718 it found its way to
the university of Utrecht as a gift from a Dutchman of the name
of de Ridder.

Finally, something should be said about the way in which
Cotton handled the manuscripts that came into his possession,
more particularly as he has been at times rather severely criticised
in this matter. It must be remembered that the greater number of
Cotton's manuscripts came to him not only unbound but in fact
in the form of quite unrelated tracts or even fragments of tracts,
amounting sometimes to but a few leaves. These Cotton arranged
generally by size, or if size and subject happened to harmonise by
subject. There was in fact nothing reprehensible in this unless we
insist that every single item, however small, should be separately
bound—a wasteful and expensive proceeding and one indeed not
normally followed even today. The only important thing to
remember in studying the manuscripts is that we must not attribute to a volume of miscellaneous material the provenance of one

of its items; the fact that, say, twenty leaves in a manuscript are known to come from Reading is no good ground for attributing the rest of the volume to the same place. For example, folios 4 to 22 of Vitellius C. viii, which contain verses, including some of Abelard's, and are of late twelfth-century date, came from the Cistercian house of Rievaulx, but in the same volume six leaves from St Paul's Epistles (ff. 85–90) in an eighth-century hand (which fifteenth-century tradition attributed to Bede himself) are from the cathedral priory of Durham, and yet another portion (ff. 91–130) came from Bury St Edmunds. To add to the complications of this particular volume the six leaves from St Paul's Epistles belong in fact to a manuscript the rest of which is now at Trinity College, Cambridge (B. 10. 5, James no. 216). The majority of the volumes in the collection under the press-marks they now bear are in fact 'make-up' volumes.[74] Sometimes a manuscript that is substantially a single volume may have had inserted in it a quite unrelated item: a good example is the manuscript acquired by Cotton in 1599 and known as St Augustine's Psalter (Vespasian A. i) from the belief that it was one of the manuscripts sent to St Augustine by Pope Gregory as recorded in Bede's *Historia Ecclesiastica* (i, 29); this manuscript had at one time at the beginning a charter of King Æthelbald as is shown by the list of contents by Richard James who was Cotton's librarian; this charter however was no longer in the manuscript when Smith catalogued it in 1696 and its presence under the press-mark Augustus II. 3 shows that Cotton must have removed it when he made up the Augustus portfolio, having only inserted the charter in the manuscript as a matter of temporary convenience, its edges being clipped to make it conform to the size of the psalter. This manuscript illustrates another practice of Cotton's; the first leaf is a single folio from an illuminated psalter of thirteenth-century date while on the verso of the last leaf is pasted a cutting from an illuminated border of late fifteenth-century date, which contains the arms of Charles, duke of Burgundy impaling those of his third wife, Margaret, sister of Edward IV. In another manuscript (Claudius B. v) there is pasted down on the verso of the last leaf, presumably by Cotton, a tiny miniature, which is of the very greatest artistic importance, being an example in the style of the

Ada school. As a last example, let me cite a small volume (Nero A. ii) made up of several manuscripts all early in date: one written in pre-Caroline minuscules of eighth- or ninth-century date perhaps from North Italy, one (a Calendar) of eleventh-century date from some house in Wessex, and the third a twelfth-century manuscript having material relating to St Cuthbert and others. To give this volume a decorative frontispiece Cotton has utilised a leaf from a late fifteenth-century Flemish illuminated manuscript, which has a border composed of a gilded background decorated with flowers, fruit, and butterflies, with in the central panel only a decorated initial, the remainder being devoid of contemporary writing; to the right of the initial Cotton has had his arms painted, and the blank space is used for this inscription, the U coming in very handily for the first letter of the first word: 'Uolumen hoc fragmentorum a Roberto Cotton collectum, continet diversos Tractatus quae proxima in Pagina sequuntur', that

Plate 16 is, 'This Volume of fragments collected by Robert Cotton has various treatises which are to be found on the next page.' There is not much doubt that it was Cotton's own work or done under his immediate direction, as we know that much of the binding was. Several manuscripts still contain in Cotton's handwriting

Plate 14b directions to the binders. One such example, the MS Vitellius A. xiii, contains a history of Abingdon which came from Abingdon itself and Nennius' *History of the Britons* from Rochester cathedral priory; at the beginning were four folios containing portraits of kings—probably French illumination executed in the thirteenth century. On the flyleaf is this direction by Cotton: 'Bind this very fair and strong/ cut it smoth on all sides . . . and Fillett it Fair with Flowers/ and press it well and smoth'; the phrase 'Fillett it Fair with Flowers' means decorate the binding with gilt floral designs. Of particular interest in this is the fact that Cotton has used in the word 'fillett' the proper technical term, and one may note generally about this direction that it would convey to the binder a precise and clear impression of what Cotton required.

Everything—the autograph loans list, inscriptions and memoranda in the manuscripts, correspondence—points to the fact that Cotton took a personal interest in the formation and the contents of his library and it would be pleasant to conclude this account of it on a happy note. But in fact Cotton's life ended in tragedy, a tragedy that arose out of his political activities. Cotton aligned himself with Sir John Eliot and the other members of the Parliamentarian party; so long as James I lived Cotton was comparatively secure for there seems to have been some close bond between them. With James's death however and the intensification of the Parliamentarians' activities Cotton could count only on the enmity of the court, an enmity which was stimulated at the beginning of the new reign by Buckingham and later by Laud. A hint of what might be expected was supplied by the incident on the day of Charles I's coronation. Cotton House had access to the Thames from its garden by Cotton Stairs. On the morning of the Coronation, 2 February 1626, Charles went by river from Whitehall Palace to Westminster; the earl marshal had given orders for carpets to be laid at Cotton Stairs where it was expected that the king would land and then pass through the garden to the palace, and there, in the words of Sir Symonds D'Ewes who accompanied Cotton, 'Sir Robert stood readie . . . to receave him with a booke of Athelstone's, being the fouer Evangelists in Lattine . . . upon which for divers hundred yeares together, the Kings of England had solemnlie taken their coronation oath'.[75] 'But', continues D'Ewes, 'the royall barge bawked those steppes soe fitlie accomodated, and being put forward, was run on ground at the Parliament Stairs, by which both his Majestie and the Lordes were faine to use the neighbour boates for ther landing'—the fact of the 'royal barge's dashing into the ground and sticking fast a little before it touched the causeway' did not escape notice. This clumsy and hasty avoidance of Cotton Stairs by the royal barge with its insult to Cotton was attributed by D'Ewes to instructions issued by Buckingham. Less than five years later the final blow fell, the occasion being the distribution of a pamphlet distasteful to the Court party, the original of which it was discovered had been in Cotton's library. As a result proceedings were begun in the Star Chamber against Cotton and his library was sealed, 'two or more of the guard being set to watch his house continually'. The effect of this on Cotton's health was catastrophic and he died on 6 May 1631 without recovering the use of his library.

The debt that later generations, and not only of scholars, owe to Sir Robert Cotton's efforts is enormous. If Archbishop Parker's remark to Cecil about the attempts to be made to preserve the manuscripts scattered far and wide by the dissolution of the monasteries—'if this opportunity be not taken in our time, it will not so well be done hereafter'—was true of 1568, it was true with even more force in Cotton's lifetime, for those years were indeed the very last during which this material could have been rescued. In the disturbances of the forties and fifties of the seventeenth century chances of destruction were increased tremendously and the new generation of collectors that was to appear about 1700 brought very different tastes and interests to the formation of their libraries.

NOTES TO CHAPTER IX

1. John Earle, *Microcosmographie*, 1628 (quoted from Edward Arber's *English Reprints*, London, 1868, pp. 28, 29).

2. *Diary of John Manningham . . . 1602–1603* (ed. J. Bruce, Camden Soc., 99, 1868), p. 103. The portrait was first reproduced as an engraving in *The Gentleman's Magazine*, n.s. vii (Jan. 1837), opp. p. 48, and appears as the frontispiece to C. L. Kingsford's edn. of *A Survey of London by John Stow*, i, Oxford, 1908. The portrait is not dissimilar from the famous bust of Stow in the church of St Andrew Undershaft in Leadenhall Street, which was executed by Nicholas Johnson in 1605 (see *Hist. Mon. Comm., London*, iv, *The City*, 1929, p. 7, and pl. 55).

3. *The Autobiography and Correspondence of Sir Simonds D'Ewes, Bart.*, ed. J. O. Halliwell, ii, London, 1845, p. 38.

4. Quoted by T. Corser in his introduction to James' 'Iter Lancastrense', *Remains Historical and Literary connected with the Palatine Counties of Lancaster and Chester*, (Chetham Soc., vii, 1845), p. civ.

5. On the 'Wunderkammer' see F. H. Taylor, *The Taste of Angels*, London, 1948, Book iii.

6. On the importance of the results of this tour see F. Haverfield, 'Cotton Julius F. vi. Notes on Reginald Bainbrigg of Appleby, on William Camden and on some Roman Inscriptions', *Trans. Cumberland & Westmorland Antiq. & Arch. Soc.*, n.s., xi (1911), pp. 343–78.

7. Quoted by Rose Macaulay, *Pleasure of Ruins*, London, 1953, p. 355; the portrait of Lithgow is reproduced at p. 456.

8. See my paper 'Sir Edward Dering: a Seventeenth-Century Antiquary and his "Saxon" Charters', *The Early Cultures of North-West Europe*, ed. C. Fox and B. Dickins, Cambridge, 1950, pp. 369–93.

9. John Twyne died 1581; and the book in which this is recorded, *De Rebus Albionicis Britannicis atque Anglicis*, was not published until 1590 (by his son Thomas). The date and subject matter of the conversation are discussed by Sir Thomas Kendrick, *British Antiquity*, London, 1950, p. 106.

10. Robin Flower, *Laurence Nowell and the Discovery of England in Tudor Times*, Brit. Acad., Gollancz Memorial Lecture, 1935.

11. On this subject generally see A. R. Wagner, *The Records and Collections of the College of Arms*, London, 1952, and the same author's *Heralds and Heraldry in the Middle Ages*, revised edn., Oxford, 1956.

11a. Since this chapter was written the official history of the Society of Antiquaries has been published (see Dr Joan Evans, *A History of the Society of Antiquaries*, 1956; see chaps. I and II on 16th- and 17th-century antiquarian activities).

12. *Catalogus Librorum Manuscriptorum Bibliothecae Cottonianae*, Oxford, 1696, pp. vii–ix. As to the printing of these two works of Spelman it may be noted that *The Original* was first published in 1684 by John Gillyflower but without 'The Occasion': 'The Occasion' was first published in 1695 by Edmund Gibson as a separate piece in his 'Life of Camden' (which he placed at the beginning of his English edition of Camden's *Britannia*), and was reprinted with the treatise itself (i.e. *The Original*), also by Gibson, in his *Reliquiae Spelmannianae*, 1698. Both were reprinted in Spelman's *The English Works*, 1723 (and 1727), part 2, pp. 69–104, and the treatise was printed again by Sir Joseph Ayloffe in his edition of Hearne's *Curious Discourses*, ii, Oxford, 1771, pp. 331–75, but Ayloffe only paraphrased parts of 'The Occasion' in his general introduction, ii, p. 331, and i, pp. xiii–xvi.

13. See *A Survey of London by John Stow*, ed. C. L. Kingsford, ii, Oxford, 1908, pp. 16–17; and see A. R. Wagner on the College of Arms, *The Times*, 18 July 1955.

14. Linda van Norden, 'Sir Henry Spelman on the Chronology of the Elizabethan College of Antiquaries', *Huntington Lib. Quart.*, xiii (1950), pp. 131–60.

15. It is preserved in the British Museum in Stowe MS 1045. It is now a composite volume; Tate's journal, ff. 6–89, had originally a separate existence. Folios 90–108 are from a much later volume (18th century), and when we revert to Tate's hand again at ff. 109–64 we are dealing with one of his commonplace books quite unrelated to the journal at the beginning of the MS.

16. The first seventeen names are numbered 1 to 17. Against ffletewode, Bouchier, Cliffe and Strangman is written 'mort'.

17. On Beale see B. Schofield, 'The Yelverton Manuscripts', *Brit. Mus. Quart.*, xix (1954), pp. 3–9.

18. Yet another list is that printed by Hearne in the introduction to his *Curious Discourses*. This is from a Bodleian Ashmole MS and is dated merely 41 Elizabeth (17 November 1598–16 November 1599): it is headed 'The names of all those which were somoned att this time', and contains the following names: Garter [Sir William Dethick], Doderidge, Tate, Clarentius [Camden], Cotton, Agard, Paton, Holland, Stowe, Thynn, Doc. Doyley, Carew, Bowyer, Hennage, Leigh, James Ley; at the end is this note 'and I left a summons with Mr Clarentius for Mr Erswicke. Not sommoned, Mr Spilman, and Mr Broughton, nor Mr Lake/ per me Ch. Lailand'.

19. From transcripts in his own collections (vol. LXXXVII, p. 5); in Ayloffe's edition of 1771 they are printed in vol. i, pp. xv, xvi.

20. The summonses to Ley are in Cotton MS Faustina E. v, ff. 203–8 (pencil foliation); that quoted is on f. 206.

21. This is Miss Van Norden's view; she refers to the *Encyclopedia Britannica*, 11th edn., 1911, xxi, p. 694, but this only partially supports her contention.

22. Preserved in Cotton MS Faustina E. v, ff. 53, 54 (pencil foliation).

23. Miss Van Norden has drawn up a table of the meetings and the subjects discussed: see pp. 147–9 of her paper.

24. 'Vita Cottoni', p. viii (summarised by Smith); the original is preserved in Cotton MS Faustina E. v, f. 57 (pencil foliation).

25. B.M. Cotton MS Julius C. iii, f. 30b; printed *Original Letters of Eminent Literary Men* (ed. H. Ellis, Camden Soc., xxiii, 1843), pp. 98–100.

26. Hearne, *Curious Discourses*, ed. Ayloffe, i, p. 76.

27. Hearne, op. cit., i, pp. 45, 46.

28. Hearne, op. cit., i, p. 47.

29. Hearne, op. cit., ii, pp. 160, 161.

30. Trinity Hall MS 1; see M. R. James, *Catalogue of the MSS. at Trinity Hall, Cambridge*, Cambridge, 1907, pp. 1–4. It was given (with a remarkable stipulation) to the College by Hare in 1603 with a number of other MSS.

31. Note that Thynne in his long and fully documented account of the history of the Inns of Court cites *inter alia* with reference to the New Temple 'The author of an annual written chronicle in French belonging to the Abbey of St. Mary's in York, which lived at that time' (that is, 4 Richard II, with reference to the destruction of records) (Hearne, i, p. 72). This is probably a reference to the late 14th-century MS of the Anonimalle Chronicle which belonged to St Mary's, York, and was formerly in the possession of Sir W. Ingilby at Ripley Castle (see N. R. Ker, *Medieval Libraries of Great Britain*, p. 119) (now in that of H. L. Bradfer-Lawrence); cf. also Galbraith's edition of the Anonimalle Chronicle.

32. Hearne, op. cit., i, p. 9.

33. The more complete copy is in B.M. Cotton MS Faustina E. v, ff. 89–90b (printed in Hearne, op. cit., ii, pp. 324–6); at the foot of this copy is written in a contemporary hand 'Mr. Cotton. Mr. Doderidge. Mr. Ley'. A fragment is preserved in B.M. Cotton MS Titus B. v, f. 210. See also on this petition *Archaeologia*, i (1770), pp. iii–v; Dr Thomas Smith in his 'Vita Cottoni', p. vii, and Pierre Des Maiseaux, Life of Richard Carew of Antonie (dated 1723), prefatory to Carew's *Survey of Cornwall*, 1811 edn., p. xvii. It is also referred to in the *Catalogue of Western MSS. in the Old Royal and King's Collections* (ed. G. F. Warner and J. P. Gilson), i, London, 1921, p. xvii.

34. B.M. Cotton MS Vitellius C. vii, f. 310.

35. See above, chapter viii.

36. *The Autobiography and Correspondence of Sir Simonds D'Ewes, Bart.*, ed. J. O. Halliwell, i, 1845, p. 80.

37. See *Vict. Count. Hist. Hunts.*, iii, pp. 148, 149.

38. *The Diary of John Evelyn*, with introduction and notes by Austin Dobson, Globe edn., 1908, p. 262. The Normandy journey is recorded under 18 March [1644]: 'I went with Sir J. Cotton, a Cambridgeshire knight, a journey into Normandy' (ibid., p. 38). Evelyn's opinion of Sir John was not high: under 2 July 1666 he writes: 'When they [Sir John Duncombe and Mr Thomas Chicheley] were gone, came to see me Sir John Cotton, heir to the famous antiquary, Sir Robert Cotton; a pretended great Grecian, but had by no means the parts, or genius of his grandfather.' (ibid., p. 245.)

39. See V. H. Galbraith, 'The Chronicle of Henry Knighton', *Fritz Saxl: A Volume of Memorial Essays*, ed. D. J. Gordon, London, 1957, pp. 136–45.

40. For a MS list of 17th-century date see B.M. Add. MS 5161, ff. 1–7, arranged alphabetically under the places. This belonged to Thomas Astle who

presented it to the B.M. in 1787. It has also notes of loans made from the Cotton Library in 1638 (on f. 9 recto and verso).

41. The presses in Cotton's library were named after the twelve Caesars, with Cleopatra and Faustina, whose busts surmounted them.

42. For their position and their relationship to Cotton House see William Capon's 'Plan of the Ancient Palace of Westminster', drawn between 1793 and 1823. This plan gives details of all the offices and houses, including Cotton's and Ben Jonson's; it was published by the Society of Antiquaries 23 April 1828 (B.M. Map Room 3615/1622). In Strype's edition of Stowe (*John Stowe's Survey of the Cities of London and Westminster 1598, Revised by Strype to 1633*, London, 1720, book vi, p. 55) the position of Cotton House is thus described: 'In the passage out of Westminster Hall into the old Palace Yard, a little beyond the stairs going up to St. Stephen's Chapel (now the Parliament House) on the left hand, is the house belonging to the ancient and noble family of the Cottons; wherein is kept a most inestimable library of MS. volumes, formed both at home and abroad.' Cotton House was sold to the Crown by Sir John Cotton for £4,500 in 1706/7. It is worth noting that Charles I was lodged in Cotton House for his trial in Westminster Hall.

43. *Cal State Pap., Dom., James I*, 1611–18, p. 305.

44. *Cal State Pap., Dom., James I*, 1623–25, p. 548.

45. *Cal. State Pap., Dom., James I*, 1623–25, p. 553.

46. Mr Frantz Fussner, of Reed College, Portland, Oregon, has very kindly supplied me with the following reference to material bearing on this in the P.R.O., viz.: SP Dom. 45/20, no. 73: 'Papers which SRC [Sir Robert Cotton] hath perused and transcribed at divers times out of the office of his majesties papers partly byfore I had the office and partly while he got license for from his majesty for the verifying of the story which Mr. Camden hath set forth, or under that pretext' (written by Thomas Wilson?). There follows a long list of papers, mostly having to do with Scotland, which Cotton had used. Also the papers for 1578–85: 'Of all these years he hath the originals' (fol. 134).

47. See B. M. Harley MS 1858, ff. 1–57, and Hatton Collection of Earl of Winchilsea and Nottingham, *Hist. Man. Comm.*, 1st Report, 1870, Appendix p. 32.

48. *Cal. State Pap., Dom., James I*, 1611–18, p. 295.

49. *Cal. State Pap., Dom., James I*, 1611–18, p. 127.

50. Published in Dublin in 1639 under the title *Britannicarum Ecclesiarum Antiquitates*.

51. When Ralph Starkey died in October 1628 D'Ewes immediately set to work to acquire his collections, though 'Mine own wants, and divers other men being about the acquiring of it likewise, made me fear I should miss it,' he writes. (Was Cotton one of the rivals?) D'Ewes was successful; see *Autobiography*, ed. Halliwell, i, pp. 391, 392.

52. *Autobiography*, ed. Halliwell, i, p. 84, s.a. 1615.

53. On these French collectors see C. I. and M. A. Elton, *The Great Book-Collectors*, London, 1893, *passim*.

54. On Peiresc's friendship with Cotton see C. T. Hagberg Wright, *Nicholas Fabri de Peiresc*, Roxburghe Club, 1926, p. 6, especially on the loan to Peiresc of the Cotton Genesis, two of the pictures of which Peiresc fortunately had copied.

55. Camden's will is printed in Ayloffe's edn. of Hearne's *Curious Discourses*, ii, 390–2: 'As for my books and papers, my will is that Sir Robert Cotton of Conington, knight and baronet, shall have the first view of them, that he may take out such as I borrowed of him; and I bequeath unto him all my imprinted books

and manuscripts, except such as concernes armes and heraldry, the which with all my auncient seales I bequeath unto my successor in the office of Clarencieux.' The will was proved 10 November 1623.

56. Cotton also owned at least one MS that had belonged to Leland, namely, a MS of Giraldus Cambrensis' *De Instructione Principum*, Julius B. xiii, ff. 48–173, in which marginal notes occur throughout in Leland's handwriting; this is almost certainly the Leland MS referred to in J. Bale, *Index Britanniae Scriptorum*, ed. R. Lane Poole and M. Bateson, Oxford, 1902, p. 425.

57. *John Aubrey's Brief Lives*, ed. A. Powell, London, 1949, p. 221 (from the portion relating to John and Arthur Dee); also the same work ed. O. L. Dick, London, 1949, p. 90.

58. i.e. *A True & Faithful Relation of what passed for many years between Dr. John Dee . . . & some Spirits*, published in 1659 (from the MS in Cotton's Library).

59. Quoted in S. W. Singer's edn. of Selden's *Table Talk*, London, n.d., p. 19.

60. Thus, 57 is described again under 59 (this is Caligula A. xii), 81 is entered again as 264 (this is Claudius B. iv, the Anglo-Saxon Heptateuch), 109 appears later as 388 (Galba A. iii), 110 as 389 (Galba A. ii), 114 as 330 (Galba A. xviii), 134 is redescribed as 338 (Vitellius D. iv), 143 as 367 (Julius A. vi), 209 as 270 (Vitellius F. xvi), 277 as 368 (Julius D. i), 306 as 386 (Otho D. vii), 310 as 395 (Vespasian E. iii), 314 as 377 (Vespasian A. xxii), 328 as 385 (Claudius D. vii), 351 as 393 (Julius B. xii), 372 as 411 (Nero A. v).

61. B.M. Cott. Julius C. iii, f. 189b: printed *Original Letters of Eminent Literary Men*, ed. H. Ellis, 1843, pp. 144, 145.

62. B.M. Cott. Julius C. iii, f. 199: printed *Original Letters*, ed. Ellis, pp. 134, 135.

63. B.M. Cott. Julius C. iii, f. 185b: printed *Original Letters*, ed. Ellis, pp. 138, 139.

64. For text of this letter and Dering's Anglo-Saxon charters see Wright, 'Sir Edward Dering: A Seventeenth-Century Antiquary and his "Saxon" charters', cited above.

65. *Summary Catalogue of Western MSS. in the Bodleian Library at Oxford*, i, ed. R. W. Hunt, Oxford, 1953, p. 77; the MSS are nos. 297-307 in the list at pp. 86, 87, i.e. *S.C.* nos. 2321, 2336, 2310, 2406, 1953, 1978, 1995, 3002, 2606, 2698, 3086. One MS with this votive altar and inscription is now in B.M. (Harley MS 988); it bears the date 1602 (see Plate 15). Another Harley MS (513) belonged to Cotton and has signature: 'Ro: Cotton Bruceus.'

66. B.M. Cott. Julius C. iii, f. 12.

67. See Harl. MS 6018, f. 159b and Add. MS 35213, ff. 34, 34b.

68. See Harl. MS 6018, f. 154b.

69. See Harl. MS 6018, f. 172.

70. See Harl. MS 6018, ff. 149b, 149.

71. Interesting letters from Lisle to Cotton are in Julius C. iii, ff. 238, 239.

72. This MS was also lent to Sir Symonds D'Ewes who made a copy of it (see *Autobiography*, i, pp. 294, 295, 299, 301, etc.): D'Ewes was lent other MSS by Cotton (op. cit., i, pp. 272, 373, 374). These loans were in 1625, 1626, and 1628.

73. See B.M. Cott. Julius C. iii, f. 51.

74. A good example is Cotton MS Tiberius B. v, the make-up of which is discussed by Dr M. R. James in his *Marvels of the East* (Roxburghe Club, 1929), pp. 2–6.

75. Sir Symonds D'Ewes in his letter to Sir Martin Stuteville, 4 Feb. 1626, *Autobiography*, ii, pp. 173–4, and supplemented by the passage in his autobiography, op. cit., i pp. 292–3.

11. MS of Pseudo-Dionysius annotated by Robert Grosseteste (see page 126)

12. Leland's list of MSS in Lincolnshire monastic houses (*see page* 162)

A Book of the Order in Counsell and divers other things &c. was in shortye in 4º — Sr Rich St Georg

A rolle of the Erle of Gloucester armes wth from out a list of this that was wthin whom in St Georg a knight was — Sr Richard Scud St Georg

A Book of the Statute of the knights of the Garter and of ther fees and the Creation of divers noblemen in H8 his tyme all in vellom being in black it was wrytty book after Disback — 4º Sr Rich St Georg

A book of divers matters Concernyng of Armes as the Solemnitie betwen H8 and of the french king Chr Instruction to Richmont Herald sent to the lady Margarett wth Badges it was wall wrap a bar Richmons herald Book it fell in a parchment Cover — Sr Rich Scud St Georg Herry

Gregory martins book of the proty and charitie of Rome a full discryption of that place in foll — Lord Will Howard

Cronica reram Anglia ad Ed 2 a monasticc mona tery &c Lt knorcast in foll bound in Black it was one of Mr Henry Sauell Booke — L note Howard

An old psalter limmed that was Eliz the Duke of Norfolks daughter old bond in foll — L wittia Howard

A Book of the Saxon Lawes in latin wth the lettr of Hows to pep passali and the Convention of Amy St Jan wth How this in the end it was recev Dr Flemyng that and lent by So mr Depate and from him to father Doderidge at large in a parchment cover — Mr father Doderidge

Gemma in Greek all in picturs most auncient lent So Menebore in pency betwen Ducus intit same bond in red parchs Lettr wth my armes in — Mr Read Grenham for the latin wnf

A prayer book bound in grene velluet wth 22 picturs fowle limmed in 8 Sl clspet — [blank]

A Book of Records gathered concernyng the Sinkinge ports especially yarmouths and Sandwich in ed lim in foll — Mr Borow the my Cosen

parlament Book of Rich 2 the 4 Hen the 5 bond in vellom and lent to Mr Attorney — Mr Berough

A great book of Abridgment of parlaments from 18 Ed prim to 30 Eliz bound in red lether and fronps — Sr Edward Cook

Articles against Cardinall wolsy so exhiton in vellom and Signed wth St the mors hand the Duk of norfolks and the rest of the lords and Judges a thin brokes — Sr Ed Cook

Collections out of the pip rolls of Hen the 2 in a vinam hand vnhll 20 anno of his raign vnlimd — Sr Edward Cooke

Gervasius Tilberiensis de otiosment Seery that Mr Selden falls Grenill bound of in Agar bound olde in 8 — Mr Selden

Knightons Historia Leicestriensis bound wth my armes foll — Mr Selden

Ingulphus and petors Bleccensis Historia Crouland senses bound with my armes foll — Mr Selden

vita Henri quinti per pilum limd and a great bondsall of Orignall things of then co vnlimd — Beniamin Jonson

Croniceu monastery St Angustini Cantuarii cum rogesteu Contarum otc bound with my armes in — Mr Bradshaw

Henricus Huntingdon Historia et liber lamfei in quo letera Baro wthwch papa centra Epu wintoy in 4 — Mr Selden

Cronica Anglie a monachio Cestrie et vita Edw ard 2 in qla legislatures Stuauers nittuntur ad ed 2 bond no us Ordinatiens bond wth my armi foll — Mr Selden

Book of the Steward Marshall and Constable bond wth my Arm foll — Mr Borough my Cosen

13. Cotton's loans-list (*see page* 198)

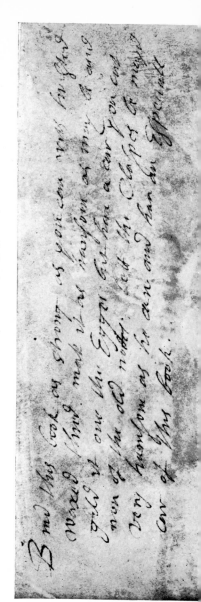

14a. Cotton's signature (*see page* 200)

Kinoatus salomon fuit. edida. id ÷ dilect.
ecclesiastes. i. contionator. i. contionum con
gregator. salomon. i. pacificus. q sedm hunc nu
meru tria composuit uolumina singula inse con
tinentia qq; terna uocabula. Primu scilicet para
bolas grece. puerbia latine. Masloth ebraice. inq
ipse ÷ ethicus. Secdo ecclasten grece. contionatore
latine. Celeth ebraice. inq ipse ÷ phisicus. Tertio.
cantica canticor sermone greco. romano. laudem
laudu. ebraico. seraserim. inq ipse e. theologicus.
In puerbis paruulu docens. & quasi de officiis p
sentib; erudiens. In ecclaste. mature etatis uiru
instituens ne qcq in mundi reb; putet ee ppetuu.
s; caduca & breuia oia que cernim. Ad extremu
ia consumatu uiru. & calcato scto pparatu in cantico can
ticor sponsi iungit amplexib qa n pri relinqui uicia
& pompis huis scli renunciem. n possum dicere osculet
me osculo oris sui. Hoc ordine & philosophi sectatores
suos erudiunt. ut pmu ethica doceant deinde phisica
& que inhis pfecisse pspexerint. ad theologica usq;
pducant. Hoc notandu ÷ qd p tres libros auctoris diui
sus÷ titulus. In puerbis annotat puerbia salomonis

15. Cotton's presentation inscription to Bodley (*see page* 202)

olumen hoc fragmento-
rum à Roberto Cotton
collectum, continet di-
versos Tractatus quæ
proxima in Pagina
sequuntur.

16. Decorative title-page made up by Cotton (*see page* 206)

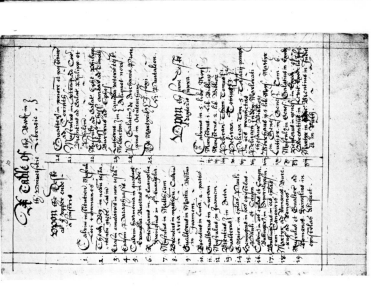

(a) Written in 1582 (see page 214)

(b) Written by Jonathan Pindar, 1650 (see page 224)

17. University Library, Cambridge, shelf-lists

18. Library of St John's College, Cambridge, 1623–8 (*see page 217*)

19. 'Pragi' Binding (*see page* 222)

20. South Room of the old University Library, Cambridge *(see page 223)*

21. Library of University College, Oxford, 1668–70 (*see page* 245)

22. Library of Jesus College, Oxford (*see page* 246)

X

The Libraries of Cambridge, 1570–1700

J. C. T. OATES

IN 1424 the University Library at Cambridge possessed 122 books; fifty years later the number had risen to 330, and by 1530 to between 500 and 600. In 1574 it possessed no more than 175 volumes, of which about 120 were manuscripts. Thus, at Cambridge, as elsewhere, the university's pre-Reformation collection had largely disappeared; the 'Common Library', which had been completed with its fittings about 1470, had been abandoned to the study of theology; and the surviving books had been moved into the 'Little Library', or rare-book room, which Archbishop Rotherham had built and endowed with books between 1470 and 1500.

The man who first resolved to restore the library to usefulness was Andrew Perne, master of Peterhouse, himself a great preserver of books during the dangerous years of the Reformation, for he is believed to have taken into his own safe keeping a number of the university's manuscripts, restoring them later when the danger had passed.[1] He naturally turned first for support to an even greater preserver of books, Matthew Parker, archbishop of Canterbury; and Parker himself set about arousing the enthusiasms of other lovers of learning. 'And it was', says Strype, 'by the Archbishop's means and incitement, that Bacon, Lord Keeper of the Great Seal, gave many books more to the library. And by the same Archbishop's motion, Sir William Cecil, Chancellor of the same University, gave to it many more, both Latin and Greek, concerning the canon and civil law, and physic. And so also did the Bishops of Winton and Durham.'[2] Parker himself gave 100 volumes, of which twenty-five were manuscripts. These were

P

from his own shelves; nearly all the remaining seventy-five were probably bought specially for the occasion—the latest works of scholarship from the great printing-houses at Basle, Geneva, Antwerp, and Frankfurt. They were uniformly bound with the initials MC upon their covers, and were placed in a special desk at the north end of the room, farthest from the door, 'to the great delectation', in Perne's words, 'of the eye of every man that shall enter into the said library'.[3]

Parker's books were for the most part theology and biblical commentary. Bacon's books, in each of which was placed an armorial gift-plate, believed to be the earliest English specimen of its kind,[4] included astronomy, geography, music and mathematics. The fifty books given by Robert Horne, bishop of Winchester, were principally Fathers of the Church; and the twenty books given by James Pilkington, bishop of Durham, were principally history. The library was rearranged to accommodate these great accessions and its furniture was mended or modified. A 'frame for my Lorde of Canterburies armes' was constructed at a total cost of 12d., and chains, rings, wire, and nails were bought for the proper securing of the books. John Sheres was paid 2s. for 'setting one 72 chaynes', and a certain Hillary, whom we find earning a shilling a year for sweeping the floor, augmented his income by no less than 4s. 2d.—8d. for helping John Sheres, and 3s. 6d. for 'setting on my lorde kepers armes and wryting the names of the bookes and figures'.[5] He wrote them very well, if we may assume, as we surely may, that they are the titles and numbers which appear on the fore-edges of those volumes which still survive in their original state; and, since we still possess the detailed catalogue

Plate 17a

of the library which was drawn up in 1582,[6] their identification is certain and their arrangement can to some extent be reconstructed. On the reader's left-hand as he entered the library was a cupboard in which lay Parker's manuscripts and a few others; and on the cupboard were a few of the manuscripts which the library had owned since before 1574. The rest of the pre-1574 library was disposed in six classes or stalls on either side of the room, each class standing in the normal way at right-angles to the wall between each pair of windows. Then came seven classes containing the printed books given by Parker's fellow-benefactors, and, finally at the north end, Parker's own books. The catalogue speaks impartially of classes and stalls and uses both English and Latin, but each stall was in two divisions and since in one instance one of these divisions is described as 'the further side' we may reasonably conclude that each stall was double-sided; and this is confirmed by the numbering of the books, for there are two sequences of numbers in each stall, one roman and one arabic, with an average of fifteen volumes in each sequence. All the printed books save some of Parker's were chained, some sequences at the tops of the books, some at the bottoms; but those books which were chained at the bottom stood, as the numbers on their fore-edges show, upside-down, and so were virtually chained at the top. The latter method is clearly an improvement, since it reduces the length (and hence the weight) of the chain; and since it is an improvement it is perhaps odd that the opportunity was not taken to install it throughout the room. Possibly this would have entailed modifications to the existing furniture greater than the university was prepared to undertake. At any rate the library (which at this stage contained 451 books) was fairly crowded, and since these benefactions quickly attracted others—including in 1581 the fifth-century manuscript of the Gospels and Acts given by Theodore Beza—it was soon found necessary to restore to use as a library the room which had been evacuated in 1547.

Similar revivals took place in the college libraries during the last thirty years of the century, though three of them—Gonville and Caius, Peterhouse, and Pembroke—had fortunately preserved a large portion of their pre-Reformation collections. Robert Horne gave printed books and manuscripts to St John's, while to Peterhouse passed a large part of the library of Andrew Perne at his death in 1589. Edmund Grindal, archbishop of Canterbury, left books to Pembroke College (and to Queen's College, Oxford) in 1583, and William Smart of Ipswich gave the same college many manuscripts from Bury St Edmunds in 1599; and Trinity acquired nearly 300 manuscripts from the scriptoria of Canterbury, conveyed to the college by a Trinity dean of Canterbury, Thomas Nevile, and a Trinity archbishop, John Whitgift. At King's College the provost, Roger Goade, fitted up the chantries in the south side of the chapel with cases, and turning his Protestantism to good account sold the papistical vestments of the chapel and bought books with the proceeds. Most important of all, Matthew Parker bequeathed the bulk of his library to his college of Corpus Christi, ordaining that the library was to be inspected annually on 6 August by the masters of Gonville and Caius and Trinity Hall. They were empowered to fine the college 4d. for every leaf of a manuscript which was found to be missing, and 2s. for every missing quire; and if it should be found that six folio manuscripts, or eight in quarto, or twelve of smaller format had been lost, then the whole collection, along with the plate which Parker had also bequeathed to his college, was, with the consent of the vice-chancellor and one senior doctor, to be surrendered to Gonville, and if Gonville should prove similarly negligent, to Trinity Hall, and thence, in the last resort, back to Corpus—a bibliothecal merry-go-round which it has not yet been found necessary to put into motion. Of equal importance, though for different reasons, is the library of Trinity Hall, built and furnished about 1600. This has survived with very little alteration and represents, in Canon Streeter's words, 'the climax in the evolution of the Lectern-system in Cambridge'.[7] Hitherto library furniture in the colleges had progressed as far as double-sided lecterns with two sloping desks on each side. At Trinity Hall a flat shelf, on which the books stood upright, took the place of the lower desk, and by this arrangement, says Streeter, 'the number of books which the lower storey of the lectern could accommodate was multiplied by four'. Between each pair of lecterns at Trinity Hall stand back-to-back seats, and all the seats and lecterns on either side of the library are, by a device common in libraries arranged on this system, set at both ends into heavy beams running the whole length of the room. Thus all the furniture on either side is a single structure fixed firmly to the floor. The 'stall-system', which follows the lectern-system in library evolution, is in effect an open cupboard with a sloping desk on which the reader placed his book while he sat on a fixed bench. This system is no longer represented at Cambridge. It appears to have been used, and then abnormally without chains, in one college only—Clare College—from 1627 to 1687, when the stalls were modified and rearranged around the walls of a new library-room in the style of a 'gentleman's library'.[8]

Thus the year 1627 appears to mark the first general unchaining of books at Cambridge (though we have seen that some of Parker's books in the University Library were without chains as early as 1574); and Clare's example was soon followed in the great library completed at St John's College in the following year. Thereafter the books in the other college libraries were progressively un-chained, save only at King's, which followed the Oxford example and kept its chains until late in the eighteenth century, probably from motives of security rather than mere conservatism, since the chantries which housed the library must have been difficult to supervise.

The library at St John's[9] was built between 1623 and 1628 at the cost of an anonymous benefactor, John Williams, bishop of Lincoln, though his desire for anonymity was not ultimately proof against the temptation to place on the exterior wall of his library his initials in letters some three feet high. It is fitted with bookcases *Plate* 18 of unusual beauty in a style which some call Jacobean Gothic and others Jacobean Renaissance. They stand, as usual, at right-angles to the walls between the windows, but they are no longer, as in the older examples, detached from the walls, their cornices being continuous with the panelwork which lines the room. Dwarf cases with lectern-tops stand between each pair of cases, taking the place of the old back-to-back benches; and since the readers no longer had anything to sit upon they were provided instead with elegant portable stools. The first duty of this noble library was to accommodate the 200 manuscripts and 2,000 printed books prom-ised to it some years earlier by Henry Wriothesley, earl of Southampton and patron of Shakespeare. His collection included many books from the library of William Crashaw, father of the poet Richard.

We left the University Library in 1574 fairly provided with books and prospering, and though the library's history from 1420 to 1840 is a story of brief enthusiasms alternating with long periods of inactivity, for a time all continued to go well. In 1585 there were delivered to the library 'certayne written bookes from peter-howse gyven by mr dr Perne';[10] and when Perne died four years later his bequests included forty shillings yearly 'to the augmenta-tion of a stipend of a learned scholar that shall be appointed for the

safe keeping . . . of the University Library'.[11] Two years after
Perne's death died Thomas Lorkin, Regius professor of Physic
bequeathing to the university his books of medicine, about 140 in
number, to be kept in the library in a great cupboard, and in 159
John, Lord Lumley, fulfilled a promise made ten years earlier by
presenting such duplicates from his collection as the University
Library required. They numbered eighty-seven volumes and included several which had once belonged to Thomas Cranmer.[1]

These busy years were followed by a quarter-century of inactivity punctuated only by disappointed hopes. A plan to build a
new library in imitation of the one at Oxford was canvassed and
received much support, only to be abandoned on the assassination
in 1628 of its prime mover the duke of Buckingham, chancellor
of the university; and when it was revived in 1640 it was again
frustrated, this time by the outbreak of the Civil War. There were
no great accessions of note, and the only donations of consequence
were Bacon's *De Augmentis Scientiarum* and *Instauratio Magna*, presented by their author, and a copy of his own *Works* presented by
James I in 1620. The king also gave a copy to Oxford, both pre-
sentations being made by a deputation headed by the royal
librarian Patrick Young. At Oxford, according to Young's account,[13] the book was handed over at a Convocation in St Mary's
and then carried in solemn procession by the vice-chancellor and
twenty-four doctors to the Bodleian, where Bodley's librarian
John Rous, 'made a verie prettie speech and placed it *in archivis* . . .
with a greate deale of respect'. 'In this', Young says, 'they far surpassed Cambridge.' Nevertheless Cambridge men may beg leave
to doubt whether Rous's speech was any prettier than the one
made on their behalf by George Herbert, in which he asserted that
'now that we have been sprinkled with the royal ink . . . we shall
cut our way through all disputations and defeat all comers.
Would some Jesuit might be given to us that by rubbing him
against your book we might straightway grind him to powder.'[1]
No Jesuit having offered himself for this curious experience, the
book was presently laid up in a special desk trimmed with grass-
green velvet and gold fringe, at a total cost of £23 19s. 10d.[15]

After these frivolities the library entered upon a period of solid
achievement with the appointment as librarian in 1629 of Abraham

Whelock, professor of Arabic and reader in Anglo-Saxon—
the first occasion on which the post was considered one proper to
be filled by a scholar of eminent reputation. Of him it was said
that he was fit to be 'the Interpreter generall not only for the
Queen of Sheba to Solomon, or of ye wise Men to Herod, but to
mankind, and to serve instead of the Universal Character'.[16] He
held office until his death in 1653, when he was worthily succeeded by William Moore, a kindly and conscientious man, whose
merits were extolled by his successor, Thomas Smith, B.D., of
Christ's College, in a sermon preached at his funeral.

Tis well known [said Smith] that he was through his whole life a diligent collectour & transcriber of the choicest Manuscripts which he
could possibly purchase by love or money; All these he gave to Caius
Colledge. While he was in the University library, how diligent he was
for the publick good from first to last, what incredible pains he took
there for you, and for how trifling a recompense ye all sufficiently
know . . . he cannot want a monument or a remembrance while *Caius*
Colledge stands, while we have an *University* or publick-*Library*, of
which we never *before* had such a *custos*; and I believe *hereafter* never
shall.[17]

Smith also was a man of some calibre—a lively controversialist
(Venn calls him 'learned and pugnacious')[18] and a collaborator in
Walton's polyglot bible. He held office for two years only (1659–
61), and saw the end of a period when the library was better con-
ducted than at any time before the régimes of Mayor and Bradshaw.

Whelock's librarianship saw the beginnings of the library's collection of orientalia, when the dowager duchess of Buckingham
presented to the university in 1632 the manuscripts which had belonged to the Dutch scholar Erpenius. They had been acquired by
her husband the duke, in order that he might present them to the
university, in 1625 when the duties of public life took him to
Holland in an unsuccessful attempt to pawn the crown jewels. The
story is told by Sir Henry Wotton in his *Short View of the Life and
Death of George Villers*.[19]

Here, it were iniurious [he writes] to overslip a Noble act in the Duke
during this imployment . . . there was a Collection of certain rare
Manuscripts, exquisitly written in Arabique and sought in the most

remote parts by the diligence of *Erpinius*, the most Excellent Linguist, these had beene left to the Widdow of the said *Erpinius*, and were upon saile to the Iesuits at *Antwerpe*; Licourish Chapmen of such Ware. Whereof the Duke getting knowledge . . . Interverted the bargaine, and gave the poore Widdow for them five hundred pounds, a summe above their weight in silver, and a mixed act both of bounty and charity, the more laudable being much out of his naturall Element.

Buckingham had hoped to secure Erpenius's printed books as well, as also the matrices for his oriental types, but these had already been sold, the latter to the printer Elzevir. The presentation of the manuscripts had not been made when Buckingham was assassinated in 1628; and the university allowed a decent interval of four years to elapse before it ventured to send the duchess a letter of condolence together with a petition that she fulfil her husband's known intention. This she did with very little delay, and the books were placed in a case made specially for their reception and bearing a commemorative inscription written on vellum.[20]

The most important occasion however of Whelock's librarianship was the presentation to the university by parliament of the collection of Hebrew books known as the Isaac Pragi collection.[21] These had been imported from Italy by George Thomason, bookseller and collector of the 'Thomason Civil War Tracts', and were offered for sale in a catalogue issued in 1647. Its title-page bears Thomason's device (a crowned rose) and the imprint of John Legate, afterwards university printer at Cambridge. On the verso is an address to the reader, ending with the familiar formulae—albeit in Latin—that no such opportunity is likely to occur again and that intending purchasers are advised to read the catalogue right through as the items have been listed in no particular order. The Pragi books occupy ten pages at the end of the catalogue, and in front of this section Thomason chose to place a reproduction in type of the title-page of one of the books contained in it—the polyglot Bible published in Paris in 1645; and in this reproduction Legate chose to insert, incongruously but prophetically, the device of the Cambridge University Press.

The plan for the purchase of this collection by the state and its presentation to Cambridge originated with John Selden, member for Oxford University in the Long Parliament, but nonetheless a loyal friend of Cambridge, where he had been offered the master-ship of Trinity Hall. The Journal of the House of Commons prints a resolution of 24 March 1647/8 'that the sum of two thousand pounds be forthwith advanced and bestowed upon the University of Cambridge, to be employed towards the Building and Finishing of the Publick Library there', the money to be paid out of the estates and lands of deans and chapters. It was also ordered on the same day 'that the sum of Five hundred Pounds be charged upon, and forthwith paid out of, the Receipts at Goldsmiths Hall, unto Mr George Thomason, Stationer, for buying . . . a Library, or Collection of Books, in the Eastern Languages . . . late brought out of Italy . . . and that the said Library . . . be bestowed upon the Publick Library in the University of Cambridge'. The resolution for the grant of £2,000 appears to have been dropped, for it was never presented to the Lords; the Pragi proposal however passed both Houses.

This transaction provoked the author of *Mercurius Pragmaticus* to some heavy and allusive satire in his issue of 28 March–4 April 1648. In it he painted a gloomy picture of the future if this anti-clerical parliament continued to interest itself in higher education.

Alas poore *Cambridge*! [he writes] the *jeere* of *Ignoramus*[22] returnes home upon thy selfe now, since thou art damned to *Presbytery* and *six penny Pamphlets* . . . It must needs bee a rare *Library*, when it shall be said, that *Will Pryn* was brought out of *Captivity* to be chained among the *learned*, and that the Commentaries of *Austin*, and the Homilies of *Chrisostome*, were jostled out of the *Range*, to make roome for the more glorious *Revelations* of threepenny *Non-sence* in *Fast-Sermons* . . . Yet I'le assure you the *Rabbins* of *Reformation* pretend high towards *Learning*, and therefore have importuned the *Houses* to make a purchase of certain *Bookes* written in *Syriack*, to bee beestowed likewise on the aforesaid *Library*; where, if the Members can spare money, you may chance to find *Rabbi Isaac*, and *Rabbi Moyses*, led in *couples* with Rabbi *Marshall*, and Rabbi *Calamy*, and all the *Rabble* of *Smec* . . .[23]

As for the recently intruded puritan heads of houses at Cambridge,

Is it not sad then such *mushromes* as these should spring up in an *University*, when the more noble *Plants* are rooted up, by the speciall care of my good Lord of *Manchester*? for, there are such *Animals* in Authority at *Cambridge*, as no *Naturalist* ever owned in *Story*, and therefore at the best are *Monsters*; Creatures that are but half *Codled* in *Scholarship*.

The business of completing the transaction was entrusted to Selden and John Lightfoot, the Cambridge biblical critic who shortly afterwards became master of St Catharine's. The collection contains over 400 separate works bound in a little over 150 volumes. They are in uniform, though not identical, bindings of reddish calf ornamented in gold, and, in some instances, stamped with Pragi's name in Hebrew characters.[24] Most of the books are sixteenth- or seventeenth-century editions, though there are a few incunabula.

Plate 19

These accessions and numerous smaller donations had by 1649 raised the number of volumes in the library to about 1,000 printed books and 400 manuscripts. In that year its holdings were suddenly multiplied eightfold by the temporary addition of the Lambeth Library.

This complicated episode had its beginning in the will of Richard Bancroft, archbishop of Canterbury, who died in November 1610.[25] He bequeathed

all the Bookes in my Studdy over the Cloysters unto my Successor and to the Archbushoppes of Canterbury successively for ever yf he my nexte Successor will yealde to such assuraunces as shalbe devised by such learned counsell as my Supervisor and Executor shall make choyce of . . . otherwise I bequeath them all unto his Maties Colledge to be erected at Chelsey if it be erected within theis six yeares or otherwise I give and bequeath them all to the Publicke Library of the Universitie of Cambridge.[26]

And so the Lambeth Library passed from Bancroft to Abbot, and from Abbot to Laud, until in 1640–41 Laud was impeached and committed to the Tower and his Palace and possessions appropriated by the state.

The university showed no great alacrity in taking advantage of the opportunity thus afforded it. Bishops had been abolished, the projected college of controversial divinity at Chelsea had not materialised, and the university, it was clear, had a reasonable title by default. Nevertheless it was not moved to action until after the Commons in September 1644 had made an ordinance granting the Lambeth books to Sion College at the petition of its president and fellows. No steps appear to have been taken to put this ordinance into effect, and the university's petition, presented in February 1646, was eventually granted after twelvemonths' to-ing and fro-ing between Lords and Commons. Those books which had been added to the library since Bancroft's death were also given to the university,[27] which had received John Selden's vigorous support in urging its claim. Selden received the thanks of the vice-chancellor, Thomas Hill, and senate of the university in official letters written to him on 2 April and 12 April 1647;[28] and Hill's own zeal in the matter is acknowledged in the sermon preached at his funeral in 1654 by Anthony Tuckney.[29] It was also, says Tuckney, at Hill's instance that a 'noble Knight' gave money for the provision of new cases worthy to hold this embarrassingly large accession. This anonymous benefactor afterwards proved to be Sir John Wollaston, an ardent Roundhead, alderman of the city of London, and one of the commissioners for the sale of royal and episcopal estates;[30] and it is indeed fortunate that his benefaction was translated into timber, for the scholarships which he founded at Emmanuel College came to nothing when the estates from which they were to be derived reverted at the Restoration to the bishop of London.

The Lambeth Library, which numbered about 11,000 books, arrived towards the end of 1649. The manuscripts and rare books were placed in the 'Little Library', which was so rearranged that the Lambeth books stood on one side of the room and the Cambridge ones on the other. Wollaston's cases were erected in the South Room, and here the Lambeth and the Cambridge books *Plate 20* were sorted in together on the shelves. In both rooms the cases were distinguished by letters, A, B, C, etc., those in the Little Library being further distinguished by a sign like a musical sharp in front of the letter. The shelves in each case were assigned a Greek letter, and each book had its own number on the shelf, so that a complete class-mark ran, for example, B. α. 12 or T. γ. 8. This was the first time a notation of this sort was used in the University Library. The class-mark of each book was written inside its front cover—the Lambeth books today still retain this memento of their Cambridge excursion—and an alphabetical author-catalogue and a shelf-list were also drawn up, all by an

Plate 17b

under library-keeper of rare industry, in a hand which is a model of neat, unhurried, unvaried legibility. His name was Jonathan Pindar, one of several persons inextricably so named, two of whom were university printers.[31]

Enthusiasm for the library ran high at this stage in its career, and John Arrowsmith, Regius professor of Divinity, declared in a public utterance that it rivalled the Vatican Library and the Bodleian,[32] though it is true that John Evelyn found 'the Schooles . . . very despicable, & publique Librarie but meane though somewhat improved'.[33] Evelyn, we must remember, was an Oxford man; and we may perhaps rely more confidently on a man of wider loyalties, Thomas Fuller, who, though Cambridge was his Alma Mater, constantly referred to Oxford as his Aunt.

At this day [he wrote] the *Library* (or *Libraries* shall I say?) of three successive *Archbishops*, *Painfull Parker*, *Pious Grindall*, *Politick Bancroft* . . . are bestowed upon *Cambridge*, and are beautifully *shelved* . . . so that our *Library* will now move the *Beam*, though it cannot *weigh it down*, to *even* the *scale* with *Oxford*. As for the *Schools* themselves, though our *Aunt* boasteth, that it is not worthy to *carry the books after Oxford Library* for the *statefulness* of the *Edifice*; yet sure the *difference* is more in the *Case* than in the *Jewells* therein contained.[34]

The bookcases which Wollaston provided are typical and handsome examples of the fittings which were installed in several Cambridge colleges during the latter half of the seventeenth century.[35] The type first made its appearance at Peterhouse in 1645. By this time, it will be remembered, chaining was being abandoned at Cambridge, and with the abandonment of chaining the need for fixed benches between the cases also disappeared. Thus at St John's in 1628 stools had been provided for the readers to sit upon. At Peterhouse the reader's seat was transferred to the case itself, the base of which was transformed into a kind of box-seat 2 feet high and 12 inches broad, on which the reader sat with his back to the shelves. Wollaston's cases resemble those at Peterhouse very closely, save that the box-seat has sunk to a mere pedestal or plinth 8 inches high and 7 inches wide; and this became the typical Cambridge model, adopted at Jesus College between 1663 and 1679, Gonville and Caius in 1675, Emmanuel in 1679, Pembroke in 1690, and at an unknown date at Christ's. It was also adapted between 1659 and 1680 to the requirements of a chained library at King's, where the small area of the chantries which housed the library posed a special problem and found an ingenious solution. A tall double-sided press on the Cambridge model, but incorporating the sloping desks necessary in a chained library, stood in the middle of the room, with half-presses of the same kind facing it against the walls; and on either side of the whole press, mid-way between it and the half-press opposite, stood a dwarf bookcase, as at St John's, with its base extended into a box-seat, as at Peterhouse. These cases were made with money bequeathed by Nicholas Hobart and Thomas Crouch, whose names, arms and initials are incorporated in their decoration. Hobart was a benefactor of the University Library also, giving it in 1655 oriental manuscripts which he had acquired while he was secretary to the British ambassador at Constantinople.

The year in which the Lambeth books arrived at Cambridge was also the year of the death of Richard Holdsworth, master of Emmanuel; and Holdsworth's will rivalled Bancroft's in complexity. He bequeathed his library

upon the University of Cambridge Provided that it please God within five years to make a settlement of the Church, and that they do restore the Lambeth library . . . to the See of Canterbury: which if it shall not be done I would then have it bestowed upon Emanuel College in Cambridge, provided that they erect a room, or case fit to retain it: for default whereof, and if it shall fall out there be no happy resettlement I would have it bestowed on the College of Dublin in Ireland.[36]

Neither Emmanuel nor the university had fulfilled their respective conditions—nor indeed had the Almighty—and when Archbishop Juxon asked for the return of the Lambeth books in May 1662 the university was in danger of losing one library without gaining the other, since Emmanuel was prepared to dispute with the university for the possession of Holdsworth's books. Juxon died with the difficulty unresolved, but a renewed claim by his successor Archbishop Sheldon was admitted and the Lambeth Library reverted to its original owners in February 1664. Ten months later the archbishop of York and the bishops of London and Ely, who had been appointed to arbitrate between Emmanuel and the university, pronounced in favour of the latter, with the provision that it pay the college £200 in compensation towards the building of a new library. The fellows of Emmanuel—who to this day feel somewhat cheated—preferred to build a new chapel and to convert the old one into a library instead, thus removing that 'great mark of singularity',[37] a chapel which ran north and south. The college also received a number of Holdsworth's duplicates and enjoyed during the next thirty years a succession of benefactions, culminating in Archbishop Sancroft's gift of over 6,000 volumes just before his death in 1693. As for the University Library, Jonathan Pindar, who had catalogued the 11,000 volumes of the Lambeth Library so admirably, appears not to have relished the prospect of cataloguing Holdsworth's 10,000 replacements. He disappears from the records late in 1664 and the task of sorting and shelving Holdsworth's books was performed by John Houlden, a Cambridge stationer and bookbinder.[38]

Three other events notable in the library's history occurred before the end of the century: the bequest in 1664 of some 4,000 volumes by Henry Lucas of St John's College, founder of the Lucasian professorship and member of parliament for the university; the bequest of 1,000 volumes in 1670 by John Hacket, bishop of Coventry, who also endowed Trinity College library with £50 a year; and the gift of £1,000 in 1666 by Tobias Rustat to be laid out in lands whose rentals were to be applied to the purchase of the 'best and most useful books'.[39] The enthusiasms of the middle years of the century were however by this time waning, and for the rest of our period the library was not well ordered. Isaac Dobson, who had succeeded Thomas Smith in 1661, made such heavy weather of the arrangement and cataloguing of Holdsworth's books that in December 1667 the university officially called upon him to finish the task by the following Candlemas—that is to say, in seven weeks. His resignation on 16 March 1668 need not, perhaps, surprise us, though he appears to have done his best meanwhile, for it was agreed on the same day that he be given £40 in four quarterly instalments, 'if he doeth live soe longe'; which indeed he contrived to do. Dobson's successor, Robert Peachey, began diligently enough, for after eleven months in office he was granted £10 above his stipend 'for the paines which he hath taken

in setting the bookes in order. And for the writeing of the Catalogues the University will take those into consideration when they
shall bee finished'. Six years later he was still hard at it, so much
so that he was granted special permission to defer his divinity
exercise. Yet all his efforts were finally in vain. By the beginning
of 1679 the confusion was such that a syndicate was appointed to
examine the library, recall books which were absent, and guard
against future losses. Five years later, in January 1684, so many
books were missing from the shelves that their return was ordered
by a grace of the university, and a few days later another syndicate
was appointed to take whatever steps they might think fit in this
sorry situation. Peachey, meanwhile, had resigned on 19 January,
putting his hand to the sad statement that he did 'most thankefully
and willingly recede from the place of publick library-keeper'.[40]
His successor, James Manfield, held office for two years only, and
it was left to John Laughton, librarian from 1686 to 1712, to
remedy the disorder which he had inherited. He may certainly be
said to have turned the library inside out, for it was during his
régime that the books were reversed on the shelf so that their
spines faced outward.[41]

The prime cause of the library's troubles during this period was
without doubt a general want of respect for the library throughout
the university, and hence the want of a continuous tradition of
pride in it and affection for it. Excellent rules for its management
were drawn up in 1581–3, 1659, and 1684; and we may hazard
that if the university had desired to respect its own rules it would
not have been necessary to draft them so often. The first set[42] of
'Orders' decreed that a three-fold inventory of the books was to
be kept, and that all manuscripts and 'all other bookes of Imagerie
with colors', all mathematical and astronomical instruments, and
all books of mathematics and history were to be locked up; the
librarian was bound by a surety of £200 to preserve safely all
books which were not locked up, to give an account of them once
a year, and to replace any missing or mutilated, 'or elles lose his
office and paye the triple valewe'; he was to attend in the library
throughout term, except on Sundays and holidays, from 8 to 10
a.m. and from 1 to 3 p.m.; he was to report to the vice-chancellor
within three days all necessary repairs to chains, clasps, or bosses,

and he was to close all books and put them in proper order before he left the building morning and afternoon; he was to hold office for three years; and his annual remuneration was to be £3 6s. 8d.[43] Only masters of arts, bachelors of law or physic, or persons of higher degree might use the library, 'so that at one tyme there be not above Ten in the sayde Librarie togither (Except they be strangers that come onlye to see and not to tarrie) and that none of them tarrie at one booke above an houre at one tyme if enye other shall desire to vse the sayde booke'; and no book or instrument was to be allowed out of the library but by special licence and grace of the university. The rules of 1659 introduce some changes.[44] There was to be an under library-keeper as well as a chief library-keeper, the latter was to be a Master of Arts at the least, and the respective duties of each were clearly defined; readers were to take an oath not to take away or misuse the library's property, and a register was to be kept of persons so sworn; 'bookes of comon use' might only be borrowed with the consent of the vice-chancellor and 'manuscripts and other of speciall note' only with the consent of the Regent House, and in either case the borrower was to deposit 'reall caution of double value'. The rules of 1684[45] are similar in their general tenor, but the rules for borrowing are elaborated: 'Noe one shall borrow any book without express leave from ye Vice-chancell^r . . . or his Lawfull Deputy, and a note under his owne hand expressing ye name of ye Book or Bookes soe borrowed. The bookes soe lent to be return'd within one Moneth: The Under Library-Keeper or some other person to bring ye note to ye Vice-Chancellour for that purpose'; and the library-keepers were to keep a register of borrowings. That successive rules so excellent in intention should have fallen so rapidly into contempt is indeed lamentable; yet at least one visitor to Cambridge found the system (or the lack of it) agreeable enough. 'The Cambridge Gentlemen', wrote Humfrey Wanley in 1699, 'are extremely courteous and obliging . . . I can borrow what books I please.'[46]

Thus the University Library grew painfully from small beginnings. For many years it must have been smaller than many college libraries. It had no Sir Thomas Bodley to give it a glorious renaissance after the English Reformation, nor did it enjoy, as the

Bodleian Library did, a private though admittedly imperfect agreement with the Stationers' Company for the deposit of new books. It is true that the university passed a kind of local Copyright Act in 1622, by which the university printer was called upon under penalty to supply to the library a bound copy of every book printed by him within a month of publication,[47] yet there is a pathetic memorandum of 1659—'some course to be thought on for the procuring of moderne Authors, of which there have been none added these 20 last yeares'.[48] From 1662 to 1679 and from 1685 to 1695 the library shared with the Royal Library and the Bodleian the privilege of deposit embodied in the Licensing Acts, and during the earlier of these two periods at any rate the university made strenuous efforts to enforce its rights, sending its agents to London and extracting from the unwilling stationers a total of some 800 titles. The second period of the Acts' operation coincided with Laughton's attempts to make good the deficiencies in the work of his predecessors, and it would appear that during these years the university was content merely to receive such books as the stationers cared to send to it.[49]

What might have been accomplished if the University Library had been directed by men of vision and determination may be seen in the library at Trinity College, built between 1676 and 1695.[50] Tradition says that Isaac Barrow, master of the college, urged upon the university the propriety of building a theatre for secular meetings, 'it being a profanation and a scandal that the speeches should be had in the University church'. He visualised a building somewhat grander than the Sheldonian at Oxford, and asserted that financial support would not be wanting if only the university aimed high enough. Caution however prevailed in the councils of the university and the scheme was rejected; whereat Barrow returned to his college in a fit of pique and, summoning his gardeners and servants, that very afternoon staked out the foundations of a building which, he declared, would be more magnificent and costly than that which he had proposed to the university. He then applied to his friend Christopher Wren for a design for a library to cover the site, and Wren not only agreed to do so but also gave his services free. His first design envisaged a circular building rising from a square plinth and covered with a dome and

Q

cupola. This did not find acceptance, and Wren then submitted his second design, based on Sansovino's library of St Mark at Venice, for an oblong library built over a pillared arcade. Wren also designed the interior woodwork and furniture, and introduced an important innovation in his disposition of the bookcases by placing the windows high in the walls, so that the cases might stand not only at right-angles to the walls but also along them beneath the windows. The library thus comprises two series of three-sided book-lined 'cells', as Wren called them, on either side of the central aisle. Four are 'lesser cells' with carved doors for the reception of rare books; for each of the others Wren provided a table with a pyramidal revolving book-rest and two stools. On the tops of the cases Wren had planned to place full-length statues, but this scheme was abandoned and busts were substituted. These were put up by Grinling Gibbons, who also executed, in lime-wood, the coats-of-arms, wreaths, and arabesques which decorate the ends of the cases. These commemorate the benefactors who responded to Barrow's appeal for their help.

There is one other collection of books at Cambridge which may be legitimately included in this survey—that of Samuel Pepys, who died in 1703 leaving his library to a nephew for his lifetime and then, by a complicated codicil, to Magdalene College, whither the books came in 1724.[51] There they still stand in Pepys's own exquisite glass-fronted bookcases in the precise order in which he arranged them. They number exactly 3,000 volumes and are arranged within their cases by size, each book being numbered 1–3,000 from the smallest up to the largest; and books which are slightly shorter than their neighbours are brought up to the required level by means of elegant little platforms. Pepys provided them with an alphabetical catalogue, a subject-catalogue, and a shelf-catalogue; and there is a table by which the location of any volume can be determined by its number. Pepys's crest and name were stamped on the front cover of every volume when it was practicable to do so, and his arms, crest and motto were similarly stamped on the back. Nearly every volume contains two bookplates, at the front an engraving of Kneller's portrait of Pepys, at the back a device of ropes and anchors with the initials SP and motto. The library is especially remarkable as a repository

Plates 1, 2

of fine bindings by the master-binders of Pepys's own lifetime, but, bindings apart, it contains books of the highest importance in a great variety of subjects: mediaeval manuscripts and early printed books; a large collection, both manuscript and printed, on naval matters, ranging from an illustrated roll of Henry VIII's navy and Francis Drake's nautical almanack to fair copies of Pepys's official correspondence; a collection of prints and drawings and another of ballads, including over 950 unique broadsheets; a calligraphical collection and another on systems of shorthand; and the six volumes of the immortal *Diary*.

For a general view of the Cambridge libraries at the end of this period we may turn to the journal of Zacharias Conrad von Uffenbach, a learned but splenetic German, much given to pejorative comment, who visited Cambridge in 1710.[52] He seems to have been determined to dislike whatever he saw, if at all possible, and some of his criticisms can certainly be discounted. When he said of the University Library that the books were 'very ill arranged, in utter confusion' he was most probably right; but when he says that 'there seem to be at most barely 6 to 8,000, as far as I can judge by my own collection', he was certainly wrong, for the number which he had been told it possessed (14,000) was quite accurate. The library of Trinity Hall he found 'very mean, consisting only of a few law books'. Of Trinity College library he said that 'it could not be handsomer or more convenient'; but 'the arrangement . . . is not at all good, as it is not according to subjects . . . but according to benefactors. This is probably done in order to allure others'—a reason some might find perfectly adequate. Of St John's (where he was shown a box containing 'all kinds of florentine marble, a fine fossil *fungus marinus*, and an English cheese petrified') he says that 'the books are more tidy than we have found elsewhere in England, but mostly *theologica*'. Of Cambridge itself he says that 'were it not for the many fine *collegia* here, it would be one of the sorriest places in the world', which is to say that *Hamlet* would be but a poor play, were it not for the Prince. He was indeed unfortunate in that so many librarians proved to be away from their colleges when he called upon them; but perhaps they had heard of his coming.

NOTES TO CHAPTER X

1. See N. R. Ker, 'Medieval Manuscripts from Norwich Cathedral Priory', *Trans. Camb. Bibl. Soc.*, i (1949–53), pp. 3–5.

2. Strype, *The Life and Acts of Matthew Parker*, ii, Oxford, 1821, p. 475.

3. Letter from Perne to Parker (Strype, op. cit., ii, p. 407). For a list of twenty of the twenty-five MSS see C. E. Wright, 'The Dispersal of the Monastic Libraries and the Beginnings of Anglo-Saxon Studies', *Trans. Camb. Bibl. Soc.*, i (1948–53), pp. 224, 225.

4. See G. H. Viner, 'The Origin and Evolution of the Book-plate', *The Library*, 5th ser., i (1946–47), pp. 40, 41.

5. These items (and other financial details mentioned in the course of this essay) are taken from the original Audit-Books and Vouchers of the university, now in the university archives.

6. H. R. Luard, *A Chronological List of the Graces, Documents, and other Papers in the University Registry which concern the University Library*, Cambridge, 1870, no. 60. This item and all other items to which Luard gives a reference beginning with the number '31' are now in the University Library.

7. *The Chained Library*, London, 1931, p. 38. On Trinity Hall see also R. Willis and J. W. Clark, *Architectural History of the University of Cambridge*, i, 1886, p. 226; iii, pp. 448–51.

8. Streeter, op. cit., pp. 64–9; Willis and Clark, op. cit., i, pp. 107, 113; iii, pp. 453–4.

9. See Streeter, op. cit., pp. 69–71; Willis and Clark, op. cit., ii, pp. 263–71; iii, pp. 451–3.

10. University Audit-Book, 1584–5.

11. See the extract from his will in Charles Sayle's *Annals of Cambridge University Library, 1278–1900*, Cambridge, 1916, p. 56, a work to which the present writer is immeasurably indebted.

12. For a list of the surviving volumes of Lumley's gift see Sears Jayne and F. R. Johnson, *The Lumley Library: the Catalogue of 1609*, London, British Museum, 1956, pp. 298–300.

13. See W. D. Macray, *Annals of the Bodleian Library*, 2nd edn., 1890, pp. 60, 61.

14. 'Nos nunc conspersi atramento regio, nihil non sublime et excelsum cogitabimus, perrumpemus controversias omnes, superabimus quoscunque. Jam dari nobis vellemus Jesuitam aliquem, ut ex affrictu Libri vestri hominem illico contundamus' (*The Remains of George Herbert* (*Works*, vol. i), Pickering, 1836, p. 218).

15. University Audit-Book, 1619–20. The detailed bills, receipted by Edward Woodroofe, carpenter, and Henry Moody, university school-keeper and bookbinder, are also in the university archives. On Moody see *Trans. Camb. Bibl. Soc.*, i (1949–53), pp. 410, 395–421 *passim*.

16. University Library MS Mm. 1. 44 (Thomas Baker's collections), p. 476: a brief 'Life or Character' of Whelock, at the end of which Baker has written, 'This I had from Mr Whelock's Daughter, by whome it was drawn, I do not know.'

17. *The Life and Death of Mr William Moore ... As it was delivered in a Sermon preached at his funeral-solemnity, April 24, 1659. In St Maries Church in Cambridge; by Tho. Smith, B.D. his successour*, Cambridge, John Field, 1660.

18. *Alumni Cantabrigienses*, pt. i, vol. iv, p. 111.

19. 4°, London, for William Sheares, 1642. The quotation occurs on p. 16.

20. Both case and inscription have long since disappeared. The wording of the latter has however been preserved by Zacharias Conrad von Uffenbach in his posthumously published *Merkwürdige Reisen* (3 vols., Ulm and Memmingen, 1753–4), iii, pp. 38–9; cf. Sayle, *Annals*, p. 72. Uffenbach's visit to Cambridge in 1710 is discussed at the end of the present chapter.

21. For what follows see I. Abrahams and C. E. Sayle, 'The purchase of Hebrew books by the English Parliament in 1647', *Trans. Jew. Hist. Soc. Eng.*, viii (sessions 1915–17), pp. 63–77.

22. The celebrated Cambridge comedy by George Ruggle, first printed in 1630 (W. W. Greg, *A Bibliography of the English Printed Drama to the Restoration*, ii, 1951, no. L8).

23. A reference to *An Answer to a Booke entituled, An humble Remonstrance . . . Written by Smectymnuus*, London, 1641. This work (an attack on the political rights of bishops) was written in collaboration by Stephen Marshall, Edmund Calamy, Thomas Young, Matthew Newcomen, and VVilliam Spurstowe.

24. 'Pragi', though now recognised as an incorrect transliteration, is the traditional form in the University Library and has therefore been retained here.

25. This episode, and the related episode of the Holdsworth Library, is described in detail (partly from material supplied by the present writer) by Miss A. Cox-Johnson in *Trans. Camb. Bibl. Soc.*, ii, part ii (1954), pp. 105–26.

26. University Library MS Mm. 1. 43 (Thomas Baker's collections): a transcript of the relevant clause supplied to Baker by Peter Le Neve, 14 April 1719.

27. For the progress of the business through Parliament see *Journals of the House of Commons*, iii. 646; v. 9, 35–6, 83–4, 88, 121, 156; *Journals of the House of Lords*, viii. 171–3; ix. 16–17, 69–70, 75, 93, 98, 102.

28. Printed in David Wilkins's edition of Selden's works, London, 1726, vol. i, pp. xli–xlii of 'Vita Authoris'.

29. Θανατοκτασία, or, *Death disarmed: And the Grave swallowed up in Victory. A Sermon preached at S. Maries in Cambridge, Decemb.22. 1653. At the publick Funerals of Dr. Hill . . . By Anthony Tuckney*, D.D., London, 1654, pp. 42–3.

30. The identity of the anonymous benefactor appears to have been first revealed in print by Thomas Fuller in his 'History of the University of Cambridge', p. 79, annexed to his *Church-History of Britain* (1655). Samuel Clarke's 'Life and Death of Doctor Hill' (first printed in his *Collection of the Lives of 10 eminent Divines*, 1662) is an adaptation, often verbatim, of Tuckney's Θανατοκτασία, pp. 35–41. There he adds after Tuckney's 'noble Knight' the words '[Sir John Wollaston, Alderman of the City of London]'. For further information on Wollaston see A. B. Beaven, *The Aldermen of the City of London*, 2 vols., 1908–13, and R. E. C. Waters, *Genealogical Memoirs of the extinct family of Chester of Chicheley*, ii, 1878, pp. 552–6.

31. See my *Catalogue of the Fifteenth-Century printed Books in the University Library, Cambridge*, 1954, p. 8, n. 4.

32. 'Alma Mater . . . novâ ditescens bibliothecâ *Vaticanæ, Bodleianæve* æmulâ' ('Oratio Prima Anti-Weigeliana', p. 1, annexed to his *Tactica Sacra*, Cambridge, 1657).

33. *Diary*, ed. E. S. de Beer, iii, 1955, p. 140.

34. Fuller, loc. cit. Grindal's books were never in the University Library (cf. p. 215, above).

35. For what follows, see Streeter, op. cit., pp. 70 and 279–85; Willis and Clark, op. cit., iii, pp. 455–65.

36. From a transcript of the relevant clauses in 'Bishop Bennet's book' in Emmanuel College.

37. Letter of William Sancroft, master of Emmanuel College, 1662–5; quoted in Willis and Clark, op. cit., ii, p. 703.

38. University Audit-Book, 1663–4: 'Paid to John Houlden for severall weekes attendance in removing frō place to place, and ordering Dr Holsworths Booke[s] according to Direction in the University Library 02–00–00.' On Houlden see *Trans. Camb. Bibl. Soc.*, i (1949–1953), pp. 405–21, esp. 410–11.

39. On Rustat and his numerous charities and benefactions (which were not confined to Cambridge), see W. Hewett, *Memoirs of Tobias Rustat, Esq.*, 1849.

40. For the events summarised in this paragraph see Luard, *Chronological List*, nos. 115, 117–18, 129, 133, 136–7, 139–40.

41. On 30 October 1706 Cornelius Crownfield printed '20000 Capital Letters, and 2 sorts of Figures 20000 of each, for ye Books in ye University Library'. These are clearly labels denoting the class ('Letter'), the shelf-number, and the running-number of the book on the shelf, to be affixed to the spine, as is still done in the library today. Before this date a single label, denoting the running-number, had been pasted upon the fore-edge of one of the covers. Payments for writing such labels and pasting them on the edges of the books were made to Jonathan Pindar on 22 February 1674/5 and 24 January 1684/5.

42. Luard, op. cit., no. 58.

43. The librarian's stipend had originally been fixed in 1577 at £10. In 1581 he was also granted by grace certain dues payable by Bachelors, Masters and Doctors on admission to their degrees, and in 1589 Perne bequeathed an additional 40s. yearly. An under library-keeper (at £6 p.a.) is first mentioned in 1640. From 1643 onwards Whelock received an additional £6 'ex nova concessione Academiae', until in 1648–9 the old and new stipends were combined and rounded off at £10. In 1668–9 the stipend was raised to £35 *plus* dues from persons admitted to degrees, but the librarian had to pay his own under library-keeper out of it. The total dues payable to the librarian varied of course from year to year but the average total stipend, excluding Perne's bequest, was about £10 from 1600 to 1621, £16 from 1621 to 1659, £20 from 1660 to 1669, and £43 for the rest of the century. The dues, though payable to the librarian from 1581, are not so shown in the accounts until 1603–4; thereafter until 1628–9 the accounts show payment of the dues but not of the official stipend. With the first year of Whelock's librarianship (1629–30), the matter appears to have been regularised. (Luard, nos. 51, 54, 55, 69, 90, 92, 120.)

44. Luard, op. cit., no. 107.

45. Luard, op. cit., no. 140.

46. *Original Letters of eminent literary Men* (ed. Sir Henry Ellis, Camden Society, 1843), p. 289.

47. Luard, op. cit., no. 84.

48. Written at the foot of the draft 'Orders for the Library' of 1659 (Luard, no. 107).

49. For details and additional information see my recent article in *Trans. Camb. Bibl. Soc.*, ii, part iv (1957), pp. 290–304.

50. Willis and Clark, op. cit., ii, pp. 531–51; iii, pp. 465–8.

51. See *The Pepys Library*, by F. McD. C. Turner, an excellent brief description, obtainable at the college.

52. See above, n. 20. The quotations are from J. E. B. Mayor's edition of selected portions of the *Reisen* published for the Cambridge Antiquarian Society in 1911 and entitled *Cambridge under Queen Anne, illustrated by Memoir of Ambrose Bonwicke and Diaries of Francis Burman and Zacharias Conrad von Uffenbach*.

XI

Oxford Libraries in the Seventeenth and Eighteenth Centuries

J. N. L. MYRES

I N the history of Oxford libraries the seventeenth century forms a definite unit. It is the age of the chained stall library, a system which presupposes a long library room, normally on the first floor, lighted on both sides with a row of windows. Between the windows and at right-angles to the walls stands a double row of back-to-back presses containing two or three fixed shelves on each side above desk level. A central gangway runs from end to end of the room between the two rows of presses. In the window alcoves formed by the presses are placed seats or benches parallel with them: seated on these the readers can study the books by opening them on desks which are attached to the presses at the level of the lowest shelf. This is the only position in which the books in such a library can be read, for they are chained to the presses by chains of sufficient length to enable them to lie open on the desks but not to be removed to any other part of the room. The books when not in use stand upright on the shelves with their fore-edges outwards, and the chains are normally attached to the front edges of their upper or lower covers, a position in which the clips which fix them are least likely to damage the bindings of neighbouring books.

Nearly every Oxford library of which the history is known was fitted or refitted on this principle some time in the years between 1585 and 1700. The earliest certain examples, at Merton, All Souls, and Bodley's work in Duke Humphrey's library, were structurally complete before 1600;[1] they were closely followed by the pre-

Laudian wing at St John's,[2] New College, and Corpus: the series
continues at Magdalen,[3] Oriel,[4] Christ Church,[5] Jesus,[6] Trinity,[7]
and elsewhere during the first twenty-five years of the seventeenth
century; it culminates with the magnificent library at Queen's
built and furnished on this pattern between 1692 and 1696.[8]

Apart from the refitting of Lincoln College library in 1739,[9]
apparently the last to follow the chained stall system, all libraries
built or refurnished in the eighteenth century in Oxford followed
an entirely different model. They had wall-shelving, generally
with galleries, and the books were not chained. This system of
wall-shelving appears first in Oxford a century earlier in Bodley's
work in Arts End (1610–12) and it was copied thence at Selden   *Frontis-*
End (1640), and apparently at St Edmund Hall (1680).[10] But in   *piece*
all these seventeenth-century examples, the books below the galleries were chained, and seats and desks exactly similar in principle
to those required in the stall system were therefore provided.
Wall-cases of this type are used in fact in most chained stall
libraries in the form of half-presses set against the end walls of the
room. It is not until the eighteenth century that in Oxford the
abandonment of the principle of chaining made possible the full
exploitation of the possibilities of wall-shelving, as it is seen for
example in the Codrington Library at All Souls (finished 1756),
at Christ Church (1716–61), at the Radcliffe Camera (1749), at
Worcester (1746), and at Oriel (1791). The splendour of these
palatial libraries, though anticipated at Queen's, is in marked contrast with the domestic simplicity of the earlier chained stall
libraries. It is made possible by two radical differences. In wall-
shelved libraries the longer and higher are the walls the greater is
the number of books that can be shelved. Moreover the books,
being unchained, can be taken out and read anywhere in the
building: hence such seating as is deemed necessary can be provided inconspicuously without either encumbering the lower parts
of the walls with desks and benches or interfering with the
spaciousness of the main floor area. In some of these libraries indeed no seating for readers, other than a few stools, was supplied
at all, the ample floor space either remaining entirely empty or
forming the setting for some suitable statuary or other works of
art.

Thus the seventeenth and eighteenth centuries are marked in Oxford by two quite different fashions in library building and equipment, fashions which are in a sense peculiar to Oxford. In particular the almost universal adoption of the chained stall system in the seventeenth century has no real parallels elsewhere. At Cambridge, for example, where similar conditions might have been expected to produce similar library arrangements, the development in fact took quite a different turn (see chapter x). It is therefore worth while to look more closely into the circumstances in which this system evolved and became popular in Oxford.

There is no mystery about the practical problem which the chained stall library was intended to solve. Mediaeval libraries had been designed for the storage and study of manuscripts, all more or less individually valuable and comparatively few in numbers. The chained lectern system in its various forms was the obvious way to give access to a limited number of books with reasonable comfort for the reader and complete security for the books.[11] But the invention of printing gradually upset the balance of this arrangement. Books without ceasing to be valuable became much more numerous in the first half of the sixteenth century, and it was physically impossible to chain them all to existing lectern fittings, however the latter might be adapted by various devices to accommodate more books lying either on the lecterns themselves or on low shelves above or below them. Nor was it possible in most cases to expand the library room (for this, in most of the earlier colleges, had been provided as an integral part of the structural layout, surrounded by other essential elements of the collegiate complex), or to make radical alterations in the arrangement of its windows. These rigidities of size, shape and fenestration compelled the adoption of an evolutionary rather than a revolutionary solution to the problem presented by the need to house books counted in thousands rather than in hundreds.

The stall system is this evolutionary solution. The top of the mediaeval lectern has, so to speak, burst open like a bud putting forth two and later three superimposed back-to-back shelves on which chained books can stand upright to be read on the desks which, like the calyx of a flower, remain below as vestiges of the split-open lectern tops.

In view of its obviously evolutionary nature it is probably futile to seek for an originator, or indeed a clear-cut origin, for this development. Canon B. H. Streeter, to whose ingenious researches on the structural details of early library fittings in Oxford and elsewhere all students of this subject must remain deeply indebted, was certainly wrong in claiming that two-decker presses were part of the original fittings of 1480 at Magdalen.[12] At that date the pressure on space produced by the multiplication of printed books was still in the future; it can hardly have been foreseen as a factor determining a radical departure from fifteenth-century library practice.[13]

It is at present impossible to say with certainty what were the first examples of the new system in Oxford. Streeter thought, and he was certainly right in the case of Merton, that both there and at Corpus the surviving structural evidence proves that a stall system existed before the alterations were made in 1623 and 1604 respectively which brought the presses in those two libraries to substantially their present condition. At Merton the evidence from the college accounts points to 1589–90 for the first introduction of stall presses, and that may be their earliest appearance in Oxford, although it is possible that the new joinery put into the New College law library in 1585–6 may have been of the stall type. The next certain case is the conversion of All Souls library from the lectern to the stall system in 1597–8 when it was adorned with the elaborate plaster ceiling and the splendid presses, many of whose decorative details survive, as Streeter has shown, in the present panelling of the old library room.[14] The older wing of the library at St John's was also fitted up on the stall system with material brought from Beaumont Palace between 1596 and 1602.[15] At just this time too Sir Thomas Bodley was carrying out his epoch-making re-establishment of the university library in Duke Humphrey's room. His proposal 'to make it fitte, and handsome with seates and shelfes, and Deskes and all that may be needfull, to stirr up other mens benevolence to helpe to furnish it with bookes' was made to the vice-chancellor in March 1598, and by the early months of 1600 the fitting up of the existing presses was complete.[16]

It should be emphasised at this point that the history of the university library had taken an entirely different course in the

sixteenth century from that followed by the libraries of the richer
colleges. The latter were already beginning to become interested
in the systematic acquisition of printed books before the death of
Henry VIII. There is evidence that some of them, notably Merton,
New College, Magdalen and All Souls, were for the first time
buying printed books extensively between 1530 and 1550, in what
has recently been described as 'a valiant attempt to catch up with
the new learning'.[17] After the accession of Elizabeth the process
was stimulated, for the increasing interest in doctrinal controversy,
and the need to be well-equipped with the new Protestant theological writings, encouraged those who controlled college finances
to adopt a more expansionist policy in the acquisition of books.

But the position of the university library was entirely different.
Unlike the colleges, the university had no endowment income to
spend on new books, no material assets which could be sold to buy
them and no permanent officials to look after what it had.[18] Its
existing manuscript collections, though extensive by late mediaeval standards, had been acquired almost entirely by gift and
became increasingly inadequate to the needs of renaissance scholarship owing to the lack of the essential up-to-date printed books
which it was nobody's business to provide. Moreover, the whole
emphasis and initiative in academic study and teaching was passing
away from the university and into college hands. For these economic and administrative reasons, and also because the university
collections were peculiarly vulnerable to the successive purges
which the religious controversies of the age imposed on public
institutions, the university library languished in the second quarter
of the sixteenth century, while college libraries grew, and after
1550 it actually ceased to exist. The manuscripts of Duke Humphrey and other benefactors were dispersed, the old fittings were
apparently sold to Christ Church in 1563,[19] and when Sir Thomas
Bodley determined in 1597 to 'set up my staffe at the library doore
in Oxford' he found nothing left but 'a greate desolate roome'.

The almost simultaneous equipment of college libraries on the
one hand and of the university library on the other with stall
presses at this time was thus due to quite different causes: in the
one case to the increasing congestion of continuously growing collections which could not otherwise find room for more books, and

in the other to the absence of any fittings or books at all, and to the determination of Sir Thomas Bodley to provide both the one and the other in the most modern method, which would allow, as he hoped, ample space for future growth.

However the argument for priority in the introduction of the stall system may eventually be resolved, it is certain that Bodley's re-equipment of Duke Humphrey's library became itself the model for direct imitation not only in Oxford but elsewhere. It is now known that the close similarity between Bodley's presses and those of Hereford Cathedral library is due not to Bodley copying Hereford work of 1590, as Streeter thought, but to Hereford copying Bodleian work in 1611.[20] It is also known that the refitting of the Old Library at Christ Church by Otho Nicholson in 1610–1611 was with presses 'equall for substance, forme, and workman-shippe to the . . . publique Library of . . . Oxford'.[21] The very close verbal similarity in the contracts for the work at Hereford and Christ Church is almost certainly due to the influence of Thomas Thorneton, who was himself a canon of both foundations, was personally concerned with the work at Hereford as librarian from 1595 to 1629 and had also been vice-chancellor of the university in the year when Bodley first offered to restore Duke Humphrey's library. He is clearly a key figure in the development of library fittings in these critical years. It may well be that other personal links with Bodley and his first librarian, Thomas James, also helped to determine the shape of these developments in Oxford. Although Dr Hovenden, warden of All Souls when the library there was refitted in 1597, does not seem to have been connected with Bodley, Sir Henry Savile, warden of Merton 1585–1621, was a close personal friend, and his influence may well have inspired the introduction of stall presses in his own college library in 1589–90 and 1623. John Rainolds, president of Corpus 1598–1607, was a notable benefactor both of the Bodleian and of his college library, and so close a personal friend of James as to be portrayed in a most conspicuous position on the painted frieze designed by him for the Bodleian Gallery in 1618–20.[22] It was almost certainly due to Rainolds that the Corpus presses were reconstructed in such close imitation of the Bodleian pattern in 1604.[23] James himself had been a fellow of New College and, though proof is lacking, it is reasonable to suppose that he took a personal interest in the extensive refitting of his own college library between 1602 and 1606.

The immediate acceptance of Bodley's work in Duke Humphrey as a model to be followed at Christ Church and Hereford, and even by colleges such as Corpus which had perhaps already embarked on stall fittings, was due in part no doubt to the general interest aroused by Bodley's activities and to his own genius for what would nowadays be called 'public relations'. But in part it was due also to a fortuitous circumstance arising from the shape and size of the 'greate desolate roome'. Duke Humphrey's library is 86 feet long and no less than 32 feet wide, considerably larger, especially in width, than any of the library rooms built for mediaeval colleges in Oxford. Thus the width of Merton library is only 20 feet 6 inches, that of Corpus library 22 feet, that of the Old Library at All Souls 19 feet 7 inches. The exceptional width of Duke Humphrey is due not to any grandiose notion in the fifteenth century that the university library should be larger than the libraries of contemporary colleges, but solely to the accident that it was built over the divinity school, whose dimensions had been settled before the idea of placing the library over it had occurred to anyone. Had the library been conceived as a separate building at this time it would almost certainly have been considerably narrower, and perhaps shorter also, than the ample measurements of the divinity school.

The spacious dimensions and the corresponding loftiness of Duke Humphrey's library made it possible, indeed almost essential from the aesthetic point of view, that Bodley's presses should be both longer and taller than would have seemed appropriate in a smaller room. At All Souls, Merton, Corpus, and St John's the presses installed at this time seem all to have had in their original state only two shelves above the desks, giving a total height of under 7 feet. Bodley's presses had from the beginning three shelves above the desks making them 8 feet 2 inches in height and were no less than 11 feet 3 inches long compared with 7 feet 6 inches at Corpus, 8 feet at Christ Church and 9 feet 9 inches at Hereford.[24] Bodley was never one to do things on a small scale, but the unusual size of Duke Humphrey's library made his work there impressive in a way that would not have been possible in a smaller setting. It is indeed very likely that, whoever first fitted up an Oxford library with stall presses, Bodley was the first to make presses three shelves in height.

But it was not only in matters of furniture that Bodley set a standard of library practice which was envied and imitated on every hand.[25] If in the sixteenth century the university had fallen far behind the richer colleges in the provision made for books and readers, Bodley's work at one stroke reversed the situation, and the speed and completeness with which he created a library which became the pride not only of Oxford but of England profoundly impressed contemporaries. As the editor of his autobiography printed officially by the university in 1647 put it, 'his single worke clouds the proud fame of the Ægyptian Library; and shames the tedious growth o' the wealthy Vatican'.

Bodley's work was indeed timely. The latter half of the sixteenth century had seen the establishment of many notable continental libraries. The Habsburg emperors, the kings of France and Spain, the pope and the Jesuit order were all forming great collections stimulated in part at least by the enthusiasm of the Counter-Reformation, while on the other side the university of Leyden was acquiring a reputation for its newly formed library of Protestant learning. But in England the royal library of Henry VIII had been starved by the parsimony of Elizabeth and the attempt of the first Society of Antiquaries to enlist her support for the foundation of a national library of history and antiquities came to nothing.[26]

The way was thus clear for Bodley to establish something which could be not just a library for Oxford but a national, indeed an international, institution. To this end he cast his net very wide in the acquisition of books and manuscripts tapping not only the resources of the London booksellers, but the continental book-markets both of Protestant Europe and of countries such as Spain or Syria where religious differences made travel for Englishmen dangerous and the purchase of books a hazardous occupation. In spite of his prejudice against books written in English, he followed the advice of his librarian, Thomas James, in arranging in 1610 with the Stationers Company for the free supply of copies of all works printed by their members, a far-sighted action which formed the basis of the library's so-called Copyright Privilege, which received statutory authority after the Restoration.

On these well-laid foundations the fortunes of the Bodleian Library grew and its reputation increased throughout the seventeenth century. Under Thomas James and his successors the books were well-ordered and their accessibility to students compared very favourably with the conditions which prevailed elsewhere. The printed catalogues of 1605, 1620, 1635, and 1674 were models of their kind, and interleaved copies of the last have served as the catalogue to many other libraries public and private not only in England but abroad, in some cases down to the present day. Throughout the seventeenth century, and at least until the foundation of the British Museum in the middle of the eighteenth, the Bodleian was in a real sense a national institution, the obvious place for the deposit of collections of importance, and a magnet which attracted scholars and visitors both from this country and from the continent. The importance attached to its preservation by both sides during the Civil War, when the possession of Oxford was strategically of great consequence, is highly significant of this unique esteem. It is indeed remarkable not only that John Rous, the Puritan librarian from 1620 to 1652, who was a friend of Milton and received benefactions from Cromwell, retained his post throughout the royalist occupation, but that Fairfax, when at last the parliamentary forces entered Oxford, should have taken immediate steps to safeguard the Bodleian from looting, although its most recent and in some ways most valuable accessions had been due to Archbishop Laud, the name most execrated by the Roundhead party. Unlike most of the established institutions of early Stuart England, and unlike the colleges of the university itself, the Bodleian weathered the storms of the Civil War not only without serious loss or damage but without even a change of leadership.[27]

In spite of the great increase in the accessions of printed books which most Oxford libraries experienced in the seventeenth century it was only at the Bodleian and St John's, where the Laudian wing of the library was finished in 1636, that a major extension to an older library building was undertaken at this time. Most colleges had to make room for their numerous acquisitions either by taking in small adjacent rooms, as happened at Corpus and

Trinity,[28] or by various expedients in adding to the height of their new stall presses, or perhaps by the addition of shelves below the desks, though the latter practice seems to have been commoner in the eighteenth century.[29] At the Bodleian however a major extension, the building of Selden End, was completed in 1640 just before the outbreak of the Civil War. The form of this extension, like that of Duke Humphrey's library two centuries earlier, was determined in part at least by extraneous considerations. The university was using the ground floor space to the west of the divinity school for a new Congregation House set at right-angles to it, and a new room opening out of the west end of the Old Library on the floor above was a natural consequence, even if it involved the destruction of the old entrance and the provision of a new access to the whole library by the reconstruction of the western staircases from the Schools quadrangle so as to reach the doorways of Arts End.[30] Selden End conforming to the spacious dimensions of the Congregation House below was thus wider and a little longer than Arts End, but it was furnished in the same style with wall-shelving from floor to ceiling on the long walls, and with galleries to give a somewhat perilous access to the upper levels.

In one or two college libraries, and also at the Bodleian at the very end of the century, further space was found by the introduction of wall-shelving above the stall presses, approached by a gallery resting on the presses themselves.[31] This expedient was only *Plate 21* possible where there was enough wall-space above the windows to make it worth while, but the absence of natural lighting to such galleries made them unsatisfactory and the additional weight led in some cases to instability. The galleries introduced in 1693 over the presses in Duke Humphrey's library to house the books of Bishop Barlow caused the south wall of the room to bulge so alarmingly that Sir Christopher Wren was called in in 1700 to devise means of holding the building together. A plan in his hand showing his massive extensions to the buttresses and the other measures he advised to strengthen the structure remains among the library records as a permanent memorial of this unfortunate experiment.[32]

At Jesus, where the library fitted up in 1622–3 with chained stall

R

presses of Bodley's type was demolished as unsafe in 1640, the old fittings were substantially re-used in the new library opened in 1679. But here too a gallery with wall-shelving was erected over the old presses on the east side of the room and plenty of light was provided for the books in this gallery by setting an upper row of windows high up in the west wall above the level of the presses below them. This experiment anticipated some of the features of the great wall-shelved libraries of the eighteenth century which also often depended for light on high windows set on one side only. Jesus library is indeed the most interesting hybrid between the two types of library which seventeenth-century Oxford produced. Much the same result was eventually achieved at Brasenose, where the library, finished in 1664 and at first apparently furnished on the stall system, later had the stalls removed, and all the windows of one long side blocked to accommodate wall-shelving. These changes however were not carried out until 1772 when wall-shelving was the normal method of furnishing Oxford libraries, and what was then done at Brasenose appears to have been simply the conversion of the library from one system to the other.[33]

Plate 22

The last great library to be built in Oxford in the seventeenth century was that of Queen's which was finished in 1696. Its construction was made necessary by the large bequest of books under the will of that same Bishop Barlow (d. 1691) whose bequests to the Bodleian had led to the insertion of the galleries in Duke Humphrey's library. There has been much uncertainty about the authorship of the splendid new building at Queen's, a problem which cannot be discussed here. More important in the present context is it to note that, as Streeter has demonstrated,[34] its layout retained every essential feature of the chained stall system, in spite of the fact that in scale, proportion, and elaboration of detail, it anticipates entirely the palatial splendour of the eighteenth-century libraries.[35] The magnificence of its carved woodwork and plaster ceiling, and the height and width of its spacious proportions are in striking contrast to the traditional simplicity of its basic plan, with the double row of three-decker presses containing books which remained chained until 1770.

But by the beginning of the eighteenth century the day of the chained stall library was nearly over. At Cambridge the chaining of books had been generally abandoned for a hundred years, and even in Oxford, where mediaeval traditions died harder, two factors contributed to outmode the chained stall system in the years around 1700. One was the increasing cheapness and multiplicity of books, particularly of books printed in the smaller sizes which even Sir Thomas Bodley had not insisted on chaining. The whole balance in book production had swung away from the folios and large quartos to house which the chained presses were primarily designed. The other factor was the social change which had come over the university in the generation following the Restoration. It was now the fashion, as never before, for the nobility and gentry to send their sons to Oxford, and the richer colleges which chiefly catered for this new class of well-to-do student, so different in its tastes and habits from the impecunious clerks of earlier times, were adapting themselves in many ways to a rising standard of comfort and convenience. New buildings like those of Queen's, Magdalen, or Peckwater Quadrangle at Christ Church were designed in harmony with an aristocratic way of life quite foreign to earlier university praotice. Magdalen's new building was set in the rural surroundings of a deer park: Peckwater Quadrangle is in appearance simply three Palladian country houses set at right-angles to one another: at Worcester a romantic lake was ingeniously contrived by Capability Brown himself. Libraries too were planned like the great libraries of private collectors, where the books had never been chained, and where spaciousness and display were more valued than security and convenience of study. Some of these new buildings indeed seem primarily designed to house the private collections of benevolent *alumni*. At Christ Church, for example, the huge new library constructed between 1716 and 1761 was filled almost as soon as it was finished with the bequest collections which it still contains: the books, manuscripts and coins of Archbishop Wake, the books, engravings and music of Dean Aldrich, the scientific and medical collections of Lord Orrery, the libraries of Dr Stratford and Dr Nicholson, the pamphlets of Lewis Atterbury and the pictures and drawings of General Guise.[36] It was obvious that where space had to be found in college libraries not only for the books deemed necessary for academic study and polite learning, but for the effective display

of pictures, drawings, engravings, statuary, coin cabinets, scientific
instruments and all the miscellaneous curios brought home by
acquisitive travellers from their continental rambles, the rigid
limitations of the chained stall system were no longer tolerable.
By freeing the books from their chains and the readers from the
fixed seats and desks which a chained library demands, the way
was clear for all sorts of experiments with wall-shelving, and the
use of novel forms, proportions and lighting effects impossible to
achieve in the long rectangular libraries with regular and sym-
metrical fenestration which the seventeenth century had inherited
from the Middle Ages.

It is not possible here to describe all the new libraries which
these conditions produced in eighteenth-century Oxford. Some
idea of their variety may be gathered by considering three only,
the new library of Christ Church, the Codrington library at All
Souls, and the library designed by James Gibbs for the trustees of
Dr Radcliffe, known since the later nineteenth century as the
Radcliffe Camera.

At Christ Church the proposal to place a library on the south
side of the new Peckwater Quadrangle is first heard of in 1705. As
late as 1716 the intention was to keep its external elevation identical with that used by Dr Aldrich for the design of the other three
sides, while the interior was to be 'the finest Library that belongs
to any society in Europe'.[37] But many hands took part in the final
design which was very different from that first intended, and the
stages in its evolution are by no means clear, although several
alternative sketches have survived, and a number of important
changes were made while building was in progress. ·

Like that of most earlier libraries, the main room extending the
whole length of the quadrangle was on the first floor, and below
was to be an open colonnade, a fashion found in many seventeenth-
century examples, and one that became very popular in the great
libraries of this age.[38] The main room 140 feet long and 30 feet
wide was to be lit from each end as well as by a row of seven tall
windows on the north side looking into the quadrangle: at one
stage stall presses seem to have been intended to stand between
these windows, but finally all save the central three were blocked
internally to accommodate wall-shelving, although they remain

unchanged (and even retain their glazing) in the external elevation. The south side of the room is entirely occupied by wall-
shelving and a massive gallery carried on Ionic columns. This
gallery is approached by a wooden spiral stair which leads from
one of the two sets of smaller rooms which flank the main central
staircase on the south side of the building. These rooms, of which
there are three on each side, have locked cupboard shelving, and
were intended to accommodate manuscripts, coin cabinets, engravings and other material deemed too valuable for the open
shelves of the main library. The great room itself had apparently
no permanent furniture but two dozen stools and a couple of
charcoal braziers, which must always have looked rather lost on
the vast empty floor. Hardly was the library finished when between 1769 and 1772 the ground floor colonnade was filled in and
made into a gallery for the Guise collection of pictures.

In this curiously haphazard way, and with the marks of constant
changes of design and intention clear upon it, Christ Church
library grew during the half-century or more that it was building
in response to the changing needs and fashions of the time. It
illustrates more clearly perhaps than any other Oxford library of
this age the supreme self-confidence of a society determined to
possess 'the finest library . . . in Europe', and proceeding through
half a century of trial and error, with wholly inadequate resources
and no professional architectural assistance, to create it.

The Codrington library at All Souls also took over forty years
to build (1715–56), and it too consisted essentially of one vast
room some 190 feet long and 30 feet wide occupying the whole
of one side of a very spacious new quadrangle. But here the design,
though not unmodified in the course of building, sprang directly
from the imaginative conception of one professional architect,
Nicholas Hawksmoor. His plan was to balance the existing lines
of hall, chapel, and antechapel on one side of the quadrangle with
the single great library on the other. This meant that, perhaps for
the first time in Oxford, a great library was set on the ground
floor, but extending upwards to the full height of the building.
Hawksmoor fully appreciated and exploited the possibilities presented by this tremendous area of wall-space, and the Codrington,
as originally designed, was the supreme example of a wall-shelved

library. Along the south side and at both ends there was room for a full range of shelving below the sills of the tall windows, corresponding to the space occupied by the stalls in chapel and the panelling in hall. On the north side there were no windows and the whole enormous wall was to be covered with book-shelves for its full height with two superimposed galleries. After Hawksmoor's death in 1736 the college dispensed with his plan for what it called the 'Attic and its gallery', so that the upper third of the north wall was left unshelved, and the bookcases stopped at this level were crowned with a heavy cornice and a great number of 'bustoes' and urns.[39] In the middle of the north side, in the place occupied at Christ Church by the main staircase, was a large shelved recess which served to break the rather bleak horizontal lines of shelving and gallery, and to provide a suitable setting for a marble statue in Roman dress of the benefactor, Christopher Codrington, to whom both the money for the new building and endowment for new books were due. Another marble statue, of Sir William Blackstone, occupied the east end of the room and a number of chairs and small sloping desks for individual readers were placed under the gallery and along the south wall. Apart from these the whole floor space was left empty. At the west end the projecting wings, corresponding to the antechapel across the quadrangle, provided space for the equivalent of the small rooms which at Christ Church had been set on each side of the main staircase recess.

In addition to his work at All Souls, Hawksmoor produced a number of designs for the library which the trustees of Dr John Radcliffe were planning to build close by. Some of these were for buildings to be attached either to Selden End or to the south side of the Schools quadrangle, and they include a variety of circular and rectangular designs, none of which was eventually adopted, although it is clear that much thought and discussion were devoted by many minds in Oxford between 1710 and 1735 to the form and the siting of the proposed Radcliffe library. Eventually however it was not Hawksmoor, who died in 1736, but James Gibbs who designed the existing building which was finished and opened in 1749. Like Hawksmoor, Gibbs had also produced a number of alternative designs, and it is curious that several of these had the traditional long rectangular form with regularly spaced lateral windows, while the model which he eventually used was for a circular library similar in general appearance to that shown in several of Hawksmoor's sketches.[40]

However the idea originated, the notion of using as a library a domed circular building of what may be termed the mausoleum type, was a highly original one. As Gibbs saw, it provided opportunities for novel experiments in the use of galleries and wall-shelving which, while retaining great spaciousness, avoided altogether the rather blank and empty effect which a huge rectangular wall-shelved room like the Codrington might give. Gibbs retained, or returned to, the traditional first-floor arrangement, and the ground floor of the Radcliffe library was at first an open colonnade with the ingenious device of a concealed internal entrance, so that the exterior symmetry of the circular structure was not broken at any point. On the first floor the central space, splendidly top-lit from the great windows at the base of the dome, was entirely open, and space for shelving books was provided on two floors in the circular aisles that surrounded it. These floors, of which the upper was really a gallery, were each independently lit not only from the central area but from their own windows, and the bookcases were set in a series of radial alcoves, so that the arrangements thus combined the features of the stall system with those of wall-shelving and galleries. From the practical librarian's point of view the waste of space for books is far larger in the Camera than in any other type of library of comparable volume, for the whole central area is entirely useless for this purpose. But although the design of the library can be criticised on the ground that provision for books appears altogether subordinate to pure architectural display and although this display itself seems centred on nothing, as though the whole building were a vast cenotaph, yet there is no denying the extraordinary skill with which the structural and aesthetic problems of the design are resolved, or the ingenuity of the lighting, or the splendid proportions of the whole. Few buildings in the world can rival the Radcliffe Camera for extreme intellectual sophistication combined with that restful sense of organic inevitability that is the hall-mark of the highest art.

It is right to end the story of Oxford libraries in the seventeenth and eighteenth centuries with the Radcliffe Camera, for it is in every sense the culmination of that story. Libraries continued to be built, as at Oriel, or to be refitted, as in Wyatt's work in the Bodleian Auctarium or the Upper Library at New College, right up to the end of the century. But there were no new ideas. From the circular form of the Radcliffe Camera, on the other hand, as well as from its ingenious fusion of elements derived both from the stall system and the system of galleried wall-shelving, sprang many new developments in the libraries of more recent times. And though some of the best features of those modern libraries may have other roots elsewhere in the past, they derive more perhaps than is sometimes realised from the line of descent that leads back from the Radcliffe Camera, the Codrington, and Christ Church, through Queen's, and Jesus, to Sir Thomas Bodley, Merton, and Corpus and so to the chained lectern libraries of pre-Reformation Oxford.

NOTE

Since this chapter was first written in 1954, the researches of Mr Neil Ker on the growth of Oxford College libraries in the sixteenth and early seventeenth centuries have greatly advanced our knowledge of the transition in Oxford from the lectern to the stall system in the furnishing of these libraries. It has been possible to incorporate in revision the information on this matter contained in his introduction to *Oxford College Libraries in 1556* (Bodleian Exhibition Catalogue, 1956), but the publication of his Sandars lectures (*Bodl. Lib. Rec.*, vi (1958)) occurred too late for reference to be made in the text to this important contribution to the subject. Mr Ker however kindly allowed me the benefit of reading these lectures before their publication.

J.N.L.M.

NOTES TO CHAPTER XI

1. See p. 239.

2. B. H. Streeter, *The Chained Library*, London, 1931, pp. 183–98: this essential book is hereinafter referred to as 'Streeter'.

3. Streeter, pp. 149–70, for Corpus; Mr N. R. Ker tells me that the college accounts for New College and Magdalen show extensive work in their libraries in 1602–6 and 1610 respectively.

4. *Victoria County History*, Oxon., iii, 1954, p. 124: this volume is hereinafter referred to as *V.C.H.*

5. G. Bill in *Bodl. Lib. Rec.*, iv (1952), pp. 145–9.

6. Streeter, pp. 213–19.

7. Streeter, pp. 221–32.

8. Streeter, pp. 232–49.

9. Streeter, pp. 249–55.

10. Streeter, pp. 75–6.

11. It is reasonably certain that all the earlier college libraries were at first fitted with lecterns, although none of these fittings now survive. At Lincoln for example the 1474 catalogue shows the books arranged on double desks (*disci*) with about fifteen books a side and half desks (*semidisci*) on the end walls (R. Weiss in *Bodl. Quart. Rec.*, viii (1937), pp. 343–59). The recent reconstruction of the Founder's library at New College revealed on the original wall-surface between the windows the triangular topped outline left by the wall-ends of the 14th-century lecterns: see A. H. Smith, *New College*, 1952, 53–4.

12. Streeter, p. 150. The library at Corpus was fitted up in 1517 with 'Dextis . . . after the maner and fforme as they be in Magdaleyn College'. Streeter argued from this that the Magdalen fittings were therefore of the stall pattern displayed by the present fittings at Corpus. But these are certainly due to a later refitting of the Corpus library, to which extensive alterations were made in 1604 on the model of Bodley's chained stalls in Duke Humphrey, then the latest thing in library equipment. Even if Streeter is right in thinking that the alterations of 1604 were to a library already fitted on the chained stall system, that does not prove that the Magdalen fittings of 1480 copied at Corpus in 1517 were of that type, for stalls may have replaced lecterns already in the last years of the sixteenth century. As late as 1589 it seems certain that the Corpus library still had lectern presses, for the catalogue compiled in that year shows the books disposed in single rows (*columnae*) on each side of each *sella*. Each side contained no more than from eleven to twenty-two volumes, and the most crowded *sella* had only forty books in all: see *The Library*, 4th ser., xviii (1938), pp. 403–16.

13. Mr Ker has shown that colleges did not set out to acquire printed books at all until the 1530s. The few incunables that reached them earlier were chance acquisitions by gift or bequest: see *Oxford College Libraries in 1556* (Bodleian exhibition catalogue, 1956), p. 6.

14. Streeter, pp. 171–9. But he is wrong in dating the All Souls reconstruction before 1572. The college accounts, of which Sir Edmund Craster has kindly given me relevant extracts, make it quite certain that both the plaster ceiling and the stall presses were put in in 1597. See also *V.C.H.*, p. 187. I am greatly indebted to Mr Neil Ker for information about the date of the changes at Merton and in the New College law library.

15. So Antony Wood, quoted by Streeter, p. 183. According to *V.C.H.*, p. 261, the material came from White Friars, near Gloucester Hall.

16. *Letters of Sir Thomas Bodley to Thomas James*, ed. G. W. Wheeler, 1926, p. 1.

17. See Mr Neil Ker's introduction to *Oxford Libraries in 1556* (Bodleian exhibition catalogue, 1956), especially pp. 5, 7, 12. Magdalen and New College bought books out of income at this time: Merton, Oriel and possibly All Souls, sold plate between 1540 and 1550 to buy books. It was a time when some plate was becoming redundant owing to the religious changes. But there is little sign of 'any real attempt . . . to protestantize the libraries in the reign of Edward VI'.

18. For the poverty of the university in the first half of the sixteenth century and its effect on the contrasting fortunes of its own and the college libraries see I. G. Philip in *Bodl. Lib. Rec.*, v (1954), pp. 27–37.

19. W. G. Hiscock, *A Christ Church Miscellany*, 1946, p. 3.

20. Streeter, pp. 50–3. The contract for the Hereford presses printed in *National Library of Wales Journal*, vi (1949–50), pp. 363, 364, lays down that they are to be 'equal for substance, proportion and workmanship to the . . . publike librarie of Oxon'.

21. G. Bill in *Bodl. Lib. Rec.*, iv (1952), pp. 145–9. Later in the 17th century the device of placing a 'squivele' or swivel in the middle of the book-chains to prevent the entangling of the chains was introduced in the Bodleian during the librarianship of John Rous (1620–52) and at once copied at Hereford: see *Bodl. Lib. Rec.*, iii (1951), pp. 117–19.

22. For the relations of Rainolds and James and the former's place on the frieze see J. N. L. Myres in *Bodl. Lib. Rec.*, iv (1952), pp. 48–9.

23. Streeter, pp. 164–70.

24. The point is discussed by Streeter, p. 204.

25. For more detail on the matters outlined in this and the four following paragraphs see *The Bodleian Library in the Seventeenth Century* (Bodleian exhibition catalogue, 1951), pp. 7–21.

26. See p. 189, above.

27. For a fuller account of John Rous and his librarianship see Sir Edmund Craster in *Bodl. Lib. Rec.*, v (1955), pp. 130–46.

28. Streeter, pp. 152–4 and 224.

29. At the Bodleian shelves were not added below the desks until 1720. See G. M. Briggs in *Bodl. Lib. Rec.*, iii (1952), pp. 213–22.

30. That the present staircases to Arts End are not original is clear not only from their style but from the fact that they cut across the lines of some of the windows and the heads of the doorways to the first-floor Schools. It is probable that the original staircases gave access to the first-floor Schools only and that a short separate stair connected Arts End with the second-floor gallery which, unlike the Schools, was always part of the library. The different alignment of the present staircases was due to the need to provide direct access from the lower stages to the doorways of Arts End after the first entrance to the library had been blocked by the building of Selden End.

31. The library of University College built 1668–70 had unlighted galleries over the presses on both sides: the charming sketch of 1674 at the beginning of the Benefactors' Register (see *Bodl. Lib. Rec.* iii (1951), p. 20 and Pl. 1) is reproduced as Plate 21.

32. *Architectural Drawings* (Bodleian Picture Book no. 7, Oxford, Bodleian Lib., 1952), pl. 9.

33. *V.C.H.*, p. 217.

34. Streeter, pp. 232–43.

35. The main difference in proportion is the greater height of the Queen's library. This makes it possible to use tall windows more than twice the height of the presses, a feature unknown in earlier libraries of this type, though the effect was anticipated in part by the double row of windows on the west wall at Jesus.

36. The coin collections have recently been deposited in the Ashmolean Museum, and Lord Orrery's scientific instruments are now in the Museum of the History of Science.

37. Canon Stratford to Edward Harley, 20 September 1716, quoted by W. G. Hiscock (*A Christ Church Miscellany*, p. 49), who discusses the stages in the development of the design.

38. The library at Jesus built in 1622 stood over a colonnade which became so unstable that the whole structure had to be demolished in 1640. Among later examples are the monumental libraries of Trinity College, Cambridge, Trinity College, Dublin, Queen's College, Oxford, and the Radcliffe Camera.

39. *V.C.H.*, p. 191.

40. The collection of drawings for the proposed Radcliffe library by Gibbs, Hawksmoor and others is in the Ashmolean Museum. Several are reproduced in *Bibliotheca Radcliviana* (Bodleian exhibition catalogue, 1949) including two designs by Gibbs for rectangular first-floor libraries, one of which was to have two parallel rooms separated by a central wall available for bilateral wall-shelving (pls. 6 and 7). There is also an ingenious, if amateurish, design 'by the honble Mr. Robert Trevor' (pl. 10) for a circular library with radial presses between the windows, as though Duke Humphrey's library had been rolled into a ball. Gibbs published his own designs for the library, as finally built, in his *Bibliotheca Radcliviana*, 1747.

SELECT BIBLIOGRAPHY

Note

The following short list of books suitable for further reading includes only works of a general nature or, in the case of catalogues, such as contain material of general importance for the history of the English library. Detailed or specialist articles in periodicals are of course omitted since references to these will be found in the footnotes to the relevant chapters.

CLARK, J. W. *The Care of Books*, Cambridge, 1901

DE RICCI, S. *English Collectors of Books and Manuscripts, 1530–1930*, Cambridge, 1930

DESTREZ, J. A. *La Pecia dans les manuscrits universitaires du XIIIe et du XIVe siècle*, Paris, 1935

EDWARDS, E. *Memoirs of Libraries*, 1859; 2nd edn. 1901

— *Lives of the Founders of the British Museum with Notices of its Chief Augmentors and Benefactors, 1570–1870*, 1870

ELTON, C. I. and M. A. *The Great Book-Collectors*, 1893

FLETCHER, W. Y. *English Book Collectors*, 1902

JAMES, M. R. *The Ancient Libraries of Canterbury and Dover*, Cambridge, 1903

— Catalogues of Manuscripts in the Libraries of the Cambridge Colleges, Lambeth Palace, Westminster Abbey, Eton College, etc., all Cambridge, 1895–1936

— *Wanderings and Homes of Manuscripts*, 1919

JAYNE, S. *Library Catalogues of the English Renaissance*, Berkeley and Los Angeles, 1956

KER, N. R. *The Medieval Libraries of Great Britain* (Royal Historical Society Guides and Handbooks, 3), 1941

LOWE, E. A. *Codices Latini Antiquiores*, vol. ii (Great Britain and Ireland), Oxford, 1935

MACRAY, W. D. *Annals of the Bodleian Library*, Oxford, 1868; 2nd edn. 1890 (enlarged and continued from 1868 to 1880)

MADAN, F. *Books in Manuscript*, 1893; 2nd edn. 1920

MERRYWEATHER, F. S. *Bibliomania in the Middle Ages*, 1849; revised edn. H. B. Copinger, 1933

MYNORS, R. A. B. *Durham Cathedral Manuscripts to the End of the Twelfth Century*, Oxford, 1939

SAVAGE, E. A. *Old English Libraries*, 1911

SAYLE, C. E. *Annals of Cambridge University Library, 1278–1900*, Cambridge, 1916

STREETER, B. H. *The Chained Library*, 1931

THOMPSON, J. W. *The Medieval Library*, New York, 1939; reprinted with supplement by Blanche B. Boyer, 1957

WARNER, G. F. and GILSON, J. P. *Catalogue of Western Manuscripts in the old Royal and King's Collections in the British Museum*, 1921

WEISS, R. *Humanism in England during the 15th Century*, Oxford, 1941; revised edn. 1957

INDEX

Aachen, 142

Abingdon Abbey, 77, 83n51

Acts of Parliament
against Superstitious Books and Images, 151, 165–6
rel. to the Court of Augmentations, 149; the Dissolution of the Chantries, 150; the Dissolution of the Greater Monasteries, 150; and the Dissolution of the Lesser Monasteries, 149
Act of Uniformity (1549), 151, 165

Adelard of Bath, translator, 110n83

Æthelstan, King, 23, 27, 30n21

Agarde, Arthur, 183, 187–9, 195–6, 197, 201

Alanus de Insulis, 102–3

Alcuin, 141–2

Aldrich, Henry, dean of Christ Church, 247

Allen, Thomas, 199

Alnwick Abbey, 150

Altar, storage-place for books, 16, 29n5

Ambrose, St, 88, 92

Ambrosius Autpertus, 92

Ammianus, 99

Ancrene Riwle MSS, 194

Andrewes, Lancelot, 186

Anglo-Saxon Chronicle MSS, 193

Anonimalle Chronicle, 210n31

Antiquaries, Elizabethan Society of, 179–91

Antonio Mario, scribe, 121

Apuleius, 143, 147

Arabic numerals, 3

Arabic works in mediaeval libraries, 95, 103, 104, 105

Aristotle, 76, 77, 94–5, 118

Arithmetic, 103

Armarium, *see* Library furniture

Atterbury, Lewis, 247

Aubrey, John, 151–2, 198

Augustine, St, bishop of Hippo, 54, 88, 92

Augustinian canons, 85; *see also* Barnwell, Bolton, Cirencester, Darley, Lanercost, Lanthony, Leicester, Merton, Taunton, Waltham
— friars, as writers, 76; *see also* York, Austin Friars

Aungerville, Richard, *see* Richard de Bury

Aupert, Ambroise, *see* Ambrosius Autpertus

Austin Friars, York, *see* York, Austin Friars

Bacon, Sir Francis, 10–11, 199, 203

Bacon, Sir Nicholas, 170, 199, 213, 214

Bacon, Roger, 68, 75, 76, 126

Baker, Augustine, 202

Bale, John, 152, 153–4, 157, 165

Bamberg, Plautus MS at, 144

Bancroft, Richard, archbishop of Canterbury, 222

Barking Abbey, 20, 21

Barlings Abbey, 150, 162

Barnwell Priory, 21–2

Barrow, Isaac, 229

Beale, Robert, 184

Beaufort, Cardinal, 116

Beaumont Palace, Oxford, 239

Beccaria, Antonio, 118, 119, 127

Bede, 91, 141, 193

Beleth, John, *Summa*, 108n29

Benedict, St, 15–16, 29n3, 138

Benedict Biscop, 3, 27, 141

Bentley, Richard, 11–12

Beowulf MS, 194, 199

Bernard, St, 90, 92

Bestiaries, 103

S